Rainer Maria Rilke

Twayne's World Authors Series

German Literature

Ulrich Weisstein, Editor

Indiana University

TWAS 796

Rainer Maria Rilke in 1926.
Reproduced by permission of the Swiss National Library.

Rainer Maria Rilke

By Patricia Pollock Brodsky

University of Missouri-Kansas City

Twayne Publishers
A Division of G. K. Hall & Co. • *Boston*

Rainer Maria Rilke

Patricia Pollock Brodsky

Copyright 1988 by G. K. Hall & Co.
All rights reserved.
Published by Twayne Publishers
A Division of G. K. Hall & Co.
70 Lincoln Street
Boston, Massachusetts 02111

Copyediting supervised by Barbara Sutton
Book production by Gabrielle B. McDonald
Book design by Barbara Anderson

Typeset in 11 pt. Garamond
by Modern Graphics, Inc., Weymouth, Massachusetts

Printed on permanent/durable acid-free paper
and bound in the United States of America

Library of Congress Cataloging-in-Publication Data

Brodsky, Patricia Pollock, 1941–
    Rainer Maria Rilke / Patricia Pollock Brodsky.
        p. cm.—(Twayne's world authors series; TWAS 796. German literature)
    Bibliography: p.
    Includes index.
    ISBN 0–8057–8226–5 (alk. paper)
    1. Rilke, Rainer Maria, 1875–1926—Criticism and interpretation.
I. Title.   II. Series.
PT2635.I65Z6287   1988
831'.912—dc19   87–29051
                                                                      CIP

Contents

About the Author

Born in Douds, Iowa, Patricia Pollock Brodsky is associate professor of German and Russian at the University of Missouri–Kansas City. She holds an M.A. and a Ph.D. in comparative literature from the University of California–Berkeley, and a B.A. in German from the State University of Iowa. She is the author of *Russia in the Works of Rainer Maria Rilke*, published by Wayne State University Press in 1984, as well as numerous articles on Rilke, Cvetaeva, Sologub, and others in various journals, including *Comparative Literature, Germano-Slavica*, and *Germanic Review*. The recipient of a Senior Research Fulbright Award, she is currently engaged in a study of images of Eastern Europe in postwar German literature.

Preface

Rainer Maria Rilke is considered by many to be the most important poet writing in German since Goethe. Certainly he exerted great influence on succeeding generations of poets, and his works have engendered a voluminous body of commentary, ranging from the critical to the hagiographical. His works, with their intense interaction of sound and meaning, and their way of stretching the possibilities of German syntax and word formation, pose a formidable challenge to translators. In the bibliography and notes, attention is drawn to the most important critical studies and translations into English.

Rilke is also known as a correspondent in the old style. His published letters now number close to thirty volumes. He kept a diary only for the years 1899 to 1902. It was his correspondence that served both as diary, confessional, and communication with friends, as a testing ground for ideas that appeared later in his works. Frequent reference is made to his letters, which are a rich and fascinating source of insight into the man and the poet.

It is sometimes dangerous to establish too direct a connection between a writer and his works. Authors cannot be depended on to tell the literal truth, since this is not their business, and many critics and readers have been led astray. But occasionally we find a writer whose life and work are so closely intertwined that to attempt to separate them is to do violence to both. Rilke was such a writer. Though his life might seem uneventful—no intrigues, no tragedies, no military exploits or Nobel Prizes—it was in its own way thrilling, intense, and surprising, as well as extremely productive; and the events that were turning points in his life also shaped his verse and prose.

Rilke's life and personality were paradoxical in a number of ways. The man who was to become a great poet of the German language was born into the German–speaking minority of a Slavic city. The singer of childhood, and a man who understood women profoundly and with sympathy, he was incapable of living in day-to-day contact with his wife and daughter, and was never able to make a permanent personal commitment to another woman. A lover of dogs, he feared owning one for the drain it would place on his emotional energies. A man who yearned for a homeland, spiritual and actual, he spent much of his adult life wandering from country to country, or as a guest in other people's homes. He produced many works extolling the virtues of poverty in the spirit of St. Francis and lamenting the state of the urban masses, but he himself preferred the drawing rooms of wealthy patrons and was obsessed by the idea that he himself might have aristocratic ancestors. In short, despite the remarkable consistence of certain themes and concerns from his earliest works to his last, there is always room for surprises for the reader of Rilke's works or the student of his life.

Rilke was an international figure, a child of many cultures, never limited or hemmed in by his origins or his accidental place of residence or citizenship. This can be seen in his linguistic skills. He wrote poems in French and Russian as well as German, and was a skillful translator from French, Russian, Italian, and English. He also knew Danish and Czech. The settings of his works mirror his wide travels, both physical and mental. In them we find the Prague of his childhood, Moscow and rural Russia, Italy, Egypt, Spain and Belgium, north German villages and the Rhône valley, and, above all, Paris, the city he first saw in 1902 and to which he returned repeatedly until shortly before his death in 1926.

Another important facet of his life and writing was his love of the visual arts. This was manifested in his study of art history, the reviews and monographs he wrote about various artists, and his friendship with many artists. Rilke was one of the most sensuously oriented modern writers; his works abound in subtleties of color, sound, light, and texture. In the following pages I will return to the features noted here: Rilke's sensitivity to art, his position as a cosmopolitan within the international culture of Europe at the turn of the century, and the contradictoriness of so many aspects of his personality and experience.

The following abbreviations have been used in the text and notes: *SW* for *Sämtliche Werke* and *GB* for *Gesammelte Briefe*. All translations are my own unless otherwise noted.

For their cooperation and generosity I would like especially to thank the Deutsches Literatur-Archiv in Marbach and Dr. Rätus Luck of the Schweizerische Landesbibliothek, Bern.

Patricia Pollock Brodsky

University of Missouri—Kansas City

Acknowledgments

Permission to quote from the following works is gratefully acknowledged here:

Excerpts from *An Unofficial Rilke* by Michael Hamburger, published by Anvil Press in 1981, are reprinted by permission.

Excerpted from *New Poems (1907)* by Rainer Maria Rilke. Copyright © 1984 by Edward Snow, translator. Published by North Point Press and reprinted by permission.

Excerpts from works published by Insel Verlag, Frankfurt am Main, are reprinted by permission.

Chronology

1902   August, Rilke moves to Paris. *Worpswede; Das Buch der Bilder*.

1903   Travels in Italy. *Auguste Rodin*.

1904   Rilke and Clara live in Rome. Travels to Denmark, Sweden. *Geschichten vom lieben Gott, Die Weise von Liebe und Tod des Cornets Christoph Rilke*.

1905   Extensive travels. Visits Lou in Göttingen. Lives in Meudon as Rodin's secretary. *Das Stunden-Buch*.

1906   Father dies in Prague. Breaks with Rodin. Second edition of *Das Buch der Bilder*. Final version of *Cornet*.

1907   *Neue Gedichte*. Final version of *Auguste Rodin*.

1907–1908   Travels, including lecture tours. Visits Capri.

1908   *Der neuen Gedichte anderer Teil*. Translation of Elizabeth Barrett Browning's *Sonnets from the Portuguese*.

1909   Meets Princess Marie von Thurn und Taxis. "Requiem für eine Freundin;" "Requiem für Wolf Graf von Kalckreuth."

1910   First visit to Duino. Travels to North Africa and Naples. *Die Aufzeichnungen des Malte Laurids Brigge*.

1911   Paris and Duino. Travels in Europe and to Egypt. Nile journey.

1912   In Venice with Eleonora Duse. Travels to Spain. Writes first *Elegy* in Duino.

1913   Ronda, Paris, Germany. *Das Marien-Leben, Erste Gedichte*.

1914   Meets Magda von Hattingberg. Outbreak of war finds him in Munich. Loses all his possessions in Paris. Translates Gide's "Return of the Prodigal Son."

1915   Lives in Munich. Drafted into Austrian Army, at age forty. *Fünf Gesänge*.

1916   Serves in army in Vienna, mostly at Military Archive. Released from service, returns to Munich.

1917   Munich. Friendship with Hofmannsthal.

1918   Translates "Die vierundzwanzig Sonette der Louïze Labé." Acquaintance with Eisner and Toller. Hopeful about the Revolution.

1919 Lou visits him in Munich. Lecture tour to Switzerland. Meets Reinharts, Nanny Wunderly-Volkart. "Ur-Geräusch."

1920 Returns to Paris for the first time since the war. Reunion with Princess Marie in Venice. Moves into Schloss Berg am Irchel (Switzerland). Close relationship with Baladine Klossowska (Merline).

1921 Encounters poetry of Valéry. End of July moves into the Château of Muzot.

1922 February, completes *Duineser Elegien,* writes *Sonette an Orpheus.*

1923 Works on translations of Valéry. *Elegien* and *Sonette.* Stays in sanatoria at Schönbeck, Valmont sur Territet.

1924 Writes poems in French. Further stays at Valmont. Visits from Clara and Valéry.

1925 Spends six months in Paris. Translations of Valéry poems published. Rilke writes his will, spends fiftieth birthday alone at Muzot.

1926 *Vergers* and *Quatrains Valaisans* (collections of poems in French). Friendship with Marina Cvetaeva. Rilke dies of leukemia on 29 December at Valmont.

1927 He is buried on 2 January in village churchyard at Raron. "Les Rôses," "Les Fenêtres," "Paul Valéry: Eupalinos oder über die Architektur." *Gesammelte Werke,* volumes 1–6.

Chapter One
Rilke: A Difficult Life

Rainer Maria Rilke was born on 4 December 1875 in Prague, as René Karl Wilhelm Johann Josef Maria Rilke. His parents were an ill-matched pair, and the tensions between them had a direct effect on Rilke's development. His father, Josef Rilke, had hoped for a military career, but circumstances had forced him to retire early and to spend his remaining years as a minor railroad official. His mother, Sophia Entz, came from a higher social milieu; her father had been a merchant and an imperial councellor, and she grew up in a palace. Her ambitious tastes outstripped what Josef could provide, and she seems to have been continually dissatisfied. She tried to create a facade of affluence: Rilke recalls her decanting cheap wine into fancy bottles for her dinner parties.

Sophia was also obsessed with the external trappings of Catholicism, which she fancied would serve to add to the image she was trying to create. She often went on pilgrimages or ostentatiously visited churches and shrines, and insisted on dragging little René along. It is due in large part to his distaste for his mother's shallow and oppressive show of religiosity that Rilke abandoned Christianity entirely and developed a personal hostility toward Christ and the Christian deity. This antipathy to established religion, coupled with a genuine and profound religious strain in his nature, were to lead Rilke to search for divinity and for a way of expressing it. The search for "God " or "god" occupied him during his entire life and contributed to some of the central metaphors in his writing. One can trace from his earliest poems both his dislike of traditional authoritarian figures—his early angels are dark and unresponsive, his Christ a helpless figure—and his attempts at finding and embodying a divine force. The latter takes many shapes in Rilke's works: the anthropomorphic God of the Russian peasants, divinities of antiquity and the Far East, art, creativity, the non-Christian angels of the *Duino Elegies*.

Rilke's personal and artistic development was seriously affected by another quirk of his mother's. Before he was born Phia Rilke had lost a female child. After Rilke's birth his mother decided to treat him in many ways as the girl she never had a chance to raise. He was given dolls to play with and often acted the part of a daughter in games with his mother that had to be kept secret from Josef, who strongly disapproved of such practices. For his first five years Rilke was kept in long curls and little lacy dresses. Only in 1882 was he sent to school, and even then he was accompanied there and back again, and had almost no contact with other children.

In the meantime, Josef and Sophia's marriage was falling apart. Both disappointed and ambitious people, the failed officer and the woman who had fallen below her class left their mark on the sensitive child. The parents separated in 1884, and in 1886 Rilke was sent to military school. One can understand Josef's wish to find an antidote to the unnatural life that Rilke had led under his mother's influence. No doubt Josef's own thwarted ambitions also played a role in the choice of schools. But it is appalling to imagine the contrast the brutal new world must have presented to Rilke's previous sheltered existence. The things that René was good at did not matter here; discipline was harsh, and the boys were crude and hostile to this odd newcomer. Physical prowess and group loyalty were everything, sensitivity and the individual, nothing. Rilke spent five years in this environment. It was here that he began to write, as much out of loneliness and self-defense as out of an urge to capture and explore the world around him.

Each of these extremes, the hypocritical atmosphere of his mother's overprotective world and the brutal and intolerant ambience of the military world to which his father had dreamed of belonging, left its mark on Rilke's personality, and produced themes, almost obsessions, that filled his works for years to come. Rilke utilized the military school as a setting in three of his prose works, and often spoke of his intention of writing a "military novel." He was never able to shake his bitterness at being forced to endure these five years of isolation and loss. When in 1920 one of his former teachers wrote to ask, with somewhat naive enthusiasm, if the now-famous poet was indeed his former pupil René Rilke, Rilke replied with barely suppressed anger. He informed his teacher, who was prepared to be proud of the poet's association with St. Pölten, that "I don't believe that I would have been able to achieve my life, if over the decades I had not denied and suppressed all memories of the five years of my military education." In the same letter he compares his school days with a Siberian prison described in Dostoevsky's *Memoirs from the House of the Dead.*[1]

What really happened at military school, and how Rilke reacted at the time, are still matters for speculation. His accounts of some events differ, depending on whom he is telling about them. He seems to have shared his father's dreams of military glory at least for a time. He tells of his pleasure, during riding lessons, at imagining himself riding into battle, and he wrote some mildly bloodthirsty patriotic poems as a young boy. His teachers recognized his poetic talents, and he was occasionally allowed to read his poems in front of the class. Whether or not his later accounts of his school days are largely exaggerated, as has been suggested, it is clear that the shock of the change in his eleventh year made a deep impression on him and turned him toward reading and writing.

Rilke felt that he had been robbed of his childhood by the combination of falsehood, coddling, alienation, and torment he had had to endure. This notion took on vast importance for him, and he came to believe that he could and should "redeem" or "perform" his childhood—that by retrieving it and living it as it ought to have been lived, he could somehow restore to his life a balance that had gone out of it at an early age. This he attempted to do in his writing. The image of a lost, spoiled, or threatened childhood recurs throughout, as do images of problematic relationships between children and their parents. Paired with these, however, we find examples of at least momentary idylls, in which children are both wise and innocent, able to communicate with one another and with the world. Opposed to Rilke's references, mostly in letters, to his own grotesque and uncomprehending mother, we find fictional figures of sensitive, ideal mothers who instinctively comprehend their children's fears and are always there when they are needed.

Rilke left military school in 1891, at the age of sixteen, ostensibly for reasons of ill health. It is probable that his parents finally realized that there was no officer's career in his future. But their next choice was equally ill-advised: Rilke was sent for a year to a trade school in Linz to prepare for a career in business. One wonders whether Josef and Phia knew their son at all. Luckily there were some well-to-do relatives who were willing to help. Rilke's Uncle Jaroslav, Josef's oldest brother, gave René a monthly stipend so that he could study with private tutors and obtain his high school diploma. However, even his Uncle Jaroslav hoped to mold young René into his own image; he envisioned his nephew succeeding him in the family law practice. In 1895 Rilke entered the Karl-Ferdinand University in Prague as a philosophy major. Within six months he had switched to law, and by September 1896 he had left Prague and set off for Munich to study art history.

But Rilke did not arrive in Munich a totally unknown, inexperienced young provincial. During the time he spent in Prague, from 1892 until 1896, he was remarkably busy, trying to establish himself as a writer and a literary man about town. He involved himself in every aspect of literary life, from writing and publishing to participating in literary clubs and cafés, to plans for founding an avant-garde theater, and in the process he became a master at self-advertisement. All this was possible because Prague was then one of the cultural backwaters of Europe. The provincial capital was so far untouched by most of the exciting and revolutionary literary and artistic events that were stirring up other cities like Berlin, Munich, and Paris. It was only in such a sleepy milieu that a young and not yet very promising poet like Rilke could make a prominent figure of himself so fast.

But this early prominence no doubt also hindered him, by allowing him too easy a notoriety, giving him no great models, creating no artistic challenges that would have required him to discipline himself sooner. He was a prolific writer and published many facile poems, essays and stories in newspapers and journals. His style was imitative and sentimental and gave no particular indication of what was to come. Passionately interested in the theater, he wrote several plays (eventually a total of nine), heavily influenced by naturalism, and even had two of them performed at the German Volkstheater in Prague. Between 1894 and 1896 he also published three volumes of poetry: *Leben und Lieder* (Life and songs), *Larenopfer* (Offerings to the Lares), and *Traumgekrönt* (Dream-crowned). The quality of his work during this period was generally not too high. One of his biographers sums it up rather mercilessly: in his poems there "triumphed a voluptuous lyricism of the soul, in love with its own affectation, a narcissistic cult of the self, of sentimental fragile-woeful-dreamy feelings; and already the structure of the verses showed signs of a musicality that was sickly, wallowing in piled-up rhymes."[2] Not, surely, an auspicious beginning for a poet with high ambitions!

Even so, Rilke found supporters. The respected poet Detlev von

Liliencron wrote him enthusiastic letters, and his professor at the university in Prague, August Sauer, encouraged him to write. The artist Emil Orlik illustrated some of Rilke's early works, and a young girl, Valerie von David-Rhonfeld, had the distinction of being the first in a long line of supportive women in Rilke's life. His fiancé for several years, she was, more importantly, responsible for getting his first book published. It was she who provided the money to pay the publishing costs.[3]

The provincial nature of Prague's German-speaking culture was not the only factor working against Rilke during his early struggles to become a poet. His family, besides providing him with a multitude of tensions and complexes, was largely lacking in culture (although his mother wrote verses and liked to cultivate an aura of refinement). Unlike his contemporaries Thomas Mann and Hugo von Hofmannsthal, Rilke did not grow up in an atmosphere where books, concerts, visits to the theater, or even spirited conversation were taken for granted. Considering the disadvantages of his childhood, the fact that he had to make up his high school studies on his own initiative and that he never finished the university, it is remarkable to see him, only a few years later, blossoming into a man of sensitivity and broad, though idiosyncratic, tastes.

Among Rilke's interests during the Prague years were his native city and the history and culture of the Czechs, an interest that earned him the disapproval of the conservative, clannish German community. The early poems, especially those in *Larenopfer,* evoke the streets, parks, churches, and panoramas of old Prague. Several stories inspired by this period, especially the two "Prager Geschichten" (Prague Tales) of 1897–99, deal directly with the social and political realities within the underprivileged Slavic majority. Another of Rilke's forays into literary politics, influenced no doubt in part by the ideals and concerns of naturalism, was his publication of a journal called *Wegwarten* (Wild chicory) that he had printed at his own expense and distributed free to hospitals, union halls, and people on the street. *Wegwarten* survived through three issues before Rilke closed up shop and moved to Munich. But this early naive gesture of solidarity with the poor illustrates a strain in his character that reappeared in *Stunden-Buch,* with its praise of St. Francis, and in his fascination with Russian peasants, north-German farmers and fishermen, and the beggars of modern Paris.

Thus by the time Rilke left for Munich in October of 1896, he was a much-published author, had made at least one romantic conquest and won himself a patroness for a time, made some tentative gestures toward the expression of some of his later themes, and attracted the approving attention of several men who were able to see through the modish poses, the derivative style, and the self-aggrandizing officiousness, to the real poet who was as yet hidden within.

Munich was intended to provide Rilke with an escape from the confines of Prague and of his family, via his studies at the university. His hopes and anxieties at this period are eloquently expressed in a novella, entitled "Ewald Tragy," written about 1898. Here the autobiographical elements are only thinly veiled, as we see young Ewald saying farewell to his disapproving family, taking a last, tense stroll with his father, and setting out for the big city on his own, insecure and lonely but excited by the future that has suddenly moved so close.

In fact, Munich was to do several things for Rilke. Through friends and fellow writers such as Jakob Wassermann, he was exposed to a new world of literary models and possibilities. Above all, Wassermann introduced him to the works of Ivan Turgenev and the Danish novelist Jens Peter Jacobsen. Rilke declared that it was only in Munich that he began to read seriously. (Already in Prague he had known the works of Maurice Maeterlinck, and declared the Belgian writer his master, but his own style had not matured, and he was apparently not yet able fully to digest and utilize what Maeterlinck could teach him.) From Jacobsen Rilke learned much about disciplined, careful writing, something he badly needed at this point in his career. He was also deeply moved by certain themes and attitudes of Jacobsen, which became the basis for his own philosophy. These included especially the idea that each person has a death of his own, just as he has his own unique life.

Most importantly, Munich brought Rilke into contact with Lou Andreas-Salomé. Fourteen years his senior, she was to become one of the most influential people in his life. She would be mistress, companion, teacher, and mother figure for three intense years and correspondent and distant confidante for the rest of his life. Luise Salomé was born in 1861, in St. Petersburg, to a German mother and a general in the czarist army, who was of French Huguenot stock. She grew up in the upper-class milieu of Russian government circles. Lou's outstanding characteristics were a critical and inquiring mind, an independent spirit, and a sovereign disregard for authority. She was well read in her native Russian literature as well as in German. By the time Rilke met her in May 1897, she already had a solid reputation as a critic, novelist, and writer of philsophical essays. She had been courted, unsuccessfully, by Nietzsche, had collaborated with the naturalists in their Berlin theater, the Freie Bühne, and in 1887 had married the Iranist Karl F. Andreas. This was a marriage that was probably never consummated but that lasted for nearly fifty years. After the turn of the century she became a pupil and friend of Sigmund Freud and one of the pioneers of psychoanalysis.

Rilke met her at a tea at the home of Wassermann and almost immediately began bombarding her with letters, flowers, and invitations to listen to him read his poetry. Despite her much wider experience of the world, something in the aggressive yet shy young poet from the provinces obviously appealed to her, and they became lovers early that summer. When Lou and her husband returned to Berlin in the fall, Rilke went with them. He rented a room in a pension and enrolled as a student of art history at the university. From the autumn of 1897 to the end of the summer 1900 Rilke and Lou were almost inseparable.

What Lou did for Rilke during these years touched the personal, intellectual, and artistic sides of his life. That this attractive, famous, and sought-after woman had chosen him as her lover and friend gave him new confidence. (Judged by the photos from this time, Rilke was not a preposessing figure. The pictures show a slender build, narrow shoulders, a shock of blond hair, large nose, receding chin, and rather thick lips. But according to his contemporaries, he had eyes of a remarkable blue, a pleasant voice, and a contagious laugh. And his spontaneous and sensitive nature, the combination of naiveté with an instinctive rightness of approach to people, must have been very attractive.)

On the intellectual and artistic levels, Lou became a sort of taskmaster, not only teaching Rilke Russian, but acting as a merciless critic for his writing, and helping him to purge his style of many sentimental self-indulgences. She also sent him to Florence, where he steeped himself in the study of art and architecture and where he wrote the first of his important diaries, *Florenzer Tagebuch* of April–May 1898. In Florence Rilke labored at learning how to observe carefully and capture precisely the objects of the world, skills that soon became second nature to him and eventually formed the basis of his unique contribution to poetry, the "Dinggedicht" (thing poem). In *Florence Journal* we see his new talents of observation, analysis, and description taking shape. Two minor but telling events from the Munich days illustrate the influence of Lou on Rilke. On her urging he changed his non-German and somewhat ambiguous name from René to Rainer. And almost overnight his handwriting was transformed from a rather ordinary, hurried scrawl to a neat angular script with personal quirks of form. It was as if under Lou's encouragement a graceful new creature, a poet-moth, had begun to emerge from the clumsy cocoon of provincialism.

Finally, Lou acted as teacher and guide, introducing Rilke to the complex paths of her native culture. Together they read and discussed Russian literature and history. Rilke delved into volumes of Russian art, folklore, religion, and philosophy, even reading a study of costumes worn at the medieval court. Lou was nearing a turning-point in her own life, as she rediscovered the variety and depth of Russian culture after many years spent abroad. Her enthusiasm was easily passed on to Rilke, who had in any case a strong attraction to Slavic things and to ancient cultures.

In the spring of 1899 Rilke accompanied Lou and Andreas to Russia, visiting Moscow and St. Petersburg. From May to August 1900 he and Lou went there again, this time without Andreas, and not only visited the capitals, but traveled through the countryside to Kiev and on the Volga to Kazan, Nizhny-Novgorod, and Yaroslavl. They stayed with peasants in a village, visited Tolstoy at Yasnaya Polyana, visited monasteries and museums, met artists and writers, bought books and icons, and in general absorbed as much of Russian reality as they could. The fact that the pious, melancholy, traditional Russia they chose to focus on was not the whole story, was indeed a dying world, did not disturb them; both found there essentially what they were looking for.

Russia—*his* version of Russia—was one of the seminal experiences in Rilke's life. Russian elements recur in all of his major works.[5] In addition, certain ideas that were already stirring in Rilke's mind, such as the relation of God and art, or the importance of humility and patience, were given form and substance in Russia.

In spite of the intensity of their shared experiences, by the end of the second trip Rilke's and Lou's affair had hit a low point. Lou saw Rilke as overdependent and demanding, and may have feared for their growth as writers were they to remain in their comfortable insular relationship. In 1898 in Florence Rilke had met the painter Heinrich Vogeler, and at the end of that year had visited him briefly in the artists' colony at Worpswede. This village in the flat bogland near Bremen had been discovered and adopted, since about 1890, by a group of German artists who sought a retreat from urban pressures. Rilke and Vogeler had become friends via their letters, and Vogeler had repeated the invitation to come to Worpswede for a longer stay. Now, upon his return from Russia, Rilke took him up on it. A visit at this time to a different set of friends in their remote village must have presented to Rilke the chance to put his recent loss of Lou into perspective.

Rilke stayed in Vogeler's "Barkenhoff," an old farm house that the artist had remodeled and filled with paintings and exquisite furnishings, and that overflowed with vital, creative people. It was the spiritual and social center of the colony. Every Sunday evening painters, sculptors, and their friends gathered there to talk, make music, show their latest work, and exchange ideas and enthusiasms. Rilke soon felt at home there and describes in letters and diaries the warmth of the community. It was the first time in his life that he had felt himself part of a group, valued for what he could offer— he often read to them, from his own works and from those of writers he loved—and accepted by people who, like him, were young and intensely engaged in their craft.

One of the most important results of his stay in Worpswede was the opportunity to be intimately involved with a group of visual artists and to discuss their work with them, watch them at work, go with them to exhibits, and learn to understand the unique land-scape that had drawn each to this place and formed his style and vision.[6] Rilke had long been interested in art, and now he deepened his appreciation of the processes involved, and his own skill at "seeing" matured. The idea of *schauen,* of looking, seeing in an active, participatory way, was to become a crucial aspect of his own art. We have already seen that in Florence he had begun to sharpen his skills. Later he always lamented that because of his visual im-maturity, he had let slip so many potentially vital experiences while traveling in Russia. But now in Worpswede he was making up for lost time. In his diaries we see that concrete visual images begin to play an important role. He begins to perceive things in terms of color, outline, contrast, and individual objects that together form a whole, a picture. This process of becoming more visually aware, more precise, is one we will observe through his works, reaching its most intense form in *Neue Gedichte* of 1903–8.

Among the people at Worpswede, Rilke's attention and affection were particularly drawn to two young women, to whom he frequently refers as "the two sisters," though they were not related: the painter Paula Becker and the sculptor Clara Westhoff. He was soon friends with both, and his diary is full of descriptions of their looks, clothes, movements, and walks with them in the moors, their visits to each other's ateliers, their talks that sometimes lasted till dawn. He saw in these talented young women an embodiment of everything that was beautiful, feminine, and alive. He became involved with Clara's art, but saw almost none of Paula's. After her exhibit in Bremen the previous year had received poor notices, Paula had been driven back into herself. She continued to work hard, developing her style, but did so privately, showing her work to almost no one. Thus it is not surprising that Rilke, who wrote about many of the Worpswede artists and in 1903 published an important monograph, entitled *Worpswede,* about five of them, seemed for years to have no impression or opinion of Paula as an artist, but only as a person and, perhaps, a symbol.

At the end of September 1900 Rilke was feeling happy and secure with his new friends and obviously considered settling down for a while in Worpswede. He had rented his own small house, not wanting to impose any longer on Vogeler's hospitality, and also needing privacy for his work. A four-day excursion to Hamburg with Paula, Clara, Vogeler, the painter Otto Modersohn, and several others seems to have cemented the harmony of feeling and purpose that bound him to Worpswede. His diary for 3 October notes how sad they all were because they were going to have to miss two of their Sunday evening gatherings, so much did they value their life together. Then on 5 October Rilke suddenly left for Berlin, without saying good-bye to anyone or leaving any explanation. And in his diary, a page has been ripped out at the end of the entry for 4 October. A number of explanations have been suggested for his actions. Rilke himself later tried to explain it by saying he felt too far away from his studies and sources in the remote village—a claim that holds little water in light of the circumstances of his leaving.

The real reason seems to be that Rilke had somehow discovered that Paula Becker was to be married to Otto Modersohn, a fact the couple had kept secret from their companions because Modersohn's first wife had died so recently. Was Rilke jarred by this news out of an as yet unspoken wish to marry Paula himself? The diaries up to this point speak of his deep affection for and appreciation of her, the "blonde painter" never mentioned by name. Or had he, as one critic suggests, seen in both Clara *and* Paula an untouchable ideal, maidenly beauty and an earnest and exclusive devotion to art, in one image?[7] In a poem from the middle of September Rilke had characterized them in that light.

> . . . Keine darf sich je dem Dichter schenken
> wenn sein Auge auch um Frauen bat;
> denn er kann euch nur als Mädchen denken,
> das Gefühl in euren Handgelenken
> würde brechen von Brokat.[8]

None may ever give herself to the poet, even though his eye begged for women; for he can imagine you only as maidens, the feeling in your wrists would break from the brocade.

He warns them against himself, against giving in to the pleading in his eyes, for he knows that deep down what he loves in them is precisely their purity. The feeling in their wrists—both are artists, whose hands are, so he suggests, dedicated to creating—would break, be overwhelmed and destroyed by "brocade," the heavy brocade of a wedding gown, or that of a matron. The poem goes on,

> Eure Stimmen hört er ferner gehn
> unter Menschen, die er müde meidet,
> und sein zärtliches Gedenken leidet
> im Gefühle, dass euch viele sehn. . . .

He hears your voices further away, among people whom he wearily avoids, and his tender memory suffers at the feeling that many see you.

Already here, in the poem, the girls go their own ways, choosing (mistakenly, he implies) to mingle with people who "see" them, share them—a knowledge that makes him suffer, since he considers them too pure for the throng. In the poem the same ambiguity exists as in the possible explanation for his flight from Worpswede: does he want them to remain unspoiled or to keep them for himself?

The next months in Rilke's life are confusing. He lived first with Lou and then in a small apartment in Berlin. He wrote to no one for two weeks—a long time, for this ardent correspondent—but then reestablished contact in a series of letters to Worpswede. He sends greetings and poems, says how he misses his friends there, and invites Clara, Paula, and Vogeler to visit him in Berlin. Rilke pursued his Russian studies and now, back in contact with Lou, made plans for a third trip to Russia. But his diary entry for 13 December reveals deep despair, with mysterious references to humiliation and self-disgust.

When Paula arrived in Berlin in January 1901 to take a course in home economics before her marriage (apparently a common custom at the time), they once more spent their Sunday evenings together. During Clara's visit in February Rilke proposed marriage. This development created a sensation among the denizens of Worpswede. Even Paula, Clara's close friend, was amazed. Rilke and Clara were married at the end of April 1901, but not before Rilke had taken a long trip to visit his mother in Italy, and, once back in Germany, come down with a severe case of scarlet fever; and not before Clara was two months pregnant.

The couple made their home in an old farm house in the village of Westerwede near Worpswede, and for about fifteen months they tried to establish and maintain a household, for themselves and then for their daughter Ruth, who was born in early December. The attempt was valiant and well-intentioned, but there was much against it. Both Rilke and Clara were essentially solitary people, artists who needed to be alone to develop and create. Indeed, their very concept of marriage underscored this need. In a letter to Paula from 12 February 1902, responding to a critical and accusing letter from her in which she lashes out at Rilke for what she sees as his possessive and harmful treatment of his wife, Rilke states, "I consider it the highest task of the union between two people: that each watches over the solitude of the other."[9]

In addition, neither was capable at the time of earning enough money to make life possible even in the modest circumstances of Westerwede. Rilke had as yet received no royalties from his books, and at about this time the stipend for university study established by his Uncle Jaroslav, and continued by his cousins in Prague since his uncle's death, was abruptly terminated, since it seemed that Rilke had given up all intentions of pursuing a university career. His father offered to find him a job in a bank in Prague, but Rilke, appalled, vowed that he would rather starve with his family than undertake such a move. It would amount to a retreat into the very world he had fled from, and he was convinced it would mean the death of his art.

Rilke appealed for help to everyone he could think of, asking for advice, for leads on jobs, for loans, even for handouts. Little came of it at first, though he did receive a commission to write a book about the Worpswede artists. This project allowed him to plunge more deeply into his study of their works, and of the landscape. It was well received and contains some of his best writing on art. Finally, however, Rilke and Clara came to the conclusion that they must break up their little household and move to a place that would provide them with opportunities for advancement in their respective arts and for making some money. The choice was Paris. Clara had studied sculpture there with Auguste Rodin and was now offered money by her parents to return to her studies. Rilke was given a commission to write a monograph about Rodin for a series on modern artists. Thus they closed their house in Westerwede. Rilke left for Paris at the end of August 1902, Clara followed a month later, and little Ruth was sent to be raised by her grandparents at Oberneuland near Bremen.

Paris was to prove a turning point in Rilke's life for many reasons. It marked the breakup of his one attempt at a traditional household. For although he and Clara remained close friends and often lived near one another in Paris, Rome, and Munich, they never again shared a home. They went their own ways, devoting themselves increasingly to their art. In addition, Paris, as represented by Rodin and later by Cézanne, became a kind of artistic apprenticeship for Rilke, at which he learned many things crucial to his growth as a poet. He perfected that skill of *schauen* that he had begun to develop in Florence and continued in Russia and Worpswede. He also acquired the conviction that poetry was not only an inspiration but a craft, a daily task that must be worked at and sweated over, even in times of despair or spiritual drought. The main source of the insight and for Rilke's subsequent efforts to achieve this ideal as a

modus vivendi was Rodin. The old man's life was a monument to
the ideal that he expressed, *travailler toujours*, to work constantly.
Rilke was impressed by the way Rodin concentrated wholly on his
artistic life while other, more purely human aspects remained subservient, on the periphery of his life.

Finally, the city itself had a tremendous effect on Rilke's consciousness. It was huge, impersonal, brusk, noisy, and apparently
uncaring. For Rilke, a poor, foreign poet of delicate health and
uncertain future, it overflowed with physical and psychological realities that seemed sometimes too much to deal with. This aspect of
Parisian life is most vividly and harshly expressed in the novel, *Die
Aufzeichnungen des Malte Laurids Brigge* (*The Notebooks of Malte Laurids
Brigge* [*SW*, 6:705–946]), written mostly in Paris and published in
1910. It also finds expression in the poems of the *Stunden-Buch* (*The
Book of Hours* [*SW*, 1:249–366]), especially in "The Book of Poverty
and Death." An aspect of Rilke's personal struggle that did not
find its way into the novel, for the simple reason that the character
Malte is unmarried, is Rilke's desperate need to support himself
and his family financially and spiritually, while managing to keep
his time his own and his energies fresh and undivided for his work.
But Paris was, on the other hand, immensely rich in stimulation,
from the works and personality of Rodin, whom Rilke saw often
in the early months during his work on the monograph, to the
history present in every street and alleyway. Rilke was strongly
attracted to the museums, galleries, palaces, and formal gardens of
the city, and these too play a major role in his works after 1902.

Rilke finished the *Rodin* manuscript in 1902, and it was published
in March 1903. Over the years his personal relationship with Rodin
fluctuated, but his admiration for the sculptor never changed. Rilke
later undertook a series of lectures on Rodin's behalf in various
European cities, and in 1907 he expanded the Rodin book by over
half by including a version of the lecture he had used on his tour
in 1905.

During the exciting but wearying winter of 1902–3, Rilke's
health had suffered. Italy had always had a salutary effect on his
body and spirits, so after completing the Rodin book he went to
Viareggio to rest. But instead he produced, in a tempest of activity
that became typical of his creative rhythm, the third part of the
Stunden-Buch within eight days. Rather than escaping from Paris,
he had brought Paris with him.

The following year he and Clara spent in Rome, Clara with a small fellowship to work on her sculpture, and Rilke trying to write. But as so often happened, he experienced a period when nothing came, nothing took form. He began to learn Danish during these months so as to be able to read in the original the Danish authors he valued, Jacobsen and the philosopher Sören Kierkegaard. His own work seemed stranded in a sea of minor irritations, not the least of which was an unavoidable visit from his mother. Among the few things he did write in Rome were the first pages of the Malte novel, and several poems, including the poignant "Orpheus. Eurydike. Hermes," a reinterpretation of the classical legend.

The next years found Rilke increasingly restless, traveling frequently, spending time at the villas of friends and patrons in Sweden, Denmark, and Capri. Through the Swedish feminist and educational reformer Ellen Key he had been introduced to a new circle of friends in Scandinavia at the end of 1904, just at the time when he had begun studying Danish and thinking intensively about Danish writers. Some of these new acquaintances were wealthy, some were artistic, some were both. But in any case, the change of scene and the fresh impressions were valuable. The images he gathered on his visit to Scandinavia in 1904 were to be used to good effect in his novel, for example, in the scenes at the homes of Malte, the young Dane's grandparents, and their family friends. Scandinavian impressions also found their way into a number of poems from this period.

Ellen Key was unusual among Rilke's friends in that she was down-to-earth, political, neither wealthy nor artistic. Almost a caricature of the bluestocking of the turn of the century, she wore sturdy shoes, never took a cab when she could walk, frequently overwhelmed people by her well-meaning but inappropriate advice, and, Rilke suspected, subsisted primarily on what was set before her when people invited her to tea. Rilke was first attracted to her because of her important book on child rearing, *The Century of the Child.* She in turn was impressed with his *Tales of God* and embarked on a lecture tour in Scandinavia to expose people to Rilke's works. Their relationship cooled eventually, as Rilke was increasingly put off, first by her bossy nature and her insistence on portraying him exclusively as a "god-seeker," and then by her rejection of his novel as a shocking and godless book.

The year 1905 saw Rilke travel to Prague and Dresden with his Rodin lecture. But 1906 brought new crises and moments of loss.

In September 1905 Rodin had invited Rilke to return to his house at Meudon near Paris to help him with his voluminous correspondence. Rilke was given room and board and 200 francs a month, and was expected to spend a few hours each day answering letters and arranging appointments for Rodin. He expected to have the afternoons and evenings free for his own work. He was happy to have the financial and material security and to be near the master once again. But the job mushroomed. Rilke was soon spending all his time at it and was forced to neglect his writing. Then in May 1906 Rodin suddenly fired him, supposedly over some letters that Rilke had answered in his own name without consulting Rodin. The reason more probably lay in the frictions between Rilke and the imperious old man, who was just at that time deeply involved in an affair and tended to be irritable. The two were reconciled the following year, but for the time being it was a shock and a disappointment to Rilke.

The other important event of 1906 was the death, in March, of Rilke's father. Despite their problems during Rilke's childhood and youth, he had been attached to the old man. In addition, for some time now a major portion of Rilke's meager income had come from his father, who had continued to send him money after Uncle Jaroslav's stipend ran dry. (Rilke was chronically short of money. It was only in this year, 1906, that things began to stabilize for him, thanks to generous loans from the publishers Samuel Fischer and Carl von der Heydt, and to advances from his own publisher Anton Kippenberg of the Insel Publishing House.)

At Christmas 1905 Rilke had gone to Worpswede for a visit with Clara, who was living there once more. Both, but especially Rilke, felt they had grown spiritually distant from their old friends. The two of them had matured and changed during their difficult life in Paris and Rome, while most of the Worpswede artists, most notably Vogeler, had, in Rilke's eyes, sunk into a kind of complacency and seemed to be going nowhere intellectually or artistically.

One exception was Paula. She had soon begun to have second thoughts about her marriage to Modersohn. In 1903 she came to Paris by herself to paint. Gradually she, Clara, and Rilke renewed their friendship, which had been dealt a severe blow and made cautious by their falling-out in 1902. Paula still tended to be critical of Rilke, both as a husband to Clara and as an art critic. She wrote home about the Rilkes' "joylessness" and complained that it could become contagious. Paula was at this time entering a crucial phase in her artistic development. She was influenced by Van Gogh and Gauguin, and Cézanne was as much an epochal experience for her as he was for Rilke in 1906. With her strong, personal style, her bold use of large, flat planes and unusual colors, and her almost mythical portrayal of the peasants and villagers of Worpswede, she soon surpassed the other Worpswede artists, most of whom got bogged down in their initial impressions and styles, and are today almost unknown.[10]

Paula felt herself growing as an artist, and feared being swallowed up, neutralized, by the traditional expectations of her family, husband, and society. In February 1906 she returned to Paris, this time seriously considering a permanent separation from Modersohn. She needed companionship and advice, but though she saw Rilke often and began work on a portrait of him, he carefully distanced himself from her and refused to get involved in her personal problems. She even suggested tentatively that she join the Rilkes and Ruth on their summer holiday in Belgium, but was discouraged by Rilke. Eventually Paula gave in to the steady pressure from home and returned to Worpswede. In November 1907 she gave birth to a daughter, and on 20 November, at the age of thirty-one, she died suddenly from an embolism.

When Rilke heard of her death he was on tour in Venice. He immediately canceled the rest of the lecture series and returned to Oberneuland to be with Clara and Ruth. It was only a year later, in 1908, that he was able to give vent to the complex of shock, guilt, sadness, and loss that her death had evoked in him. The result was one of his most personal and moving poems, "Requiem für eine Freundin" (Requiem for a friend), a poem that expressed clearly his ideas about the old enmity between life and art, which he felt so strongly himself, and which constantly made such difficult demands on him.

For seven months of 1907–8 Rilke was on the road. He returned to Paris in May, and in September moved into the sixth residence he had lived in in Paris, an apartment in the Hotel Biron, a former cloister in the Rue de Varenne. It was his home off and on till the end of 1911. Pictures of Rilke at work at his outsized desk show an austere room with no decoration and immensely high ceilings.

It is redolent of a cloister, and became a retreat in which Rilke completed the second book of the *New Poems* in 1908, and where he was finally able to bring his novel to a close at the end of 1909. The novel, which has so much the character of a confession, but is also a masterful piece of conscious structuring and careful craftsmanship, cost Rilke a great deal in terms of energy and health. Its completion was like a purgation, or the end of a long struggle with a serious illness. He felt drained, in need of a rest, healing, a change of scene. Throughout 1910 Rilke kept up a schedule of frantic travel and ferocious socializing. In this year alone he traveled to Leipzig, Jena, Berlin, Weimar, Rome, Venice, Duino, Oberneuland, Prague, and Cologne. At the end of the year, he set out on a journey through North Africa that lasted from November 1910 until the end of March 1911 and took him to Algiers, Tunis, Cairo, and the Nile Valley.

The travels brought him new faces and friends, new images for future poems. They cannot be said to have brought him rest or healing for his body and spirit. In 1910, after the great effort of *Malte Laurids Brigge,* Rilke entered another of those barren periods that belonged to the larger rhythms of his creativity. He wrote intensively for short periods, creating an artistic whole in a few days or weeks. Of the *Stunden-Buch*, for example, the first book was written in twenty-six days in 1899; the second in eight days in 1901; and the third in another eight days in 1903. *The Tales of God* came into being in eleven days in 1899. And between 2 and 23 February 1922 he completed his masterpieces: six of the ten *Duino Elegies* and the fifty-five *Sonnets to Orpheus.*

The Malte novel is something of an anomaly in this pattern, since he worked on it from 1904 until 1910. Likewise the totality of the *Duineser Elegien* stretched from 1912 until 1922, but as we have seen, over half of this cycle came all at once, at the very end. As a disturbing counterpoint to the periods of intense inspiration and energy, Rilke suffered from times, longer or shorter, when the voices were silenced, his ideas would not coalesce, the words were not the right ones, and he despaired of ever writing again. The fact that each time the drought was eventually ended by a rush of words did not make each new drought any easier to bear. There was always the thought that this time it would not end.

One event occurred in 1910 that was wholly positive. It began when Rilke was invited to tea, in Paris, by a woman who was to take her place alongside Lou, Clara, and later Nanny Wunderly-Volkart and Katharina Kippenberg, the wife of Rilke's publisher, as one of the great caring, stabilizing women in his life, amid all the more or less transitory affairs and friendships. This new friend was the Princess Marie von Thurn und Taxis, a well-read woman, a generation older than Rilke, with contacts among the artistic and aristocratic world of Europe. Sensitive and sensible, she became indispensable to Rilke as a wise, motherly, and powerful patroness. She brought him together with a new circle of philosophers, musicians, diplomats, and writers. Their relationship was so close and frank that Rilke confided to her many of his physical, emotional, and personal problems; she in turn relied on him for advice in family and business matters—a remarkable gesture of trust on both sides.

The princess's two castles, at Duino near Triest on the Adriatic and at Lautschin in Bohemia, were open to Rilke, and he made many visits to both in the years to come. Duino especially became important to him. It was an aged house on a cliff, surrounded by medieval battlements, with blooming gardens, solitary walks, and views of the sea. He first went there in April 1910 and was charmed by the lovely old building, the gardens, and the human warmth and intellectual stimulation that he always found there. Rilke spent the entire winter of 1911–1912, from October until May, alone at Duino, with only a few servants to watch out for him. It was in this welcome solitude that, early in 1912, the first of the great *Elegies* came to him. In gratitude to his hostess, he called them the *Duino Elegies*.

The next few years followed a now-familiar pattern: travels, illness, despair at his own unproductiveness, and an increasingly complex set of relationships with women. In 1912, for example, Rilke finally met a person whom he had admired for a long time: the aging Eleonora Duse, friend of Rodin and former lover of the poet D'Annunzio, and the greatest actress of her generation. Rilke was fascinated by her and saddened by the decline in her career and fortunes. When they met, she hadn't had a role in three years. For a time he tried various schemes for finding a stage and a vehicle for her for one last great role, but his efforts were in vain, and he sensed in her a reservoir of self-destructiveness. She died while on an American tour in 1924 of pneumonia contracted while forced to wait outside a locked theater in Pittsburgh.[11]

In the winter of 1912–13 Rilke also traveled to Spain—another

new realm of impressions as Egypt had been. This trip was not as
unlikely or as unprepared for as it might seem. In the early days
in Paris Rilke had become friends with the Spanish painter Ignacio
Zuloaga, who had introduced him to the works of El Greco, at that
time not well known outside Spain. Rilke reacted strongly and
enthusiastically. In subsequent years he encountered other works by
El Greco, in Rome and Munich, and gradually formed the plan to
travel to Toledo, El Greco's city. As Wolfgang Leppmann points
out, Rilke knew no Spanish and little of Spanish literature, and had
no particular interest in that country's history or culture. His feelings
for Spain were almost entirely based on his enthusiasm for a painter
who was not even Spanish but came from Crete, and who had few
ties to the Spanish artistic tradition.[12] The stark drama of Toledo's
landscape, architecture, and colors made a deep impression on Rilke,
and his description of El Greco's angels has much in common with
his own mysterious, un-Christian angels in the *Duino Elegies*. While
in Toledo Rilke began reading the Koran (he had already been
attracted to Islam while traveling in North Africa); and paradoxically, El Greco's mystical visions inspired in him a renewal of the
anger at Christianity that we saw in his works around the turn of
the century.[13]

During these years Rilke's health continued to deteriorate. He
complained of migraines, nosebleeds (he had been forced to interrupt
one poetry reading in order to bring under control a sudden, violent
attack), hemorrhoids, loss of memory, and digestive problems! His
system was so delicately balanced that he could produce swellings
and wrench muscles just by shaving. At about the same time he
seriously considered going into psychiatric analysis. Clara, who had
been seeing a psychiatrist in Munich, urged him to do so. But
Lou—oddly enough, since she was herself a convinced disciple of
Freud—discouraged him. Ultimately Rilke himself decided against
the treatment. He feared what such a "great spring-cleaning" would
do to his inner structure and said that to exorcise his demons might
also upset the "angels" of his inner motivation and talent.

One of the problems in reading the thousands of pages written
about Rilke is how to judge the objectivity, accuracy, and intentions
of the writers. Many left memoirs about their relationships with
Rilke. Of these, many were women—lovers, admirers, friends. The
number of different intimate encounters with women, usually artists
of one sort or another—poets, actresses, dancers, painters, musi-

cians—rose sharply in the years after Rilke had completed *Malte Laurids Brigge* and entered his long artistic dry spell. One of the most intense and, if one believes her, most serious of such encounters was Rilke's friendship, in early 1914, with the pianist Magda von Hattingberg, whom he met after she had read his *Tales of God* and written him an admiring letter.[14] Rilke responded with an openness, indeed eagerness, that must have surprised her. They met in Berlin and for several months were inseparable, meeting one another's friends and traveling together to Munich, Paris, and finally Duino. Rilke was then in the depths of one of his unproductive phases, almost totally unable to work. According to Magda, whom Rilke called "Benvenuta," the welcome one, he asked her to marry him, but after much soul-searching she declined. Her reasons included fear that his writing would suffer irrevocable damage from the human and emotional distractions, but also a realization that, as much as she loved him as a person and a legend, he was not the flesh and blood man whom she envisioned marrying.

It should be pointed out that since 1911 Rilke and Clara had been discussing a divorce; the idea was Clara's. Rilke had finally agreed and had written to his lawyer in Prague about it. But bureaucratic hurdles, including their different religions and nationalities, had seemed so insurmountable that they never carried through with the plan.[15] Presumably Rilke would have renewed his legal efforts had Benvenuta agreed to marry him. One of the most important aspects of their relationship was that Benvenuta was able to help Rilke to a greater appreciation of and attraction to music, an art form with which he admitted he had always felt uneasy, as if fearing its power to overwhelm the senses. Somewhat later in 1914 Rilke's liaison with the painter Loulou Albert-Lasard began. During their time together Rilke's poetic productivity revived somewhat; Loulou's contribution to the record of this relationship is a portrait of Rilke done in 1916.

In July 1914 Rilke had left his apartment in Paris for what was intended to be a brief visit to Germany. When the war broke out in August, he was caught like a hare which has been cut off from its burrow. As an Austrian citizen, he was considered an enemy alien and could not return to Paris, for his country was at war with France. The public havoc wreaked by the war was mirrored in Rilke's life, its losses echoed on many levels. Already in 1914, as fighting between Italy and Austria erupted along the Adriatic coast, his beloved Duino was badly damaged by mortar fire. In 1915 he received word that his landlord in Paris, tired of waiting for the rent (which Rilke had in fact sent, via neutral Holland) and doubtful whether his alien roomer would ever return, had sold all of Rilke's possessions at auction: furniture, books, letters, manuscripts, and all the small personal treasures which he had gathered in his wanderings and his many friendships.

In 1915 he published five poems, not in praise of Austro-Hungary or any political party, but a sort of mystical paean to a war god. But despite this brief enthusiasm for the war, Rilke was appalled and numbed by the insanity of it. The least nationalistic or political of men, he found it hard to understand the fierce chauvinism and national hatreds that were fired by events and that in turn carried those events forward. He had lived and traveled in so many countries, had friends everywhere, and knew and valued other languages and cultures besides the Germanic, and the idea of war among the people of those cultures was madness.

Rilke lost many friends in the war; a whole generation of poets was virtually wiped out. And in 1916 he himself, antinationalist, ailing, forty years old, received his draft notice from the Austrian army. The notion of Rilke as a soldier was so absurd that all his friends, including those who had themselves been inducted, captured, or wounded, agreed that Rilke should not have to serve. His powerful friends in many circles, including the government, went into action to get him a deferment. He was eventually released, but not before he had spent some weeks in basic training (where a sergeant, in scorn and disbelief at his middle name, Maria, persisted in calling him "Mitzi")[16] and further months in a government office in Vienna. There, along with other uniformed writers, he was expected to indulge in "Heldenfrisieren"—in "dolling up heroes," producing prettified and edifying versions of news reports from the front, for home consumption. He was equally unfit for both assignments.

Upon his dismissal from the army, Rilke returned to Munich, where he spent the rest of the war, with occasional trips to Berlin or other parts of Germany. Though he is often looked on as a conservative, partly, no doubt, because of his intimacy with so many representatives of the old ruling class, and because of his own aristocratic bearing, Rilke felt no regrets at the collapse of the Austro-Hungarian Empire or the disappearance of the old political alliance.

Indeed, he watched with hopeful interest and support the early activities of the short-lived Bavarian Soviet during the November 1918 revolution in Munich. His apartment was even searched twice by the police, because of his friendship with left-wing writers such as Ernst Toller and Oskar Maria Graf.[17] At the end of the war Rilke, like all of Europe, was exhausted. His productivity had dwindled again to almost nothing, except for a few translations from the Italian and Portuguese. He regarded the years spent in involuntary exile in Germany as a kind of imprisonment, and wanted only to get away.

In the summer of 1919 the opportunity finally presented itself. He was invited to come to Switzerland to give readings from his poetry. Saying good-bye to Lou, Clara, and other friends at the station in Munich, he did not know that he would never return to Germany. In Switzerland he traveled a great deal, partly in connection with the poetry readings, partly because, having no permanent home, he was forced to accept hospitality or find accommodations where they offered themselves.[18] He met many new people, some of whom became close friends. If anything speaks for the essential attractiveness of his personality, it is that throughout the years, in times of productivity or of drought, in good and bad health, he was always able to find people who valued him as a dinner guest, a conversation partner, a house guest—who were willing to do things for him and pleased to have the opportunity.

His main preoccupation at this time was to find a place to live—cheap, modestly comfortable, but most of all isolated so that he could work undisturbed. This ideal house for which he longed and searched was not, of course, an end in itself, but the minimal prerequisite for being able to settle down and write once more. The icy silence had already begun to thaw by the summer of 1919, shortly after he left Germany. In August he wrote a dense little essay called "Ur-Geräusch" (Primal sound), and in November his first poem written since the war, a sonnet for his Swiss friend Nanny Wunderly-Volkart.[19] These were good signs. But the great goal, and the implacable force that urged him on, was the completion of the *Elegies* begun at Duino in 1912. He had sensed from the beginning that they were to be his major statement, and that although by now some five poems existed that seemed to belong together, they were not yet finished. It was his faith in this ultimate wholeness, this task as yet undone, that sustained him through the darkest days of the war and of his personal despair.

His search for a home continued. The situation was complicated by the fact that when his homeland, the Austro-Hungarian Empire, to which Prague had belonged, had ceased to exist at the end of the war, Rilke had become stateless. Several times his visa for Switzerland had to be extended and only in the nick of time, in May 1920, was he granted a passport as a citizen of the newly founded state of Czechoslovakia. The years 1919–20 were spent, as usual, under way—on the speaking tour, and revisiting his beloved Venice, which turned out to be a sore disappointment. He had no desire to return to Germany, and certainly not to Prague. In October 1920 he was able to spend a week in Paris, his first visit since 1914. There his spirits revived visibly. But the exchange rate for the hopelessly inflated German mark was so bad that he couldn't afford to stay in Paris for long.

From November 1920 until May 1921 he found a temporary haven. He was offered the use of a small chateau at Berg on the Irchel. The isolated house (doubly isolated because it was quarantined during a hoof-and-mouth epidemic) was friendly, the library where he worked made him feel optimistic and near to being able to write once more. Indeed, during the months at Berg that winter he produced two strange sets of poems that he claimed had been dictated to him by the shade of an eighteenth-century gentleman, the Count C. W. But his time there was up before he had really collected himself and shaken off the pall of six barren years.

The actual discovery of the home he had been seeking was part farce, part miracle; it could so easily not have happened at all. In the fall of 1920 he had spent a brief, pleasant visit in the Valais, a stern, mountainous, wine-growing region in the Rhône valley in southern Switzerland. In July of 1921 he and his friend the painter Baladine Klossowska again found themselves in the Valais. They had gone there to follow up a lead about a small house that was for rent, but it turned out to be unsuitable. Depressed, they had returned to their hotel. After dinner, on a day that "seemed that we should cross it off entirely," the two friends went out for a stroll, "as if pulling ourselves together, for our consciences' sake. . . . In the window of the Bazar Hair Salon right next to the Belleview, where one goes by every day, we discovered the photo of a tower of a little castle 'from the thirteenth century' with . . . the caption 'for sale or rent.' My dear," he asks the friend to whom he writes the letter, "is it perhaps my Swiss château?"[20]

Rilke and Merline[21] visited the tower, and talked with the landlady. After he had finally decided it was really the right place, it seemed for a time that the cost might be too high. However, at the last moment a Swiss friend, Werner Reinhart, stepped in and rented the tower for Rilke. Later Reinhart bought it outright and gave it to Rilke to use as long as he lived. The tower was the Castle of Muzot, a small, compact, two-story medieval building set above vineyards near the village of Sierre. It took several weeks to clean and renovate the little castle and make it minimally livable. Rilke's first letter from Muzot is dated 5 August 1921. Here in Muzot he finally found the right atmosphere, the seclusion, and the security he had lacked for so long. And here, in February 1922, six months after moving in, he not only completed the *Elegies,* which he had begun many years before in the garden at Duino, but also wrote, quite unexpectedly, another book of poems as well, *Sonette an Orpheus* (Sonnets to Orpheus), all between 2 and 23 February. Rilke described the experience as a "hurricane in the spirit." Rarely in the history of literature has there been recorded a release of creative tension so explosive, a concentrated application of energy and artistic fulfillment so intense. It was also a physical and spiritual release for Rilke, who announced the news and expressed his relief and joy to many friends in letters during the days that followed. I will examine both sets of poems in a later chapter.

The remainder of Rilke's life brought a mixed set of events and emotions: the belief that he had accomplished his great task; a renewed burst of creativity in new directions; the pleasure of new and renewed friendships. But mainly it was a time of physical decline and mounting terrors, masked by a brave and stubborn refusal to give in to the disease that was devouring him. Among the poetic productions of those last years were his translations of verse and prose by Paul Valéry. Rilke met and corresponded with Valéry, to whom he felt a close kinship, largely because he recognized a kinship in their creative lives. Valéry had written and published poems as a young man but then fallen silent for two decades, only to burst on the scene again in 1920 with poems in a mature, perfected style. Rilke saw in Valéry's patient silence and sudden self-assured blossoming motives similar to those that had led him to refuse to publish the fragments of the *Elegies* over the years. Instead he had held out, in the faith that some day the right moment would come. The *Elegies* and *Sonnets* were published only in 1923, after a delay caused by currency problems in Germany, where his publisher was located. The year 1924 brought a flood of poems in French. Some, like *Vergers* (Orchards) and *Quatrains Valaisans* (Quatrains from Valais) focused on life and nature in his new homeland. Others, like "Les Roses" (The roses) and "Les Fenêtres" (The windows) returned to themes that had long interested Rilke. The first two cycles were published together in 1926, the other two in 1927, after his death.

His spirits were raised temporarily by a series of visitors to Muzot in 1924. Clara and her brother came—it was the last time Rilke saw his wife; his publisher Kippenberg visited as did his benefactor Werner Reinhart, the owner of the castle; and Paul Valéry came to Muzot. Although he later revised his opinion, his first reaction to Rilke's life at Muzot was bafflement and sadness: "A terribly lonely, very small chateau in a vast, sad mountain region; old-fashioned, serious rooms with dark furniture, narrow windows: it constricted my heart. A life so withdrawn seemed hardly possible to me, eternal winters long in such excessive intimacy with silence."[22]

December 1924 again saw Rilke in a clinic, this time at Valmont; there was no noticeable improvement in his health. On 6 January 1925 he suddenly checked out and set off for Paris. It was to be his last visit, a long one of eight months, until the end of August. He visited a few friends, walked the streets and parks of the city which had been so crucial in his work, and spent long hours with Maurice Betz, the young writer who was working on a translation of *Malte Laurids Brigge*.[23]

Rilke returned to Muzot in mid-October. Shortly after coming home he made his will, a brief, businesslike document, with Nanny Wunderly-Volkart and Werner Reinhart as executors. In it he disposes of his furniture and pictures; gives permission for his letters to be published; and requests that, should he become mentally incapacitated by his illness, he be spared the interference of a priest. "Bad enough that in my physical emergency I had to admit the mediator and negotiator in the form of the doctor; any spiritual middle-man would be offensive and nauseating to my soul as it moves toward openness."[24] Finally, Rilke made arrangements for his burial in the churchyard of the ancient village of Raron, standing on a narrow cliff above the Rhône, upriver from Sierre and Muzot.

He included in the will the verses he had written for his tombstone: "Rose, oh reiner Widerspruch, Lust / Niemandes Schlaf zu sein unter soviel / Lidern" (*SW*, 2:185) (Rose, oh pure contradiction, delight at being no one's sleep under so many lids). We see again the rose motif that reappears with such regularity in Rilke's poetry, symbol of complexity, mystery, beauty in itself which has no need to *mean*. There is also a suggestion of ambiguity in the final word, *Lidern* (lids). The German word *Liedern,* with only one letter different and pronounced identically with *Lidern,* means "songs." The poet sleeps beneath the "lids;" that is, the soft petals of the rose. He also sleeps under "so many songs"; the hundreds of poems that have made up his life's work lie lightly on him now.

The year 1926 brought one last great friendship, with Marina Cvetaeva, a young Russian poet living in French exile.[25] In May a correspondence began, instigated by the poets' mutual friend Boris Pasternak, that lasted until November 1926, just a month before Rilke's death. Though by now fully in the grip of his illness, Rilke replied to the lonely poet in long, warm letters full of understanding and advice. Out of the friendship grew two poems by Rilke, a graceful little one called "Marina: voici galets et coquillages" (Marina, here are pebbles and shells), and a longer one, "Elegie an Marina Zwetajewa-Efron." This provocative poem was a response to Cvetaeva's doubts about her role as a poet, about her ability to go on writing, bombarded as she was by mundane cares and responsibilities. The poem is both a reaffirmation and a challenge; it says much about Rilke's own views of the lonely, dedicated life of a poet that he knew firsthand. Cvetaeva, too, was inspired by the friendship; an essay and at least two long poems grew directly out of their long-distance dialogues.[26] The two never met, though they had made tentative plans to do so in early spring 1927; Rilke did not live long enough to make the journey.

On 30 November, Rilke finally could not bear his condition any longer; he was admitted once again to the clinic at Valmont. For the next month he fought a brave, losing battle against an extremely rare and painful form of leukemia. He refused to be given drugs which, while easing his pain, would also make him lose consciousness. He did not allow anyone to visit him except Nanny Wunderly-Volkart. Even Clara, who traveled to Valmont when she heard of his condition, had to leave again without seeing her husband. Rilke carried on long conversations with his doctor, who had known him for years, but he did not allow the doctor to tell him the diagnosis or to speak of death. Near Christmas Rilke wrote a few notes to close friends, including Lou. Early in the morning of 29 December, a few weeks after his fifty-first birthday, he died. He was buried, as he had wished, in a simple ceremony at the village church of Raron.[27]

Chapter Two
Major Motifs and Early Works

In the previous chapter I traced the main events of Rilke's difficult life. Before going on to examine his works, it will be useful to look at the subjects, both abstract and concrete, that form the skeleton for almost everything he wrote. Rilke has often been read as a religious poet or mystic. But we need only look at his outspoken attitude toward organized religion, especially Christianity, to know that this interpretation has to be amended. It has also been said that Rilke simply uses religious form and terminology to discuss nonreligious topics, but actually for him the topics were related to his concept of divinity.

As he matured, Rilke's works underwent a focusing process. At first he addressed some sort of anthropomorphic god, related to the Christian one but not identical with him. As time passed this god became more clearly associated with creativity; he became both an artist and a work of art. Eventually God disappeared from the works and was replaced, in the last years, by the Angels of *Duineser Elegien*: superhuman beings, aloof and all-knowing, with whom man must come to terms. The emphasis is placed increasingly on the act of making art, the nature of the artist's—especially the poet's—calling, and his relationship to the world. It is this constellation of motifs that remains central to Rilke's oeuvre. The focus varies, from the artist in the earlier works and *Malte Laurids Brigge,* to the artistic object in *Die neuen Gedichte,* to a search for the nature of man's creative task in *Duineser Elegien* and *Die Sonette an Orpheus.* But at the core are always the notions of creativity and praise.

There are, in addition, numerous specific concerns that occupy Rilke. Prominent among these is death. In subsequent chapters we shall see how these ideas developed and in how many variants death appears. It is one of the underlying motifs of *Malte Laurids Brigge;* Rilke addresses it in several requiems, for Paula and others; it takes on an almost medieval character in some works, becomes a dark figure on a path through the bog in his discussions of Worpswede, and appears as a glorious display of light and fountains in the swashbuckling "Cornet." Under the influence of Jens Peter Jacobsen, Rilke developed the idea, already referred to, that each person has a death of his own, as uniquely his as his life had been. He also frequently uses the image of death as the core or seed of a fruit: death is placed within us to ripen. For women, giving birth also implies bearing a death along with each life they create.

I have already noted the importance for Rilke of seeing—*Schauen*. This is to be expected in a writer who was so intimately involved with the visual arts and for whom the artistic act was a central concern. The poet Malte says of himself, "I am learning to see." Typical poems bear titles like "Der Schauende" (the watcher), "Der Lesende" (the reader), "Das Lied des Blinden" (the song of the blind man), or "Die Erblindende" (the woman who is going blind). There are numerous references to light and darkness, to color, and to mirrors. Rilke is a highly visual poet, emphasizing the seen world; in addition, he pointedly calls our attention to the act of seeing. For him it becomes more than just a sensory act; it is intensified into a skill to be cultivated, and finally becomes a philosophical standpoint vis-à-vis the world.

The past plays an important role in Rilke's works. He was well read in the history of Europe, particularly of Russia and France. Many works contain historical figures, some of them quite obscure, who stand for themselves within the vivid world of their day and at the same time become bearers of the author's concerns. We know the importance that the idea of lineage had for Rilke. We have seen his interest in genealogy and his half-serious belief that he was descended from Slavic nobility. The idea of descent from an ancient line plays a part in his writing as well. Malte is descended from two old Danish families, and his contacts with his own past, as well as the historic past of Europe, are vital to the novel. In some early poems we find young aristocrats, even princes, in humble conditions. Many old houses full of historic treasures and family heirlooms appear. This emphasis does not stem from any innate snobbishness in Rilke, any more than did his enjoyment of life at the houses of his patrons. Rilke himself led an austere life and had few demands beyond those he felt necessary to his creative powers. He was a vegetarian, drank very little, and had few possessions, other than his books and pictures, and a few pieces of furniture. Rather, for

Rilke the past, especially that of great families, implied a way of life that was valuable in itself: graceful, aesthetic, well-proportioned, and humanistic. This view of the past was related to another important characteristic of his works: his interest in and respect for inanimate objects. These range widely from buildings—castles, monasteries, peasant huts—to art objects—icons, ancient statues, a piece of lace—to everyday objects—a pitcher, a chair, a teacup. We also find objects from the natural world such as rain, flowers of all kinds, but especially roses. He often chose to focus on objects from the past, both as something inhuman, with a life and purpose of its own, and as a link to another era, filled with human connections, anecdotes, and experiences.

Nature and landscape are also important for Rilke.[1] He was always susceptible to his surroundings, both geographical and climatic. The first landscape that made a deep impression on him was that of Russia, with its vast spaces, huge rivers, and little villages dotting the plains. Next came Worpswede; we have seen how Rilke reacted to its flat bogland, its streams, poplars, and dramatic skies. Later travels introduced him to the peculiar personalities of other lands, and in his late French poems the vineyards and mountains of the Rhône appear in the warm glow of gratitude. Certain cities and locales recur: Moscow, Paris, Venice. Paris expecially left its mark on him, both because of its extremes of poverty and loneliness, and because of its civilization, grace, and beauty.

Many animals populate Rilke's pages: horses, cats, lions, the famous panther of *Die neuen Gedichte*, a unicorn, and countless dogs. Rilke had a special relationship with dogs; he loved to watch them and record their expressions and feelings. For Rilke, the dog was the animal closest to man, capable of affection, loyalty, and sorrow. His nearness to us in his needs, desires, and pleasures makes him poignant, but it is also a tragedy for the dog, whose animal nature is thus somehow betrayed. He is distanced from himself, his purity undermined by his having thrown in his lot with human beings. He is, as Rilke put it in a poem in *Die neuen Gedichte,*

> nicht ausgestossen und nicht eingereiht,
> . . . .
> beinah begreifend, nah am Einverstehen
> und doch verzichtend: denn er wäre nicht.
> (*SW,* 1:641)

Not banished, and not included, . . . almost comprehending, close to agreement, and yet he renounces it: for he would not exist.

When we look at a dog's face as he seems to laugh, or wrinkles his forehead in puzzlement, we feel he is "almost human," as if he were on the verge of grasping precisely what we are saying or feeling. But in the last instance he dares not cross the line to comprehension, for if he did, he would no longer exist as a dog, but would have become some lost, unnatural creature, neither dog nor man.

Despite his affection for dogs, Rilke never owned one. He declared that it was too great a responsibility, not just in the time required to care for it, but in the emotional investment he would make in the relationship. This he knew he could not afford, just as in each human relationship he always retreated from total commitment. Isolation from other creatures was the price this loving, gregarious man felt he must pay for his creativity. But the dog remained a favorite figure for expressing certain feelings. There are many dogs in *Malte Laurids Brigge,* all intimately related to human beings. They remain loyal up to and beyond their masters' death and resemble their human companions in face and personality. A story from 1907, "Eine Begegnung" (an encounter), is a parable of a failed attempt at friendship; a dog offers his companionship to a man on a path and is rejected by the man, who is anxious not to get involved. Many poems focus on dogs, and Rilke even uses dog imagery in discussing Rodin, who welcomed Rilke in 1905 "wie ein grosser Hund . . . wiedererkennend und mit tastenden Augen" (like a big dog . . . recognizing me again, and with groping eyes).[2] Elsewhere he says of a Van Gogh self-portrait that it looked "wie wenn es ein Hund schlecht hat" (like when a dog is having a rough time).[3] Rilke's feeling that dogs were very human at times overflowed into a perception that people could also be very doglike.

Certain human types recur frequently. Children are for Rilke the vehicle of innocence, but they are also victims of adults. In his works we find children lost among uncomprehending adults, stuck in schools that distort them, but also sometimes left to themselves to explore, experience, and create their own world. It was his strong feelings about what children need that led initially to his friendship with Ellen Key, who approached the same problem from a professional, pedagogical point of view. Rilke's desire to recapture and "achieve" his own unsuccessful childhood is closely related to the figures of children in his works. Nor is it surprising that we find many references to and variations on the theme of parents and children. Given Rilke's own problematic relationship with his parents, it is logical that he continued over the years to struggle with this problem.

Lovers too were important, particularly young women, and particularly those whose love is unrequited or impossible. Over the years Rilke developed a vision of an ideal love, the *gegenstandslose* or *besitzlose Liebe* (objectless love, or love without possession). This was a state in which the lover is so strong and sure in his, or more often her, love that the object, the specific person, becomes superfluous. The lover loves outward, as it were, in an expenditure of pure energy, of pure, intransitive loving. Rilke was fond of certain historical and literary figures who seemed to fit this pattern. These included a Portuguese nun named Marianna Alcoforado, whose letters he translated; Mary Magdalene; Heloïse; Bettina Brentano, ignored by the aging Goethe; and Louïze Labé, a sixteenth century French poetess. It has been suggested, of course, that in developing his theory and immortalizing the great unrequited lovers, in turning their loss into something positive, he was providing a poetic and philosophical defense for his own inability to receive and reciprocate love in an ordinary fashion. Indeed, this remains one of the most problematic areas of his life and thought.

The poor and humble, too, were important, especially in Rilke's earlier works. In his poems and stories from Prague we see the downtrodden working-class Czechs who aroused his sympathies. In Paris the homeless and poverty-stricken came as a shock to his senses and are recognized in some of the key passages of *Das Stunden-Buch* and *Malte Laurids Brigge.*

The generally undistinguished quality of Rilke's earliest works, stemming from his Prague and Munich days, has already been mentioned. The first collections of verse, *Leben und Lieder, Larenopfer, Traumgekrönt,* and *Advent,* were followed by two more collections, written between 1897 and 1899. *Dir zu Feier* (In your honor) remained unpublished and was sent to Lou, the "you" of the title, in a hand-written copy. The previous collections had been dominated by an attention to mood: an imaginary, fairy-tale world exists, separated from reality.[4] As Lou began to have a positive, liberating effect on Rilke, he began to unite life and art in his poems. *Dir zu*

Feier is characterized by an emphasis on the acts of giving and receiving. The first poem begins, "Ich möchte dir ein Liebes schenken" (I'd like to give you something dear).[5] After all that Lou had given him and done for him, the poet feels that he would like to reciprocate; his gift is the book of poems. In *Dir zu Feier* the creative impulse is seen as coming from outside, like a gift. This attitude of openness and patience accompanied Rilke for many years, strengthened by his experiences in Russia. It is expressed in many works and in his letters, and in some sense reflects his creative process. We know how often and for how long he waited for inspiration, only to be overcome by words that had been ripening somewhere, seemingly outside himself. He often spoke of his poems as having been "given" to him.

An opposite idea is expressed in *Mir zu Feier* (In my honor), first published in 1899. Here the artistic act appears as an expression of the creative will of the individual. The material of the poems, the external subjects and situations, are seen as merely an "Aufwand," an excuse for the author to express different, more personal concerns. His own situation as a developing poet is central, and his words are seen as willed, not given. *Mir zu Feier* was later thoroughly revised and published in 1909 as *Die frühen Gedichte* (Early poems). Rilke was later critical of these early works and refused to allow *Leben und Lieder* to be included in the collected works.

The language in the early works, from 1896 through 1899, especially, has been compared to the ornamental elements in *Jugendstil*. *Jugend* (youth) was a magazine published in Munich beginning in 1896. The *Jugend* style is the style favored and made popular in its covers and illustrations. *Jugendstil* was particularly widespread and influential in posters and book design. Like art nouveau, it emphasized graceful and voluptuous lines, and made much use of plant forms. The relation of Rilke's verses lies in the sinuous, decorative quality and the sensuous feeling of motion found in both.[6]

The language is characterized by the use of neologisms. In Rilke's case these often arose out of the combination of several existing words to suggest a new relationship. In *Larenopfer,* for example, we find "Lichtgetänzel" (the dance of lights, *SW,* 1:12) or "Dämmerdustgeschwel" (a dusky, dark smouldering, used to describe the effect of the evening, falling on urban streets, *SW,* 1:18). This tendency to try to burst the bounds of the language by creating new words lasted well past the turn of the century. We still find such experiments in *Das Stunden-Buch* and *Das Buch der Bilder*. In later works Rilke uses it much more sparingly and to greater effect, preferring to make use, instead, of the untapped, unrealized power within existing words. (But even late in life Rilke lamented that certain words or concepts simply did not exist in German. The palm of the hand, for example, must be gotten around in German by *handteller* (hand plate). And he could find no satisfying German equivalent for the French *vergers* [English orchard].)

Other early idiosyncrasies include the overuse of certain parts of speech. In a poem from *Mir zu Feier* there are six present participles in ten lines, intended, apparently, to create a sense of motion. There was also a tendency toward a somewhat tortured syntax, usually for the sake of the rhyme. The following example from *Larenopfer* can stand for many others.

> Ein Riesenspinngewebe, zieht
> Altweibersommer durch die Welt sich;—
> Und der Laurenziberg gefällt sich . . .
> (*SW*, 1:66)

A giant spiderweb, wends Indian Summer through the world its way;—
And on Mount Lawrence there holds sway. . . .

This is not intended to be an exact translation; considerable liberties have been taken with the last two lines in order to make the point: the clumsiness required to make lines 2 and 3 rhyme. In order to do this, Rilke split a verb form that would ordinarily be written together and placed the reflexive pronoun *sich* at the end of the second line. Having achieved this, the resultant rhyme is not really worth the effort. This sort of overwriting disappeared with time. But at the beginning of his career Rilke was so full of enthusiasm, so intoxicated with the sound of his own voice, and so eager to discover new possibilities, but at the same time so bogged down in his provincial and outmoded models, that for a time he often stumbled over his own feet.

Simultaneously with these first books of verse, Rilke was trying his hand at writing dramas. Between 1895 and 1901 he wrote ten dramatic works, some of which were finished pieces, while others remained fragments. Only three were ever performed. There is not a great deal written about Rilke's plays,[7] but they should not be ignored, if only because he was himself such an avid theatergoer and critic and put so much of his youthful energies into his own dramatic endeavors. Rilke was influenced by the prevailing modes in the theater as well as by specific dramatists. The leading movement in Central European theater since the 1800s had been naturalism, represented in Germany by such writers as Gerhardt Hauptmann and the dramatic team of Johannes Schlaf and Arno Holz. In Prague Rilke had also seen productions of plays by other, less well-known naturalists. Based on the application of empirical observation and scientific method to literature, as employed by Emile Zola, naturalism emphasized the situation of the individual within society. The task of the dramatist was to present characters as realistically as possible while focusing on the forces that had made them what they are. Favorite figures included those from the socially deprived proletariat: the poor, sick, or insane, and prostitutes and alcoholics. Plots involving incest and child killing hearkened back to the plays of the Sturm und Drang (Storm and Stress) movement of the late eighteenth century, but with the emphasis always on social and psychological cause and effect. Language was stretched, in the service of verisimilitude, to include disconnected speech, colloquialisms, poor grammar, and slang.

A number of Rilke's plays show the influences of this movement. *Im Frühfrost* (*Early Frost*), written in 1895 and performed in Prague in 1897 with the young Max Reinhardt in the cast, *Jetzt und in der Stunde unseres Absterbens* (*Now and in the Hour of our Death . . .*), also performed successfully in 1896, and *Höhenluft* (*Air at High Altitude*), written in 1897, all partake of the mood and values of naturalism. In each, individuals struggle against the circumstances that threaten the well-being or the very existence of their families. Evil is represented by lascivious moneylenders, greedy landlords, and a voracious and decadent bourgeois society. Sometimes the protagonists are ground down by their lot (the girl in *Frühfrost* who becomes a prostitute in order to save her father from prison; the dying woman in *Jetzt und in der Stunde* who dies before she can be evicted). Sometimes they are strong enough to prevail (the unwed mother in *Höhenluft* who turns down a chance to return to her destructive middle-class parents).

As time went on, Rilke succumbed to the spell of other dramatic traditions, particularly neoromanticism and symbolism, in the spirit of Hugo von Hofmannsthal and the later Hauptmann. Rilke's dramas came more and more to focus on the individual and an individual solution, rather than on social causes. In these plays there is little action; everything of importance lies, so to speak, in the air between the characters. Their problems are emotional, even metaphysical ones, and talk, not action, is their response. Sometimes there is an unreal, almost fairy-tale quality about the atmosphere. *Die weisse Fürstin (The White Princess)*, written in 1898 and published in 1900, is far indeed from the subject matter, language, and tone of *Frühfrost*. Here a princess, after years of waiting and longing, is about to slip away with her lover in a mysterious rowboat; she is prevented by an outbreak of the plague. In another play, *Ohne Gegenwart (Not Present)*, of 1897, there are qualities that may be seen as forerunners to the theater of the absurd. As in Beckett's *Waiting for Godot* and Anouilh's *Ardèle*, the main character never appears onstage. And as in the Beckett play, the emphasis is on the psychological effects of waiting for something that never comes.

Another important influence on Rilke's theater was Anton Chekhov. Rilke had read *The Seagull* and *Uncle Vanya* in Russian, during or shortly after his first trip to Russia in 1899. He decided to translate and find a stage for them. In this way he hoped to introduce Chekhov to German audiences, who knew only his short stories, if they knew him at all. By the spring of 1900 Rilke had completed his translation of *The Seagull* and had been able to interest the Secession Theater in Berlin in mounting a production. But then his plans began to unravel. Rilke had second thoughts about using *The Seagull* as Chekhov's introduction to the German stage. He was afraid it would be too earnest and slow-paced for the audience, and so he shifted his hopes to *Uncle Vanya*. Here too there were problems. The play was out of print in Russia, and Rilke had to wait for a copy from which to do his translation. Then a Russian friend warned him that *Uncle Vanya* was even less suitable for production than *The Seagull*. (It is interesting to note that even in Russia Chekhov had an uphill battle at first; the first performance of *The Seagull*, in 1896, had been a failure.)

In any case, Rilke never translated *Uncle Vanya*, and the manuscript of *The Seagull* has been lost. But Rilke was pleased and excited by getting to know and work with Chekhov's plays, and said that they had taught him a lot. It was only a few weeks after he had completed his *Seagull* translation that he wrote his play *Das tägliche*

Leben (Everyday Life), whose protagonist is an artist who has gone off the track in his art and his life and can only be brought back by the advice of a wise woman and the love of a humble one. The influence of Chekhov is present on many levels.[8] Unlike its Russian model, however, the stage career of *Tägliche Leben* was short-lived. The premiere at the Berlin Residenz-Theater in December 1901 was a flop, and a planned performance in Hamburg was called off (*SW*, 4:1055).

Rilke wrote his last dramatic work, a sketch called *Waisenkinder (Orphans)*, in 1901. But he did not abandon his interest in the theater entirely. In the early part of 1901, after his precipitous flight from Worpswede to Berlin, he was invited by Lou to meet Gerhart Hauptmann. The two were attracted to one another, and Hauptmann gave Rilke a signed copy of his new play *Michael Kramer* and invited him and Lou to attend a dress rehearsal. Rilke was so impressed by the play, a story set among artists and focusing on the conflict between an artistic calling and the realities and demands of bourgeois life, that he later dedicated *Das Buch der Bilder* to Hauptmann, "with love and in gratitude for *Michael Kramer.*"[9]

In 1902, while living at Westerwede, Rilke was responsible for a Maeterlinck festival held at the Kunsthalle in Bremen, which included a lecture on the playwright by Rilke himself and a production of his play *Sister Beatrix,* which Rilke directed. In his lecture Rilke reveals his vision of Maeterlinck as a poet striving to reach beyond the boundaries of truth, in whom Rilke found the message that "one must neglect and leave behind this life that surrounds us," because it is too small and circumscribed: "Maeterlinck makes the human soul into a dramatic subject."[10] *Sister Beatrix* is based on a medieval legend. Rilke staged it almost totally with amateur actors, who he felt would be more naive and more receptive to his direction. A black gauze veil was stretched across the stage between actors and audience to create the proper haziness of mood. The production was apparently well received. In later years Rilke wrote no more plays and never again attempted active participation in the theater. But he did talk about plans for a play called "Alkestis," and in Paris he made notes for a ballet for the Russian dancer Nijinsky. Certain dramatic tendencies can still be found in his nontheatrical works. For example, there is his frequent use of dialogue in the poetry and of the apostrophic form, in which the lyric "I" addresses some "thou" without getting, or expecting, an answer.

Before going on to Rilke's middle period and the appearance of his first works of lasting importance, we should look at two other areas of activity: critical prose and translation. I have already mentioned the two major monographs from 1902 and 1907, *Worpswede* and *Auguste Rodin*. Between 1893 and 1905 Rilke published a number of critical essays in a variety of journals and newspapers in Prague, Munich, Berlin, Vienna, Bremen, and Leipzig. It is interesting to note the relative openness and fluidity of the literary world of his day, in which an obscure young critic (at least for the first few years) could publish in so many cities, on topics ranging from the latest novels, dramas, and poetry, to events in painting and design, to the system of criminal justice. He was one of the first to recognize a major talent in Thomas Mann. "One will definitely have to make note of this name," he begins a 1902 review of Mann's novel *Buddenbrooks.* (*SW,* 5:577). And in two essays published in 1901 and 1902 he brought Western readers important information and opinions about what was happening in Russian art (*SW,* 5:493ff., 613ff.). After 1905 Rilke wrote comparatively little criticism. Of the other nonfiction that he produced between 1906 and 1926, only a few things, such as a small piece on the town of Furnes (Veurne) in Belgium and the essay "Ur-geräusch," appeared in print during his lifetime.

The other large area in which Rilke made a significant mark was that of literary translation. The combination of early training, frequent travel, cultivation of international friends and acquaintances, and a natural talent for languages made Rilke an excellent linguist. As a translator he is remarkable in that he manages to capture the feeling and intent of the original without overwhelming it as is so often the case in poetic translation. It is especially hard for a poet, with a highly developed style of his own, to go lightly when rendering someone else's words. But Rilke's translations are generally exemplary.

German was spoken in his family, which belonged to the German minority in Prague. But his exposure to other languages began early. His report card for 1889–90, his fourth year at St. Pölten, shows that in German and Czech he was "very good," while in French he was "excellent."[11] Rilke knew Italian from his many visits to Italy. He translated two Petrarchan sonnets and, over the course of ten years, between 1913 and 1923, over fifty poems by Michelangelo, with whom he was fascinated and to whom he devoted a story in

Geschichten vom lieben Gott. He learned enough English to be able, with the help of a friend fluent in the language, to translate Elizabeth Barrett Browning's "Sonnets from the Portuguese," although he always declared that the Anglo-Saxon world was alien to and unattractive for him.[12] We know that he studied Danish in order to read Kierkegaard and Jacobsen. He began to translate Jacobsen's poetry, but did not complete the project. According to Ernst Zinn, Rilke also translated from the Swedish, Latin, and Flemish[13] and he apparently picked up enough Arabic in his travels to North Africa to read the Koran.

The language and culture that had perhaps the most profound influence on him was Russian. In preparation for his trips to Russia in 1899 and 1900 he took Russian lessons from Lou, in addition to immersing himself in the study of Russian literature and history. Though he was never fluent, he learned enough to have simple conversations, to read literature in the original, and even to write poems in Russian.[14] His secretary at Muzot reports that during the last months of his life she read aloud to him in Russian from Turgenev and other writers.[15] Many of his translations from the Russian are lost, including, besides *The Seagull,* Tolstoy's play *The Living Corpse* and excerpts from Dostoevsky's *Poor Folk.* Some of the extant translations are little more than exercises in the language, but others, like a ballad by the romantic writer Mikhail Lermontov, are noteworthy. Rilke had published several translations of works by the peasant poet Spiridon Drozhzhin before his second trip to Russia, and it was this contact that provided the opportunity for him and Lou to visit Drozhzhin in his village.

By far the most important Russian translation was his version, done between 1902 and 1904 in rhythmic prose, of the medieval epic *Slovo o polku Igoreve (The Lay of Igor's Campaign).*[16] It is the tale of a disastrous military campaign in the twelfth century against a pagan tribe and the death of all but two members of the army of Prince Igor. The anonymous work is starkly beautiful, with its evocation of a pre-Christian Slavic vision of man and a world of magic and animal spirits.[17]

Of all the foreign languages that Rilke encountered, he felt most at home in French. From his move to Paris in 1902 until the outbreak of war in 1914, except for a year spent in Rome and Scandinavia, he lived in France for at least part of every year. When he moved to Switzerland in 1919, he once more had the opportunity to speak French regularly. And as we know, he spent eight months in Paris in 1925. In addition to his many French poems, particularly after 1923, there is a large body of translations from French authors. These include, apart from the Valéry poems already noted, Gide's "Return of the Prodigal Son," twenty-four sonnets by Louïze Labé, and poems and sketches by Verlaine, Mallarmé, Baudelaire, Jean Moréas, the Comtesse de Noailles, and Maurice de Guérin. The "Portuguese Letters" of Marianna Alcoforado were done from a seventeenth-century French version.[18]

Rilke's translations underscore several important facts. First is his phenomenal talent for languages. Second is the sensitivity to others' work and the control of his own language that allowed him to produce such accurate, yet poetic, renderings. Perhaps most important was the international character of his mind and art revealed in these activities. He thought of himself as a European, not as an Austrian or a Czech. He valued the interaction of many cultures that was possible until 1914 and which he tried to keep alive through his own efforts even after the collapse of the old world. He was fascinated by other cultures and their poets. By spending so much time and energy in translating them, he was both making them available to many more readers and in the best sense, making them his own. As J.R. von Salis put it, "His cosmopolitanism is naive, natural, aristocratic, he wasn't aware of national barriers to other cultures and people."[19]

Chapter Three
Short Prose Fiction, 1893–1922

One striking fact about Rilke's career as a writer is that he tried his hand at all the major genres—poetry, drama, essays, epistolary prose, and prose fiction—and showed talent in all of them, while rising to undoubted heights in some. His best-known works of fiction are the novel *Die Aufzeichnungen des Malte Laurids Brigge (1910)*, to which chapter 6 of this monograh is devoted; the collection entitled *Geschichten vom lieben Gott* (1904), first published under the title *Vom lieben Gott und Anderes* (About God and other things) in 1899; and a poem in prose, *Die Weise von Liebe und Tod des Cornets Christoph Rilke* (The Lay of Love and Death of the Cornet Christoph Rilke), which appeared in 1904.

Interspersed among these are numerous other works of fiction. Some were published as collections of stories, such as *Am Leben hin* (Alongside of life, 1898), the *Zwei Prager Geschichten (Two Prague Stories*, 1899), and *Die Letzten* (The last ones, 1901). Rilke planned two further collections, "Totentänze" (Dances of death) and "Was toben die Heiden" (How the heathens are raging), neither of which materialized. Stories intended for these collections appeared separately in journals. The highly autobiographical "Ewald Tragy" and "Die Turnstunde" (The gym lesson), both written between 1898 and 1899, were not published until 1929 and 1942, respectively. It has been suggested that Rilke refrained from publishing *Ewald Tragy* out of respect for his family, which is satirized in the story.

The forms most frequently used by Rilke are the short story and the sketch. These can vary in length from one or two pages to twenty or thirty. Several stories, notably "Ewald Tragy" and the two "Prague Stories," "König Bohusch" (King Bohusch) and "Die Geschwister" (Siblings), stretch to the length of novellas, each being close to sixty pages. Some stories have a real plot; others, like the plays and much of his early verse, emphasize mood and emotions. Still others are philosophically oriented and serve as illustrations for

Rilke's literary and artistic tenets. Such, for example, is "Im Gespräch" (In conversation) from the collection *Die Letzten*. It consists entirely of a conversation about the nature and meaning of art.

It has been noted that Rilke's works often reflect events and processes in his life. It is also of central importance to note that in terms of content and emphasis Rilke was amazingly consistent throughout his life. The major themes discussed at the beginning of chapter 2 were there almost from the start. They undergo many transformations and recombinations but remain at the center of all his inquiries. Once he had recognized the problems that were vital to him personally, he spent the rest of his life addressing them with ever-greater precision and force. The changes we can trace in his fiction have to do with artistic experience, increasing stylistic maturity, and influences from outside—from the people whom he met and whose works he read, the countries and cities he visited, and the unavoidable events of life and history, such as deaths and births, partings and wars.

Rilke's first prose products, like his earlier verse, show a precocious young man not yet in possession of a personal style. In *Am Leben hin* we find a combination of the humorous and the heartrending. The stories abound in fated lovers, moribund old ladies, blind girls, and even an abused child dying in the snow on Christmas Eve. The decadence and sentimentality of the period are very much in evidence. At the same time, the young writer gives us protagonists who manage to resist the attractions of disease or ill-conceived rebellion. In "Das Familienfest" (Family celebration) he presents a sly, sharp-eyed look at bourgeois life that prefigures the longer treatment in "Ewald Tragy."

Rilke never got around to writing a planned "military novel," but in at least two stories and a sketch, as well in parts of *Malte Laurids Brigge*, he gave form to memories of and reactions to his years at military school. "Pierre Dumont" (1894) shows the return of a young boy to school after a vacation. He spends his last free afternoon with his mother, eating so much cake in anticipation of his return to the school diet that he makes himself sick. His mother delivers him at the gate, where he is greeted by a harsh voice telling him to "report to duty, damn it!" (*SW,* 4:414). The story "Die Turnstunde" (1899) shows much greater artistic control. In lucid, spare prose it presents Gruber, a weak, unathletic student who is usually among the worst in his gym class. In the story he suddenly climbs easily to the top of a metal pole, something he had never been able to do before. For a few moments he is the center of the surprised and admiring attention of the others, but they return to their exercises and Gruber is forgotten. He then faints and is carried off to a dressing room, where he dies of a heart attack. The news is announced by an unfeeling lieutenant and classes go on as usual.

It is clear that Rilke was portraying Gruber's suffering out of his own experiences, intensified by having them lead to the child's death. Rilke obviously didn't die at the military school; but he may sometimes have felt that he was going to, or wished he could. Over and beyond his profound resentment of the atmosphere and the ethos of the place, he was frequently sick, missing hundreds of classes during his five years there. In addition, his report card for 1889–90 shows that he failed gymnastics and fencing the first time around, although he passed them by special examination later on.[1] His unsentimental portrayal of the interaction between pupils and officers shows that he had to some extent been able to bring his hatred under artistic control. But it also shows that the bitterness was still alive.

One cannot totally ignore, however, the other side of Rilke's attitude toward the military. It had a certain romantic glamor for him, at least when seen at a safe distance, transported, for example, into another century. Of all of Rilke's works, the one which established his fame was *Cornet*.[2] This tale in rhythmic prose is a sensitive and sympathetic, even glorifying, treatment of the life and death of a young soldier. Written in 1899, reworked in Sweden in 1904, and first published that year, it served as the first volume of the new Insel-Bücherei in 1912.[3] In the 1660s a soldier is riding to the front to join his regiment. After many days he arrives at the place where armies from all over Europe are rallying to fight the Turks. There the general honors him by promoting him to the rank of cornet, the flagbearer. That night a ball and banquet are held at the castle; the Cornet meets and falls in love with the lady of the castle and finds his love returned. The next morning the enemy attacks suddenly, the Cornet leaps from his lady's side, and, grasping the flag, plunges into battle, where he is killed by a horde of Turks.

The principal source for Rilke's tale was a document that his Uncle Jaroslav had found during his research into the family history. The paper concerned an inheritance of land by one Otto Rülke after the latter's brother Christoph is reported dead in battle. Despite his feelings about military school, Rilke's imagination must have been fired by the discovery of an ancestor killed in a famous battle. It has also been suggested that his interest in the genre of the epic poem or heroic tale stemmed in part from his reading of such works in Russian during and after his first visit.[4] It is certainly true that Rilke knew the old Russian heroic songs and folk tales. We shall see that they found their way into *Das Buch der Bilder* and *Geschichten,* which were written about the time Rilke was first working on *Cornet.*

In any case, Rilke was attracted by this sparse reference to the fate of young Christoph Rilke and succeeded in endowing his simple story with flesh and color, portraying it in lyrical language and with great emotional appeal. Various scenes portray stages of his long ride: the monotony of the road and countryside, the friendships that grew among the soldiers thrown together by circumstance, the horrors of war. One scene at the campfire shows how, despite their differing nationalities, ages, and natures, the soldiers are united and tamed by thoughts of their mothers. Christoph is twice exposed to sexuality in a threatening, brutal form: when he rescues a girl found tied to a tree, and when soldiers and camp followers grapple on top of the huge military drums. It is significant that only in the clean, civilized, and graceful world of the castle does he succumb to the enticements of love.

The poem begins, "Reiten, reiten, reiten, durch den Tag, durch die Nacht, durch den Tag. Reiten, reiten, reiten. Und der Mut ist so müde geworden, und die Sehnsucht so gross"[5] (Riding, riding, riding, through the night, through the day, through the night. Riding, riding, riding. And courage has become so tired, and yearning so great). The monotony of the ride is there, but so are its subtly changing rhythms. The noisy brutality of the baggage train emerges in the compactness of the description, the many sentences without subjects, and the violent verbs: *blendet, raufen, rufen, packen, zerreissen, drücken* (dazzles, scuffle, call, grab, tear, press [15]). Rilke also makes use of vivid neologisms in similes like "Kommen Knechte, schwarzeisern wie wandernde Nacht" (there come servants, blackiron like a wandering night [15]).

The festivities at the castle contrast strongly with the discomfort and the subconscious feeling of danger of the previous days. The sounds of the banquet are portrayed through onomatopoetic combinations such as "die Stimmen schwirrten, wirre Lieder klirrten aus Glas und Glanz" (The voices buzzed, confused songs clinked from glass and glitter [22]). The effect is much more marked in German, with the repeated *r* sounds and high vowels. Objects are personified deftly in passing; cottages squat thirstily by a marshy spring, the regimental flag dreams uneasily, and in the morning the windows of the burning castle "shout, red, into the midst of the enemy"(30). When the Cornet, after his longed-for night of love, rides into the midst of the Turks, his reckless and joyful perception of death is reflected in the imagery: "die sechzehn runden Säbel, die auf ihn zuspringen, Strahl um Strahl, sind ein Fest. Eine lachende Wasserkunst" (The sixteen curved sabres that leap toward him, ray upon ray, are a festival. A laughing fountain [33]).

This prose poem, delicate and sensuous, was for long Rilke's most widely read work—to his displeasure in later years. Immensely popular during World War I, it was carried to the front by young German soldiers in their rucksacks. At one point during the war, an Austrian government official asked Rilke whether he would do an updated version, with the Cornet as a fighter pilot. Rilke had a hard time convincing him to drop the idea. As he wrote to Princess Marie about the "flying Cornet," "not even God can do such transpositions; when he decided to make a flying dog, it turned out a sadly exaggerated bat."[6]

In September 1914, a few weeks after the war had begun, Rilke wrote a short sketch about life at St. Pölten entitled "Erinnerung" (Memory). It was apparently called forth by the combination of the war and Rilke's visits, during that time, to Wilhelm Schenk von Stauffenberg, his Munich physician. The doctor was trying to use psychoanalytical methods to reach to the root of the poet's illness. It was natural that precisely this epoch in his life should surface under these methods. But what is as least as significant is that in "Erinnerung" Rilke reaches a decision to which he would ever after adhere, namely, that a true course of psychoanalysis would be disastrous for him as a writer. In the sketch he admits that he can imagine some people being relieved "if one produced in them a kind of spiritual nausea and made it possible for them to get rid of the unusable or misunderstood bits of childhood in chunks" (*SW*, 6:1079). But for himself, he feels it his task and fate to use precisely those unlivable, premature, frightening aspects of his childhood, "to create angels, beasts, if it must be, then monsters" (*SW*, 6:1079).

In Rilke's prose, children and childhood form one of the central sets of images. Often the children are orphans, or are abused or neglected by their parents. These can be seen as a projection of Rilke's feelings about his own childhood, for although not literally orphaned, he was often treated by his mother as a sort of amusing toy to be shown off to guests and then left to his own devices. And when his parents separated in 1884, he was sent to live with various relatives until being sent off to boarding school in 1886.

Eventually, childhood and a childlike quality came to have positive connotations for Rilke. He applied these criteria to all sorts of subjects. To be considered childlike (unspoiled, naive, spontaneous, simple, open) was a good thing, whereas to be called grown-up was not. One scholar suggests that he even applied these criteria to entire nations and cultures.[7] Those he judged childlike in his terms—Russia, Denmark, Sweden, the Czechs, and even the French (in the sense that he considered the latter spontaneous and emotionally honest)— were the countries he loved most. The ones he considered grown-up—Germany, England, and the United States— he disdained or avoided. They embodied negative values: efficiency, mechanical expertise, an aggressive go-getter mentality. These peoples were best at things military, industrial, and financial, achievements to which Rilke attached no importance.

The positive nature of childhood is expressed in other ways. In "Die Letzten," a young man has consciously distanced himself from his past and his mother by his involvement in political agitation. But during a serious illness he reevaluates his motives and actions, and retreats totally from the social world into one of aesthetics. Childhood appears to him as a symbol of that ideal world. He declares, "Childhood is a country, independent of everything. The only land where there are kings. Why go into exile? Why not get older and more mature in this land? . . . Why get accustomed to what *others* believe?" (*SW*, 4:276). In the story "Im Gespräch" the practical world is again compared to other possible worlds. The preferred one is a place where art and beauty are never complete, but always in the process of creation. It is a life both active and aesthetic, and again childhood functions as its symbol. "Art is childhood. . . . Art means not knowing that the world already exists, and making one. Not to destroy what you find, but simply not to find anything finished. Nothing but possibilities. Nothing but wishes" (*SW*, 4:229).

Like a child for whom the whole world is new and full of endless surprises, the artist in Rilke's view is one who is constantly discovering and creating in naive joy. His task is never over, so long as he goes on creating, just as a child, so long as he is allowed to remain a child, lives in a world of infinite newness. When a child is forced by adults to learn their ways and think and act as they do, he soon leaves the world of childhood and becomes someone different. In Rilke's eyes, growing up is a process of loss. When an artist begins to think as others do, to value applause, to heed criticism, to follow fashion, or to aim not at the process of creativity for its own sake but at finished products, he undergoes a process of loss similar to that of the child forced out of childhood.

Rilke also emphasizes the relations between children and parents. *Ewald Tragy* most clearly addresses the problem of a son and his father whose views are incompatible. It also points out the emotional threads that must be broken if the younger person is to free himself. Generational differences are sometimes portrayed through characters who are not literally father and son, as in the conversation between a young, eager clerk and an older, jaded, and conservative one in "Im Leben" (*SW*, 4:568–74). More often stories focus on sons and mothers. Mothers fall into two basic, related categories that reflect Rilke's deep ambivalence. One type is the loving, caring mother whose universe revolves around the happiness of her son and who is prepared to make whatever sacrifices are required for his sake. In "Pierre Dumont" the mother has a "pale, good face and lifeless, bleak eyes" (*SW*, 1:407). She concerns herself with the details of his daily life, is saddened that the customs of military school have reduced him to a cipher, "No. 20," worries about his studies, and tells him not to catch cold. She indulges his gluttonous desires on his last day of vacation and seems willing to meet his every wish. This is a gently humorous, rather traditional portrayal of mother as mother hen. But she is shown in a fully positive light. The mother in "Die goldene Kiste" (The golden box [*SW*, 4:426–32]), like Pierre's mother a widow, but unlike her living on the edge of poverty, works day and night to provide for her little son, only to have him die suddenly of a fever. The mothers of the soldiers in *Cornet* are elevated to an almost mythic level. There the youths listen respectfully as a German soldier speaks of his mother, and are brought together by his tale, for "what one relates, they have all experienced, and in just the same way. As if there were only one mother" (10).

The other type is not so much the opposite of this one as its intensification to an extreme. The mother of Harald, the political agitator in "Die Letzten," loves her son. But her love takes the form of a "stubborn battle operating with all kinds of sentimentality, in order to bring him back to the dependence of a child."[8] She resents his political life, which pointedly excludes her, and she rejoices when he rejects that life and the girl who was his partner in it, for a return to home and roots. That there are dangers in this retreat is shown by the denouement. Harald and his mother have been discussing Walpurga, the legendary "white lady" of their hereditary castle, who was killed by her jealous husband and who is said to appear just before a member of the family is to die. Indulging a wish of Harald's expressed in his delirium, the mother appears before him in her white wedding dress. Harald screams, thinking it is Walpurga come to announce his imminent death. The beauty of the rejuvenated mother, the beauty of their closeness and of his dreams of becoming an artist, congeal at the end into ugliness and terror.

In "Einig" (United), as in "Die Letzten," a son returns to his mother ill and embittered. He had left years before in order to free himself from the slavery of her love and oppressive piety. Now, suffering from a serious heart defect, he has come home to die, but first he wishes to have it out with his mother. With heavy irony he says, "I love all the paths on which you led me, those quiet, noiseless paths around the edge of life, to your god. . . . What is piety? . . . Love that has lost its way and searches and gropes in boundless space. And a yearning which folds its hands instead of spreading its wings" (*SW,* 4:91). In the young man's disgust at how his youth was squandered, we recognize Rilke's horror at the insidious influence of his mother. It is significant that Rilke's son-protagonists return to their mothers in a state of illness and defeat, though they do not always recognize this fact. They have rebelled and tried to lead a life of their own, but find themselves helplessly bound to the claustrophobic world of their mothers. Rilke often referred to Sophia in terms of anger and despair. Writing to Lou in 1904 about an impending, dreaded visit from her, he says "Every meeting with her is a kind of regression. . . . When I have to see this lost, unreal woman, connected with nothing, who cannot grow old, I feel how even as a child I strove to get away from her, and I fear deep within me that even after years and years of running . . . I am still not far enough away from her. . . . And that I am yet her child; that some time or other a barely perceptible secret door in that faded wall that belongs to nothing was my entrance into the world."[9]

It can be seen that many topics in Rilke's works are presented from more than one angle. He detested the contemporary military world, but glorified bravery in battle. He presented mothers who are saintlike and others who are selfish and destructive. Childhood is a time of joy and innocence, but it can also be one of deprivation and despair, made so by unfeeling adults. This sense of balanced opposites is typical of Rilke, who carefully juxtaposes different views of each question, not usually in the same work, but in complementary works that reflect and illuminate one another; at times he even gives multiple possibilities.

The single most important prose work next to *Malte Laurids Brigge* is the collection of stories entitled *Vom lieben Gott und Anderes,* republished in 1904 as *Geschichten vom lieben Gott.* It was subtitled "An Grosse für Kinder erzählt" (Told to grownups, for children). Children play an important role both in the stories themselves and in the narrative frame.[10] Rilke relates that they were written in seven nights in November 1899. This was just after his first journey to Russia and the stories are permeated with impressions of Russian literature, history, and folklore. It is here, and in the poetic cycle *Das Buch der Bilder,* that the most Russian references and influences are to be found. I shall return to this subject later.

The collection consists of thirteen stories told by an unnamed first-person narrator to a variety of listeners. These include people from the mundane world of the town: a teacher, a neighbor, an official, a member of an artists' association. Each of these is to a certain extent satirized as the representative of a traditional, unreflected, trite, or self-satisfied point of view. The most important frame listener is Ewald, a lame man who sits at his window and watches the world go by. Four of the thirteen stories are told to him, and Rilke endows him with many positive characteristics: patience, curiosity, sensitivity, the art of watching, and a childlike simplicity. The narrative frame is complicated by the fact that all the listeners are intended only as go-betweens; for as the original subtitle indicated, the stories are meant for children. They are only told to grownups in order to be passed on to the town's children as the occasion arises. The narrator himself never meets the children, although he does write them a letter explaining why he cannot come to them directly. "Who knows if you would like me. I don't have a very nice nose," and, he goes on, sometimes it has a pimple on it, and they might be distracted from his story (*SW*, 4:296). He suggests instead that he will tell stories to the adults, who will in any case tell them better than he can.

Having thus set up his frame, Rilke proceeds to have his narrator tell tales to the various listeners. This does not happen without comment, as the adults object to things in the stories and argue with the narrator. Sometimes the children's reactions, always more straightforward than those of the adults, make their way back to the narrator. There is also a certain amount of tension between the narrator and the various members of his audience. Frequently the stories arise out of a situation or event within the frame. Sometimes a character in the frame refers back to a previous story, or asks for one about a particular topic (this happens several times with Ewald). Thus the fiction of a series of conversations among adults is preserved.

A word should be said about the implications of the title: *Geschichten vom lieben Gott*. The phrase "der liebe Gott," literally "dear God," is used mainly by children and simple people. In German it has a certain familiar, affectionate tone; this quality is lost in the English translation of the title as "Stories about God." In his letter to the children the narrator promises that, since he knows how interested they are in God, he will try, whenever possible, to include something about him in the stories; this then takes place on several levels. The listeners discuss, and react to, the presence or absence of God in various tales. The pompous teacher disapproves of the narrator's apparently flippant use of biblical texts. Once the children complain that God was missing from a tale. On another level the stories are "about God" in that Rilke, through a multitude of possible images, suggests a theology of creativity, in which God emerges as both artist and work of art.

These images of God change from one tale to the next, moving from a humorous, anthropomorphic figure to an ever-more distant and abstract one, until in the last story he no longer exists at all, but is only an idea and a promise. These gradually retreating images are held together mainly by the motifs of art and creativity. These are in turn interwoven with others that we have encountered elsewhere and that will reappear in later works: poverty, faith, humility, childhood. Let us look at how Rilke develops his images of God.

In the first three tales of the cycle God is portrayed as fallible and rather human. Most importantly, he is shown as an artist. In the first story, "Das Märchen von den Händen Gottes" (Fairy tale about God's hands), he is seen in the act of creating man. Things are not going too well; he is having trouble making the nostrils symmetrical. God's left hand accidentally drops the just-completed man to earth, before God has a chance to see what he looks like. In the second tale, "Der fremde Mann" (The stranger), God is angry and frustrated. He cuts off his own right hand and sends it to earth to take on human form, so he can see what he has created. This irascible and impatient deity is saved only at the last minute from bleeding to death. The third tale focuses on a modern apartment house; the higher up one climbs, the poorer are the inhabitants and the less they are wearing. Poverty and nakedness are developed into a positive symbol for authenticity, simplicity, and even "the Absolute," in the terms of one critic.[11] The less people are hidden by mere externals, so goes the reasoning, the closer they come to the purity in which God created them and the more the Absolute can shine through appearances. That most people do not understand or desire this state is shown by the final twist of the tale. An artist is commissioned to make a statue of the truth, but when he presents the finished figure—unclothed, as befits the truth—the "city fathers, teachers, and other influential personages" (*SW*, 4:307) demand that it be clothed before it is set before the public. And once again, as a side effect in Rilke's parable, God is prevented from seeing what man looks like.

The second set of three stories is set in ancient Russia; it is here, more overtly than anywhere, that Rilke's fascination with Russia emerges. He had studied the culture in some detail before visiting Moscow and St. Petersburg in 1899 with Lou and her husband. The stories reflect both his acquired knowledge of, and his attitude toward, Russia. Rilke went to Russia already prejudiced in its favor, partly because of his deep attraction to its literature and art, partly due to Lou's contagious enthusiasm. It is safe to say that he went seeking confirmation of his ideas and that he found it. His Russia was a vast, peaceful land peopled by religious peasants. Its history was long and slow-moving, and he saw as its main virtues the patience of its people and their childlike, unfinished nature. He foresaw a great, profound future for this country. This conviction is frequently couched in almost metaphysical language, in terms of "destiny" and "becoming." The Russians were equated, in his mental hierarchy, with children; they were positive, helpful, and unspoiled figures. In addition to the peasants Rilke was fascinated by the rites and trappings of the Russian Orthodox church and by Russia's history with its pomp, violence, and tragedy.

Among the sources for Rilke's impressions were historical songs and *byliny*.[12] Such traditional folkloric material forms the basis for all three of the "Russian" tales. In the first, "Wie der Verrat nach Russland kam" (How treachery came to Russia), God is portrayed as a peasant building a church in the steppe. He provides Czar Ivan with the answers to three riddles upon which the fate of his empire rests. But Ivan, after successfully defending his throne, cheats the old man of his promised reward. The peasant chastises him for bringing dishonesty into Russia and disappears, to the consternation of the Czar's messenger, who declares that "the supposed peasant was . . . God himself" (*SW*, 4:315).

The second Russian tale, "Wie der alte Timofei singend starb" (How old Timofei died singing), is based on Rilke's knowledge of the peasant tradition of *kobzars*,[13] village singers in the Ukraine who knew by heart all the songs of their people, and passed them on to the next generation. This tradition he combines with material from one of the byliny about a hero named Dyuk Stepanovitch. In Rilke's story, Yegor, son of one such singer, marries and leaves home instead of staying in the village to become heir to his father's songs and the responsibility that goes with them. The old man, Timofei, is so saddened by this that he stops singing, and village life becomes bleak without his songs. Yegor, hearing of these developments, leaves his wife and returns home to learn the songs and become the next bard. Timofei dies happily, singing his favorite song. Here Rilke juxtaposes two of his central themes: a son who leaves home, rejecting his parents' way of life and his own responsibility, and the confrontation of life and art, in an either-or situation. Yegor can choose his wife and child, or his art (in the role of a singer). Typically, Rilke makes him opt for art, even though it means personal sacrifice. God does not appear in the tale by name, which leads to a discussion between the narrator and Ewald. Ewald, in his simple faith, declares that it is never too late for God to enter a story, and implies that he in fact was present in Timofei, the pious musician and faithful bearer of tradition.

In the third tale, "Das Lied von der Gerechtigkeit" (The song of justice), Rilke combines his sometimes shaky knowledge of Russian sixteenth-century history with the kobzar tradition to create in a small space a story that is saturated with Rilkean and Russian motifs. We find here a son who is unable to fulfill the expectations of his father, an icon painter, and who tries in various ways to leave the village and find a niche for himself. He finally succeeds thanks to the appearance of an old bard who is walking through the country-side, urging the villagers by means of his "song of justice" to take up arms and join the Cossacks in their war against oppression. The young man slips away to join the fight. Again it is Ewald who declares, "It's like in the story about treachery. This old man was God" (SW, 4:337).

As the cycle progresses, God generally becomes less human and more abstract. In the seventh story, set in the Venice ghetto during the Renaissance, he is equated with the distant sea. In the eighth, set in Florence, he is the creative force within the stones under Michelangelo's hands, and within Michelangelo himself. Thus he becomes progressively less tangible and more of a force, a direction, or a goal. In the ninth tale Rilke's gentle humor shows through again. It is told to a group of passing clouds, who mistake the narrator for one of themselves. He tells of a group of children who express their concern for the state of the world under adult control. Among other things the adults neglect their duties; that is, telling bedtime stories. Worst of all, they do not pay any attention to God, and the children fear that the important things in life—bread, babies, the sunrise—will cease to exist if something is not done. They decide it is up to them to make sure God gets his due, and choose a small silver thimble to "be" God; they will take turns caring for it each day. Here God has lost all human form; and the radical idea is proposed that any object at all can be (or contain or represent) divinity.

It is significant that Rilke allows a group of children to arrive at this idea. It is also important to note that what they propose is not pantheism, in which divinity is present in every object. Here the emphasis is on singularity. The thimble is chosen "because of its beauty" (SW, 4:355), and the children emphasize that "anything can be God. You just have to tell it; (SW, 4:355). That is, divinity is potential in all things, but one makes God by an act of choice and by verbalizing that choice. Whereas in the earlier stories God appeared as a creator, by the ninth story the idea of God as creation is taking shape.

Not God but death is the focus of the tenth tale, a parable about the futility of excluding death from our daily lives. Here Rilke illustrates an idea that was growing in importance for him at this time—that of the naturalness and intrinsic rightness of death, which should, together with life, form a whole. In this tale God appears only in the frame, as the narrator tells a gravedigger how God was once frightened away by all the folded, praying hands and pointed church steeples that had sprung up on earth. God escapes through the back door of Heaven and rediscovers the warm darkness and roots under the earth. The image of a dark god whose realm is within the earth and within us is one Rilke develops elsewhere, particularly in the *Das Stunden-Buch*. He posits this image in contrast to the traditional God of light, of reason, and of showy outward display, emphasizing instead a humble, personal, and internal relationship. In part Rilke's dark divinity arises from his interpretation of the Russian peasant's relationship with his God and from the smoke-darkened icons of the Orthodox religion. (Rilke's extensive thoughts on the significance of icons can be found in his essays "Russische Kunst" [Russian Art] from 1901 and "Moderne Russische Kunstbestrebungen" [Modern Russian artistic endeavors] of 1902; both are in *SW*, vol. 5.)

In the eleventh tale, "Ein Verein, aus einem dringenden Bedürfnis heraus" (An association out of urgent need), and in its frame, Rilke makes fun of the institution of "Vereine"—organizations and clubs of all sorts formed to bring together people of similar interests and to bring order into their activities. This is a custom that seems to survive particularly well in German-speaking cultures. "The whole of my activity for the past five years," says the narrator in dismay, has been resigning from organizations. "And yet there are still associations which, so to speak, contain me." (*SW*, 4:368). In the tale proper this kind of artificial and somewhat oppressive togetherness is contrasted to three painters who have come together out of a genuine sense of common purpose. However, as the three develop their own individual styles and ways of seeing, they grow apart. The last we see of them, all three have set up their easels at the edge of the earth and are engaged in painting God, the ultimate work of art.

The twelfth story deals with a proud young man who learns true humility and becomes a beggar and eventually a saint. God is present by implication in the impulses of a virtuous man. Finally, in the last story, "Eine Geschichte, dem Dunkel erzählt" (A story told to the darkness), the characters discuss their conceptions of God. Klara says that for her, God existed once—she sees traces of him in paintings, statues, bells—and he will be again some day. Thus, by the end of Rilke's cycle, God has become an idea and a promise. Rilke combines in this final image the unifying force we sense in beautiful objects and the dynamic that leads us to create new ones (in this case, Klara's child and the paintings of her husband, Angelo).

Rilke's stories about God cannot, as has been the tendency, be considered Christian or even basically religious in any traditional sense. The protean divinity he is concerned with is transformed gradually from artist to artistic product to a state of mind. Rilke is mainly interested in creativity, for which his seemingly ingenuous little stories are but one attempt at finding an adequate metaphor. The transformations of God are, as we have seen, intimately connected with questions of art, beauty, and creativity. The stories are peopled by painters, sculptors, and musicians; they are also permeated by children, peasants, and simple people like Ewald. All of these factors combine in the stories to constitute, not religious parables, but experiments in prose, full of thematic tensions, that lead toward a religion of art.

Chapter Four
Das Stunden-Buch and
Das Buch der Bilder

Rilke rarely worked on just one project at a time. Thus in the fall of 1899, back in Berlin after his first trip to Russia, we find him producing simultaneously works in a number of genres. Between 20 September and 14 October he wrote the poems that were to become the first part of *Das Stunden-Buch* (*The Book of Hours; SW,* 1:249–366). In one night during this same period he wrote the first version of *Cornet,* on November 3 the first version of "Die Turnstunde," and on 8–9 November a grotesque short story set in Prague, entitled "Frau Blahas Magd" (Mrs. Blaha's maid). Between 10 and 21 November came the stories *Vom lieben Gott und Anderes,* the first version of *Geschichten.* In January 1900 he produced the essay "Russische Kunst" (Russian art). During the same time he was writing individual poems which would eventually be included in *Das Buch der Bilder* (*The Book of Images*).

It is not surprising that the subjects and attitudes central to one work turn up in other, contemporaneous ones. In its form and imagery, *The Book of Hours* is a poetic counterpart to *Geschichten,* but it is far more than that. Written over a space of more than four years, it catalogs the shifts and developments in Rilke's interests. It also represents a transition from the sentimental, decorative style of much of his early verse to the sparer and more convincing style of his mature poems. In later years, when Rilke was sternly critical of his early works, calling them imprecise and immature, he always made an exception for *The Book of Hours.*

Rilke called the first part of *The Book of Hours* "Die Gebete" (The prayers). He did not envision either adding to it, or publishing it. The poems, which "came to him" as if from outside himself, are permeated by the Russian experience as well as by the poet's interest in the art of the Italian Renaissance. Rilke sent a copy of the manuscript to Lou, who was at that time still his closest friend and confidante. In eight days during September 1901 a set of poems related to the "prayers" came to Rilke at Westerwede. This was after the second trip to Russia, after his marriage to Clara, and during a period when he was estranged from Lou. These poems were to become the second part of *The Book of Hours* under the title "Das Buch von der Pilgerschaft" (The book of pilgrimage). Then came the birth of Ruth, the first separation from his family, Paris, Rodin: hard years for Rilke. The spring of 1903 found him in Viareggio trying to regain his health after his initial Parisian experiences. Here, again in eight nights, Rilke wrote down the third part of *The Book of Hours*, "Das Buch von der Armut und vom Tode" (The book of poverty and death). He cut and revised the "prayers" extensively, and the three books were published together at Christmas 1905.

In *The Book of Hours*, as in *Geschichten*, Rilke confronts the interrelated problems of the nature of creativity and of God. We find here, particularly in the first part, a series of transformations similar to those that God underwent in the stories. In addition, a new emphasis is given to poverty, loneliness, and death—subjects that were present, certainly, in the earlier poems and stories, but that take on firmer contours and become more centrally related to the other motifs, as Rilke's life takes on more somber colors.

In its original form, the first part was considerably longer and accompanied by a prose commentary in the form of a diary, written by the lyric "I" of the poems, a monk named Apostol. The ultimate title, the "Stunden-Buch," reflects the persona of the monk and the original prayer format. A book of hours or *livre d'heures* was usually a small volume (although some were large and lavishly illustrated) carried during the Middle Ages by both clergy and laymen. It contained prayers and meditations for each hour of the day. In addition to prayers, the monk's utterances take the form of meditations, laments, and dramatic dialogues with God, with himself, and with other characters. He begins with an ecstatic outburst as he feels the surging of his creative powers. "Mir zittern die Sinne. Ich fühle: ich kann—und ich fasse den plastischen Tag" (My senses quiver. I feel: I can do it, and I grasp the malleable day[253]). He feels himself as incomplete and full of potential as his subject.

> Ich kreise um Gott, um den uralten Turm
> und ich kreise jahrtausendelang;

und ich weiss noch nicht: bin ich ein Falke, ein Sturm,
oder ein grosser Gesang.

(253)

I circle around God, around the ancient tower, and I've been circling for
thousands of years. And I don't yet know if I'm a falcon, a storm, or a
great song.

Apostol, nameless in the later version, is an icon painter. In the
Russian Orthodox church, monks were instructed in the strict traditions of icon painting and were expected to reproduce accurate
copies of existing icons for distribution in churches and monasteries
and among the people. The icon painter was usually anonymous,
much as were the builders and decorators of Gothic cathedrals in
the West. He was a humble servant of the Lord and was not expected
or allowed to instill his own ideas or visions into his work. But
Rilke's monk is beset by grave temptations. He knows something
about the art of Renaissance Italy and is fascinated and repelled in
turn by Western conceptions of art, particularly religious art, and
of the role of the artist in the creative process. The monk ponders
the differences between his artistic tradition and that of the West.
He thinks of his fellow monks, "Brüder in Sutanen" (brothers in
cassocks [254]) who paint brilliant, fiery paintings in Italy, "im
Süden, wo in Klöstern Lorbeer steht" (in the South, where in clois-
ters laurel stands [254]). There, artists express their personal visions
and achieve the "laurel" of personal glory. But Apostol's relation
to his subject and his work is different: "*Mein* Gott ist dunkel und
wie ein Gewebe / von hundert Wurzeln, welche schweigsam trin-
ken" (*My* God is dark, and like a fabric of a hundred roots that
drink silently [254]).

Both the 1899 "Gebete" and the 1905 version, "Das Buch vom
mönchischen Leben" (The book of monastic life), focus on contrasting views of art. The monk, representing Russian tradition, wishes
to remain anonymous in his schematic portrayals of an ineffable
God. The art of the West, represented by Titian, Michelangelo,
and others, is full of individual genius, rooted in life. "Ich weiss,
wie menschlich sie Madonnen planen" (I know how humanly they
plan madonnas [254]), the monk relates, half horrified at their
daring, half envious and attracted. In the earlier version, Apostol

deals stringently with his own wavering loyalty. In a letter to his spiritual father, he reveals his fears, reaffirms his resolve to follow the dictates of the church, and asks the Metropolitan to be strict with other icon painters. In the 1905 version, Rilke deleted the letter and in general softened the fanaticism of his character. In fact, the new Apostol is the bearer of Rilke's conception of God as multifaceted, a work of art in himself.

In a number of poems the monk lists the rules and expectations under which he must work, humbly, using the same colors and strokes to portray God as did the painters before him. From there he moves naturally to God himself, in his ever-expanding fantasies addressing him in a multitude of forms: as a neighbor in the next room, as the primal darkness, a cathedral, a dreamer, the law, a tree, a riddle, the earth itself. We see at work here the same impulse that infuses *Geschichten,* except that here there is a tension between the images of God and the self-perception of the poet-monk. If God is a dreamer, the monk will be his dream. If he is a neighbor, the monk knocks on the wall to be sure he is all right. The monk himself arose out of God's darkness; and in a poem that begins "Ich will dich immer spiegeln in ganzer Gestalt" (I want to mirror you always in your whole form [260]), he goes on, in the peculiar logic of the book, "Ich will *mich* entfalten" (*I* want to blossom; my italics).

The monk is one of the builders working at creating God, the cathedral. He refers repeatedly to the act of painting, and at the end of the first part he envisions himself becoming a meadow from which God will retrieve his long-lost songs. Thus the monk's role vis-a-vis God is one of artist, creator, and source. Apostol also makes it plain that this God whom he constantly addresses depends on him for his very existence.

> Was wirst du tun, Gott, wenn ich sterbe?
> Ich bin dein Krug (wenn ich zerscherbe?)
> Ich bin dein Trank (wenn ich verderbe?)
> Bin dein Gewand und dein Gewerbe,
> mit mir verlierst du deinen Sinn.
>
> (275)[1]

What will you do, God, if I die? I am your pitcher (if I shatter?) I am your drink (if I spoil?). Am your garment and your trade, with me you lose your meaning.

Rilke does not seek to diminish the figure of God, but rather to transform it. He reaffirms his conception that God is a work of art still in the process of becoming, a future reality. Without the human artist who is constantly adding to his creation, both the process and God would cease to exist, even potentially.

Two principles underlie the changing images in these poems: God is multifaceted and protean, and he is in the process of becoming. "Du bist der Wald der Widersprüche" (You are the forest of contradictions [283]), the monk tells him, and elsewhere he declares, "Auch wenn wir nicht wollen: *Gott reift*" (Even if we don't intend it: *God is ripening* [262]). In "Das Buch von der Pilgerschaft" we find some changes of tone and emphasis. The monk is alienated and uneasy; he addresses God more intensely but with less joy. He has evidently left his monastery and gone wandering, for he recounts his experiences among the pilgrims and focuses more on the woes of the human condition. The question of art has receded into the background, and there is more emphasis on the monk's relation with God, who still assumes many forms, but is now less concrete, colorful, and varied. He has, in a way, become both larger and more distant. The monk addresses him as "Erlauchter," "Ewiger," "grosser alter Herzog des Erhabenen" (illustrious, eternal, grand old duke of the sublime). He is also more obviously related to the forces of Nature. His presence is seen in storms, dawns, a river (based on Rilke's voyage on the Volga), and the dew.

The monk now vacillates in his attitude. He knows that God's very existence has been called into question, but this situation does not really disturb him, for his problem is not one of disbelief. As in *Geschichten*, the question is not whether God exists. Apostol is content to find proof of his existence in natural things:

> Tu mir kein Wunder zulieb.
> Gieb deinen Gesetzen recht,
> die von Geschlecht zu Geschlecht
> sichtbarer sind.
>
> (320)

Don't do any miracles for me. Let your laws prevail, which from generation to generation are more visible.

What does disturb the monk is his own relation to God. He is no

longer as secure in his stance as he was in part 1, where the emphasis
was on his role as artist. Now he vacillates between aggression and
humility. In one poem he declares anew his responsibility:

> Ich bin derselbe noch, der kniete
> vor dir in mönchischem Gewand:
> der tiefe, dienende Levite,
> den du erfüllt, der dich erfand.
>
> (307)

I am still the same one who knelt before you in monastic garb, the
profound, serving Levite, whom you fulfilled, who invented you.

In part 1 his concern had been for God's survival: "What will you
do, God, if I die?" Here the sense of his own importance in the
relationship becomes primary. He challenges God, demanding
recognition:

> Bist du denn Alles—ich der Eine,
> der sich ergiebt und sich empört?
> Bin ich denn nicht das Allgemeine,
> bin ich nicht *Alles*, wenn ich weine,
> und du der Eine, der es hört?
>
> (308)

Are you everything, and I the single one who submits and rebels? Am I
not the Universal, am I not everything, when I weep, and you the One
who hears it?

Rilke also returns to the subject of fathers and sons, and merges
the two central problems in a startling way. The monk reasons as
follows: I love God like a son. But do we really love our fathers?
Don't we rather disdain them, ignore their advice and experience,
leave them behind, outmoded and moribund? The idea that, as
God's son, he could behave this way frightens him:

> Das ist der Vater uns. Und ich—ich soll
> dich Vater nennen?
> Das hiesse tausendmal mich von dir trennen.
> Du bist mein Sohn.
>
> (312)

That's what the father means to us. And I—I should call you Father? That would mean separating myself from you a thousandfold. You are my son.

Rilke allows his monk to develop this reassuring idea. Of course the idea that the monk is father to God, his creation, fits with the central metaphor of part 1, in which God was the artistic product of the monk. If the monk is the father, then God the son will be the one to go forth, grow, survive, and inherit. In this strange twist, the monk tries to reassure himself that he will not abandon his God as he would have to were he caught in the role of son. He does not seem to consider that the new relationship has other consequences: that God, now defined as the son, must logically abandon *him*. Rather, he dwells on the inheritance that he will pass on to his "son":

> Du bist der Erbe.
> Söhne sind die Erben,
> denn Väter sterben.
> Söhne stehn und blühn.
> Du bist der Erbe.
>
> (314)

You are the heir. Sons are heirs, for fathers die. Sons stand and bloom. You are the heir.

We feel that, in his stubborn repetition, he is trying hard to convince himself.

Included in this inheritance are both the beautiful objects and moods of nature, and the creations of man. The monk describes some of them: Venice, Kazan, Rome, Florence, the cathedral at Pisa, the Trinity Monastery, Moscow, and the underground cave monastery at Kiev. All these represent a combination of art, architecture, and religious inspiration. In them, too, is reflected the East-West dichotomy of part 1, in their division into Russian and Italian monuments, joined here and made equal. Apostol concludes that they are all already God's by rights, for the actions and products of all creative people, whether poets, painters, or lovers, occur for his sake.

In a roundabout way we have arrived back at the idea of part 1, and also of *Geschichten:* that it is up to us to bring new things into the world. There, the creations added up to the idea of God; here, they are a sort of gift to God, who has been "invented" by the monk in the first place. Since leaving the monastery the monk has become more aware of the problems of mankind. It is true they appear here in rather abstract form, deprived of realistic details. But they nevertheless form an important part of his current worries, and he tries in various ways to convey to God what it is like to be human. (There is, perhaps, an echo here of the motif of God's attempts to discover the nature of his wayward creation.) The monk tells of the people he has seen or known, the errors men fall into. People do not really live their lives, but exist behind masks, made inauthentic already in childhood. They suffer from nightmares of imprisonment and darkness, with madness serving as night watchman. Or they voluntarily immure themselves, like the monks in the underground monastery in Kiev,[2] or the nuns who "bleiben in der Häuser Schweigen / wie in der kranken Brust der Geigen / die Melodie, die keiner kann" (remain in the silence of their houses, as the melody that no one knows remains in the suffering breast of the violin [328]).

Sometimes people arise suddenly and take to the road, to follow some dark instinctual call. The monk has seen pilgrims of all kinds, simple and calm, or searching desperately. He tells of a possessed monk at an encampment who has a seizure in front of the hospice. His body is bent, thrown about, made to dance and almost to fly, but none of this attracts the attention of God, his intended audience. He becomes a fish, a bird, a marionette, an executioner's sword, in the grip of his seizure, but only when he strips off his ragged cloak and kneels in total submission does God notice him (334–37). The key to his release and acceptance is humility, a quality that is echoed in poems throughout this section of *The Book of Hours.* The monk compares his soul to Ruth, the humble woman of the Bible. What men must learn, according to this teaching, is *"fallen /* geduldig in der Schwere ruhn" (to *fall,* to rest in gravity, patiently [321]). We have met the idea of falling, the downward thrust, as a positive thing in *Geschichten,* where God returns to mankind by way of the earth. We shall meet it again as a crucial image in the last *Duino Elegy.*

But of himself the narrator says:

Ich war zerstreut; an Widersacher
in Stücken war verteilt mein Ich. . . .
Wie hob ich meine halben Hände
zu dir in namenlosem Flehn,
dass ich die Augen wiederfände,
mit denen ich dich angesehn.

(306)

I was distracted; my self was dispersed among adversaries. How I raised my half hands to you in nameless supplication, that I might find again the eyes with which I had gazed at you.

Herein lies a clue to what has happened to the monk in the years since he first addressed God. He has lost his eyes, that is, the all-important power of observation, of sensual contact and comprehension, the mainstay of his identity as painter and poet. His hands are only "half hands," that is, he is unable to work and produce.

Significantly, the monk says that he is now recovering; "Jetzt bin ich wieder aufgebaut / aus allen Stücken meiner Schande" (Now I am reconstructed again out of all the fragments of my shame [307]), and offers himself for God's use. But in the pages that follow we find precisely that ambivalence and vacillation mentioned above; the spiritual convalescence is perhaps not as far along as he would like us to believe. This book is a book of pilgrimage in several ways. There are the pilgrims he has met who have shed their former lives and taken to the road in search of a community of the spirit; there are those whose wanderings are halting and fearful, who "mit dem Schritt von Blinden / das Dunkel treten" (tread the darkness with the steps of blind men [310]). And there is his own pilgrimage which is not yet over. His path will, in fact, lead him into ever darker places before he reaches the end.

It is useful to recall certain events from Rilke's life during the time he was working on the first two books of *The Book of Hours*. These include his estrangement from Lou, a serious illness in early 1901, his loss of Paula, and his despair at having no way to support a wife and child. The turmoil of these years is also evident in many works contemporaneous with *The Book of Hours*;[3] they are peopled with orphans, suicides, the incurably ill, and men who leave or forget their women. It would be naive simply to equate biographical and literary data. But the concatenation of distractions, losses, and

dead ends would seem to be ultimately indivisible from the mood
and obsessions of Rilke's works during this period.

The third part of *The Book of Hours*, "Das Buch von der Armut
und vom Tode," focuses primarily on the human world. Like Rilke
in 1902, Apostol has found his way to a large modern city; the
shock waves from this encounter inform the poems of this section.
The first fourteen deal mainly with death, while the remainder
portray poverty in various forms. The section begins with hard,
claustrophobic images. The monk feels as if he were trapped within
a mountain, like a vein of ore. He begs to be allowed to serve in
some other capacity, in empty lands and wide expanses of nature—
an echo of the Russian steppes and the windswept fields of
Worpswede. But Apostol realizes he is required to suffer and serve
in the gloomy cities. His main complaint against them is their
alienating and destructive effect on the inhabitants, whose smiles
are distorted to grimaces and whose work is pointless and humili-
ating. Typically, he focuses on children. People live, unaware that

> Da wachsen Kinder auf an Fensterstufen,
> die immer in demselben Schatten sind,
> und wissen nicht, dass draussen Blumen rufen
> zu einem Tag voll Weite, Glück und Wind,—
> und müssen Kind sein und sind traurig Kind.
>
> (345)

Children grow up by windowsills that are always in the same shadow, and
don't know that out there, flowers call to a day full of breadth, happiness,
and wind, and they have to be children, and do it sadly.

Rilke concentrates on two other aspects of life in the city: the
lack of a proper relation to death, and the perversion of the concepts
of wealth and poverty. I have already noted Rilke's obsession with
the idea of death as a personal and unique event. In *Armut* he develops
this idea through a series of metaphors of gardens and childbirth.
Death is natural and innate, but also susceptible to a bad harvest
or a miscarriage. He points out the weak and sick in the city who
cluster around the hospitals, waiting to be admitted.

> Dort ist der Tod. Nicht jener, dessen Grüsse
> sie in der Kindheit wundersam gestreift,—

> der kleine Tod, wie man ihn dort begreift;
> ihr eigener hängt grün und ohne Süsse
> wie eine Frucht in ihnen, die nicht reift.
>
> (347)

Death is there. Not the one whose greetings touched them wondrously in childhood. The little death, as it is understood there; their own hangs green and without sweetness within them like a fruit that does not ripen.

The clearest statement of Rilke's views on this subject comes in the lines in which he urges God to provide each person with his own death:

> O Herr, gieb jedem seinen eignen Tod.
> Das Sterben, das aus jenem Leben geht,
> darin er Liebe hatte, Sinn und Not.
>
> Denn wir sind nur die Schale und das Blatt.
> Der grosse Tod, den jeder in sich hat,
> das ist die Frucht, um die sich alles dreht.
>
> (347)

Oh Lord, give to each his own death. The dying that emerges from the life in which he possessed love, meaning, and need. For we are but the husk and the leaf. The great death that each has within him—that is the fruit around which everything turns.

Rilke will become more specific about what he means in *Malte Laurids Brigge,* where we shall find examples of the "great" and "little" deaths. This and the surrounding lines, where he compares our purposeless and random death with the natural ways of animals, also prefigure *Duino Elegies.*

The concept of a personal death is related, of course, to that of a unique life, meaningful and self-aware. This, too, is lacking in a modern city. People are confused and demoralized by the noise, the dirt, the fast pace, and the diminution of air, space, and light. Even the winds, says the poet, are confused when they wander into a city:

> . . . Deiner Winde Wehen
> fällt in die Gassen, die es anders drehen,

ihr Rauschen wird im Hin- und wiedergehen
verwirrt, gereizt und aufgeregt.

(352)

The blowing of your winds falls into alleys which twist it in a different
way, their murmuring becomes confused in going back and forth, irritated
and edgy.

Contemplation of the effects of the city leads Rilke to his next
main point: the rich are no longer rich, nor the poor truly poor.
This section of *The Book of Hours* has caused heated controversy,
because here Rilke enters an area that tends to trigger emotional
responses, and he does so in nontraditional and ambiguous terms
that have misled a number of readers and brought him much hostility. His statements on the subject deserve a closer look. He opens
his discussion with the assertion, "Viele sind reich und wollen sich
erheben— / aber die Reichen *sind* nicht reich" (Many are rich and
want to rise, but the rich *aren't* rich [353]). To illustrate his point
he lists a number of people or types who *were* rich, as he conceives
of the term. Among them are nomadic chieftains whose herds provided warmth and milk, sheikhs who lived ascetically themselves,
but had their horses' currycombs set with rubies, merchants who
poured their wealth into collecting paintings. Rilke attempts to
unite these disparate figures in the summary: "Das waren Reiche,
die das Leben zwangen / unendlich weit zu sein und schwer und
warm" (355) (Those were rich men who forced life to be boundlessly
broad and heavy and warm). They were men whose riches were
transformed into beauty and generosity; the truly rich were those
who gave their wealth away—the philanthropic, whereas by implication those who call themselves rich today are merely acquisitive.
They possess much, but do not have the impulse to share it.

Likewise, the poet continues, the poor are not really poor any
longer: "sie sind nur die Nicht-reichen" (They are merely the not-
rich [355]). In the lines that follow, Rilke portrays the urban poor
who are despised, downtrodden, and discarded by society. They are
deprived of possessions, but not poor in Rilke's sense, which is a
metaphysical, not a social, one. This is summarized in a line that
has probably caused more furor than any other in Rilke's works:
"Denn Armut ist ein grosser Glanz aus Innen . . . " (For poverty
is a great glow from within [356]). The remainder of *The Book of*

Hours is taken up with an elucidation of this statement. First Rilke illustrates it with images of God as a poor, homeless man, a rolling stone, possessionless and pure. Then he presents a series of verses praising the virtues of the truly poor, who emerge as humble, quiet, useful, and good, rooted in nature, graceful and knowing, vulnerable and open.

> Denn selig sind, die niemals sich entfernten
> und still im Regen standen ohne Dach;
> zu ihnen werden kommen alle Ernten,
> und ihre Frucht wird voll sein tausendfach.
>
> (361)

For blessed are those who never went away, and stood still in the rain without a roof. To them will come all harvests, and their fruit shall be fulfilled a thousandfold.

It soon becomes clear that Rilke's vision of poverty is related to the values expressed in the Sermon on the Mount: "Blessed are the poor in spirit; for theirs is the kingdom of Heaven. . . . Blessed are the meek; for they shall inherit the earth."

An important distinction should be made, however. These and the verses that follow emphasize life in *this* world. They emphasize physical tenacity, and foresee actual fruitfulness and earthly joys, which are not meant as a promise of future reward or compensation for current suffering. Earlier in this section the poet called out for the birth of a "Tod-Gebärer;"—a "bearer of death" whose prophet he wishes to be. Rilke pointedly contrasts this figure to Christ:

> Erfülle, du gewaltiger Gewährer,
> nicht jenen Traum der Gottgebärerin—
> richt auf den Wichtigen: den Tod-Gebärer . . .
> und mich lass Tänzer dieser Bundeslade,
> lass mich den Mund der neuen Messiade,
> den Tönenden, den Täufer sein.
>
> (350–51)

Fulfill, you mighty guarantor, not that dream of the mother of God, but set up the important man: the death-bearer, and let me be a dancer for the ark of this covenant, let me be the mouth for the new Messiad, the sounding one, the Baptist.

Elsewhere Rilke asserts the ascendancy of this world over any promised afterlife; he does not deny the possibility of survival after death, but prefers to leave open all possibilities relating to the mystery of death. As Eudo Mason puts it, "If it came to that, . . . Rilke would prefer . . . death as an absolute extinction to immortality under Christian conditions."[4] In the poems detailing his vision of spiritual poverty, Rilke emphasizes that it is impossible as long as people continue to be trapped in cities, and asks whether there is no room in nature for these humble souls.

A major figure in *The Book of Hours* is St. Francis of Asissi, the saint whose fame rests on his poverty, humility, and love of all creatures. Rilke makes him into a kind of erotic nature spirit, impregnating the world with "seines Liedes Pollen" (the pollen of his song [365]). Like Orpheus he dies singing and rises into the sky as a signal of hope for the poor, "der Armut grosser Abendstern." (the great evening star of poverty [366]).

Rilke has been accused of political conservatism, of aestheticizing the plight of the poor, and even of "latent fascistic attitudes."[5] It is true that his way of dealing with social problems was not political, practical, or even particularly engaged. But we know from his works—from the *Wegwartten* and plays, the *Prague Stories, The Book of Hours* and *Malte Laurids Brigge*— and from his letters concerning such things as the war and the 1918 German revolution, that he was anything but unaware and indifferent. Nor was his experience of urban poverty purely theoretical. But the level on which he experienced these things and the approach that he took to them always related back to his personality and his main concerns, which were basically contemplative. He was concerned about people's self-consciousness and their awareness of their relations to the whole of human life within a larger context.

Unlike *The Book of Hours*, *The Book of Images* is not a self-contained cycle focusing on a circumscribed set of topics or united by a limited set of interrelated images. Thematically, it does not lead in a particular direction, but reflects the many subjects that occupied Rilke during a time of upheaval and change, from 1898 to 1906. The first edition appeared in 1902; but the greatly expanded second edition of 1906 is the one to which I shall refer here. *The Book of Images* is divided into two books, each of which in turn has two parts. The verses in *The Book of Hours* were published more or less in the order of their composition. In *The Book of Images* this is not the case; poems from 1899 to 1906 are interspersed throughout the four sections. Thus the poems are not ordered according to chronological principles.

Neither is there a strict division by subject matter. Book 1, part 1, contains poems about a variety of familiar Rilkean subjects: loneliness, silence, perception, childhood, and death. It is peopled by young girls, knights, saints, and martyrs. Equally melancholic in tone, book 1, part 2, has two main thematic strains. One set of poems emphasizes man's alienation from himself and the world. The other considers the nature of poetry and tentatively suggests it as a task for man. The motifs of book 2 are less obviously related and less coherently grouped, but the book contains some of the most interesting poems in *The Book of Images*. Part 1 raises questions about the past and emphasizes self-perception. There are a number of poems with religious content that foreshadow other works or mirror attitudes already noted. "In der Certosa" (In the Carthusian monastery) is a skillful psychological portrait. A young man is made to enter a monastery at the wishes of his father, but finds his whole being rebelling against his fate. His dissatisfaction with his lot is a variation in a different key of Apostol's, who did not resent being a monk, but had serious misgivings about what he was required to do as a painter. "Die heiligen drei Könige" (The three holy kings) is a strange, wry treatment of the Nativity. Mary is told by the angel to be nice to the wise men, since they have been on the road a long time—and who knows what may have happened to their kingdoms by now? The tone is light, almost flippant:

> Drei Könige von Unterwegs
> und der Stern überall,
> die zogen alle (überlegs!)
> so rechts ein Rex und links ein Rex
> zu einem stillen Stall.
>
> (411)

Three kings from Underway, and the star everywhere, they set forth (just think of it!) a king to the right and a king to the left, toward a silent stall.

Both poems were written in July 1899, a few months before the "Gebete," so different in tone.

Book 2, part 2, in addition to containing further poems based
on religious scenes, emphasizes death and perception, and presents
a series of portraits of failed lives. One long poem in part 2 reflects
Rilke's feelings about Christianity. "Das jüngste Gericht" (The Last
Judgment) presents a graphic vision of the day when the tombs
open and hordes of the dead emerge, screaming and scrabbling. The
poet, the angels, the saints, and God himself are aghast at the
prospect, which was not part of God's plan, but was forced on him
by his son. Here, as in the poem in *The Book of Hours* that called
for a "Tod-Gebärer," Rilke begs God to send "einen aus uns" (one
of us) to negate and make unnecessary this "fürchterlichen Wied-
erleben" (terrible reanimation [418]). The idea of physical resurrection is seen as unnatural and horrifying. Book 2 also contains a
number of poems on historical themes based on Rilke's reading of
Russian history and literature. These focus on figures from prehis-
tory, as portrayed in the byliny; members of the Rurik dynasty,
Ivan the Terrible, and his feeble-minded son Fyodor; and Charles
XII of Sweden, who was defeated by Peter the Great at the Battle
of Poltava.

Formally the poems in *The Book of Images* are quite varied, as
could be expected in a collection that spans nine years. Rilke was
experimenting with a variety of line lengths and rhyme schemes.
We still find a tendency to use internal rhymes. Sometimes the
language has the feel of prose, and a strophe may consist of a long,
convoluted sentence merely set in lines. Rilke also attempts long
narrative poems here, such as the "Jüngste Gericht" or the poem
about Charles XII. In book 2, he inserts small integral cycles of
poems into the larger, more amorphous text: in part 1, the six
poems entitled "Die Zaren" (The Czars), in part 2 the ten poems
called "Die Stimmen" (The voices) and the nine poems of "Aus
einer Sturmnacht" (From a stormy night). He even includes a dramatic sketch, "die Blinde" (The blind woman), as well as a poem
dedicated to Paula Becker and a requiem written for a friend of
Clara's. Thus we see that *The Book of Images* was a sort of catchall,
a place in which works in various genres and styles, with a variety
of moods and subjects, found a home.

There is, however, one level on which this work can be said to
form a whole and lose some of its accidental or occasional character.
The element that binds all four sections, if not all the poems in
them, is the emphasis on the visible world and the act of seeing.

The work is called, after all, the book of *images*. Book 1 opens with a poem to challenge the reader to look at the world and, by doing so, to participate in its creation. This is an echo of the concept of the artists who continually create God:

> Wer du auch seist: am Abend tritt hinaus
> aus deiner Stube, drin du alles weisst;
> . . . .
> Mit deinen Augen, welche müde kaum
> von der verbrauchten Schwelle sich befrein,
> hebst du ganz langsam einen schwarzen Baum
> und stellst ihn vor den Himmel: schlank, allein.
> Und hast die Welt gemacht. Und sie ist gross
> und wie ein wort, das noch im Schweigen reift.
>
> (371)

Whoever you are: at evening, step out of your room, in which you know everything. With your eyes, which, tired, can barely free themselves from the worn threshold, you slowly lift a black tree and place it before the sky: slender, alone. And you have made the world. And it is large, and like a word that ripens still in the silence.

Eyes and pictures appear in many poems. A small boy's "grosses Schauen" (great watching [386]) follows his mother's hands on the piano; the poet says to his guardian angel, "du bist das Bild, ich aber bin der Rahmen, / der dich ergänzt in glänzendem Relief" (You are the picture, but I am the frame that completes you in brilliant relief [381]).

A poem written in Paris in 1903, "Die Konfirmanden," shows traces of a new direction in which Rilke was moving. Closely observed physical reality is combined with equally closely perceived inner, psychological reality, to capture both the look of a Sunday in spring and the feelings of a group of youngsters who have just been confirmed and have entered the no man's land between childhood and adulthood. Here Rilke uses light, color, and texture in ways that show clearly his attraction to modern painting. In the church, the children are showered with song, like rain, and

> . . . wie im Wind bewegte sich ihr Weiss,
> und wurde leise bunt in seinen Falten
> und schien verborgne Blumen zu enthalten—:

Blumen und Vögel, Sterne und Gestalten
aus einem alten fernen Sagenkreis.

Und draussen war ein Tag aus Blau und Grün
mit einem Ruf von Rot an hellen Stellen. . . .
(387–88)

Their whiteness moved as if in a wind, and quietly became bright in its
folds, and seemed to contain hidden flowers—flowers and birds, stars and
figures from an old distant cycle of legends. And outside was a day of
blue and green with a shout of red at the bright spots.

The children's clothes are reduced to their whiteness, and within
this color many others are revealed, like isolated splashes on a canvas,
changing with the light, building up gradually toward meaning—
the figures from a legend. The day, too, is built up by the poet as
if by a painter, adding a color at a time, highlighting it with spots
of red.

Another aspect of the subject of vision and perception and another
facet of Rilke's development are shown in a series of four poems in
book 1, part 2. Written in several places and at different times,
they are placed together in *The Book of Images,* where they reveal a
subtle but telling relationship. In "Fortschritt" (Progress), written
in 1900 at Worpswede, when Rilke was learning about painting
firsthand, he records a new stage in his growing sensitivity:

Und wieder rauscht mein tiefes Leben lauter,
als ob es jetzt in breitern Ufern ginge.
Immer verwandter werden mir die Dinge
und alle Bilder immer angeschauter.
Dem Namenlosen fühl ich mich vertrauter:
Mit meinen Sinnen, wie mit Vögeln, reiche
ich in die windigen Himmel aus der Eiche,
und in den abgebrochnen Tage der Teiche
sinkt, wie auf Fischen stehend, mein Gefühl.
(402)

And again my deep life murmurs more loudly, and as if it now moved in
broader banks. Things become ever more related to me, and all the images
ever more observed. I feel myself more familiar with the Nameless: with
my senses, as with birds, I reach out of the oak tree into the windy
heavens, and into the broken-off days of the ponds my feeling sinks, as
if standing on fishes.

He feels a growing closeness to and comprehension of objects, pictures, the tangible world, a process that will be intensified throughout the first decade of the century. Both his senses and his feelings, according to the poem, are becoming one with his surroundings; like birds, his senses are at home in the expansive regions of the sky. His emotions plunge to explore new depths naturally and smoothly, and they are so delicate and so light and sure of touch that they can balance on the slippery backs of the fish that dwell there.

In the next poem, "Vorgefühl" (Anticipation), the poet compares himself to a flag on a pole high above the ground. Nothing else yet gives a sign of coming change: the doors do not slam, the dust lies undisturbed, no gusts rattle the chimneys. But he, in his elevated isolation, senses the wind before it arrives and is "ganz allein in dem grossen Sturm" (all alone in the great storm [403]). The poet, with the heightened awareness mentioned in the previous poem, knows and feels more fully than other people. He is as unlike the ordinary man as the tossing, plunging flag is unlike the unsuspecting house before a storm.

The third poem, "Sturm" (Storm), carries on the storm imagery, but the focus shifts quickly from an actual storm to the scene that a storm evokes in the poet's mind. He envisions the rebellious Cossack chief Mazeppa, who joined forces with Charles XII to fight the Russians in 1709. By Rilke's day Mazeppa had become a commonplace of the European imagination. One facet of his legend was the story of his having been captured, in his youth, by his mistress's husband, tied naked to the back of a horse, and sent off into the steppes to die. After many days of thirst, delirium, and danger, Mazeppa was found and rescued by a Cossack girl. Rilke evokes both aspects of Mazeppa's career, but focuses on the plight of the prisoner on the racing horse. In "Sturm" the lyric "I" of the poem undergoes a series of transformations. First he identifies himself with Mazeppa: "Dann bin auch ich an das rasende Rennen / eines rauchenden Rückens gebunden" (Now I too am bound to the raving race of a smoking back [403]). The next lines focus on the deprivation of the rider's senses and the intensification of the only perception that remains to him: "alle Dinge sind mir verschwunden, nur die Himmel kann ich erkennen" (all things have disappeared for me, only the heavens can I recognize [403]). Then the "I," limited and focused like Mazeppa, merges with the landscape through which the horse carries him:

> Überdunkelt und überschienen
> lieg ich flach unter ihnen,
> wie Ebenen liegen;
> meine Augen sind offen wie Teiche,
> und in ihnen flüchtet das gleiche
> Fliegen.
>
> (404)

darkened over and shone upon, I lie flat beneath them as plains lie; my eyes are open like ponds, and in them flees the same flight.

From being a mere observer, he has become both participant—Mazeppa—and backdrop.

The final transformation takes place in the fourth poem, "Abend in Skåne" (Evening in Skåne), written in Sweden in 1904. The poet emerges from a forest into a clearing at evening and is struck by the peace and grandeur of the sunset. He steps into the wind,

> denselben Wind, den auch die wolken fühlen,
> die hellen Flüsse und die Flügelmühlen,
> die langsam mahlend stehn am Himmelsrand.
>
> (404)

the same wind that the clouds feel, the bright rivers and the windmills, that stand, slowly grinding, on the horizon.

As in "Sturm" he had become akin to the plains and ponds, so here he becomes just one more object among others in the landscape: "Jetzt bin auch ich ein Ding in seiner Hand, / das kleinste unter diesen Himmeln" (404) (Now I too am just a thing in his hand, the smallest one under these skies [404]). In four poems, the poet has transformed himself from perceiving subject to perceived object. The process of sharpening his senses, the consciousness of that process, and the ultimate hoped-for identity with the perceived world are all matters of supreme importance to Rilke during these years. In Neue Gedichte and Malte Laurids Brigge they will assume central roles.

One other set of poems illustrates Rilke's concern with the subject of perception that binds *The Book of Images* together. These are poems that focus either on a person intensely involved in the act of vision or on the blind. The latter is only an apparent paradox, to which I shall return. The first are typified by two poems in book 2, part 2: "Der Lesende" (The reader) and "Der Schauende" (The watcher). The reader experiences a feeling of comfort and serenity, of at-homeness in the world, both on his page and, when he finally looks up from his book, in the twilight world outside his window. The watching man watches a storm pass by, reshaping the world as it goes. He concludes that we should behave more like things and submit willingly to the forces that mold us. Instead, we fight petty battles and are proud of defeating insignificant opponents, rather than seeking out those greater than ourselves. To grow, he says, means "der Tiefbesiegte / von immer Grösserem zu sein" (to be deeply defeated by ever greater things [406]). For Rilke, the process of learning to see and to create must be coupled with a growing awareness of one's own incompleteness, a sense of humility, and a desire to be taught and changed.

Blindness plays an important part in Rilke's world view. Some-times it represents a negative state, reflecting traditional attitudes, but more often there is a positive, almost mystical value attached to it. In *The Book of Images* there are three works about blindness. Of these "Das Lied des Blinden" (The blind man's song) in the cycle "Die Stimmen" takes the most negative stance; but it must be seen in the context of the other "voices." "Die Stimmen," written in Paris in 1905–6, continues the concern for the poor expressed in the third part of *The Book of Hours*. The introductory poem to the cycle states that the needy have to "sing" so that people will notice them, rather than just walking by. Even so, he says, people are not attracted by the songs of the poor; only God is pleased and stays a long time to listen to them. Each of the angry or melancholy "voices" that follows is a first-person lament or a description of his lot by a member of the downtrodden: a beggar, a blind man, a drinker, a suicide, a widow, an idiot, an orphan, a dwarf, and a leper. What unites them above all is that they are outsiders, whether because of physical infirmities, poverty, their own weakness, or their lack of human bonds. The blind man calls his lot "ein Fluch, / ein Wid-erwillen, ein Widerspruch, / etwas täglich schweres" (a curse, an aversion, a contradiction, a daily heaviness [449]). Unlike most of

Rilke's blind, he compares himself bitterly with the sighted, who he says are mistakenly self-satisfied.

> Ihr rührt euch und rückt und bildet euch ein
> anders zu klingen als Stein auf Stein,
> aber ihr irrt euch: ich allein
> lebe und leide und lärme.
>
> (449)

You stir and move and imagine that you sound different from stone on stone, but you're wrong: I alone live and suffer and make a noise.

It is the paradoxical assertion that only the blind man experiences life and "sees" clearly which ties the man tenuously to the other blind people and the meaning of blindness in Rilke's works.

For Rilke, blindness is often treated as part of the process of increasing sensitivity. For Mazeppa and the poet in "Sturm," their whole sensual contact with the world was reduced to vision, and even that to their view of the sky rushing by overhead. Yet precisely through this process of reduction and deprivation they became one with that world. It is similar with the case of blindness. The loss of one sense forces the person inward, makes him concentrate his efforts on the other senses and learn new ways of awareness. This is the situation in the dramatic dialogue in book 2, part 2, "Die Blinde" (The blind woman). Here a stranger, presumably Death, asks a woman what it had been like to go blind. She tells him in calm but powerful words about her experience: from the initial feeling of loss and isolation and her resistance to her new state, to a growing keenness of her sense of hearing, to a realization that no one could follow her or be with her in her darkness, to a sense of being an island, and finally, to a vision of herself as calm. Her grief is told in terms of brutal, fundamental loss:

> . . . Die Welt,
> die in den Dingen blüht und reift,
> war mit den Wurzeln aus mir ausgerissen,
> mit meinem Herzen (schien mir), und ich lag
> wie aufgewühlte Erde offen da und trank
> den kalten Regen meiner Tränen. . . .
>
> (465)

The world, which blooms and ripens in the things, had been ripped out
of me by the roots, along with my heart, so it seemed to me, and I lay
there open, like churned-up earth and drank the cold rain of my tears.

Her gradual realization that life will go on without her is an insult
and a shock, which she then tries to imagine in detail:

> Ohne mich! Wie kann es denn ohne mich Tag sein? . . .
> Meine Blumen werden die Farbe verlieren.
> Meine Spiegel werden zufrieren.
> In meinen Büchern werden die Zeilen verwachsen.
>
> (467)

Without me! How can it be day without me? My flowers will lose their
colors, my mirrors will freeze up, in my books the lines will close over.[6]

But finally the painful process leads to a state of acceptance and
even richness of a new level:

> Dann wuchs der Weg zu den Augen zu . . .
> Jetzt geht alles in mir umher,
> sicher und sorglos: . . .
> Ich muss nichts entbehren jetzt,
> alle Farben sind übersetzt
> in Geräusch und Geruch.
> Und sie klingen unendlich schön
> als Töne.
>
> (469)

Then the path to my eyes grew over. Now everything moves around in
me, sure-footed and at ease. I lack for nothing now, all colors are translated
into sound and smell. And they ring endlessly sweet, as sounds.

In the third poem of *The Book of Images* which deals with blindness,
"Pont du Carrousel," a blind beggar standing on a bridge in Paris
becomes the pivot of all human endeavors—in the sense of T. S.
Eliot's phrase, the "still point of the turning world":[7]

> Der blinde Mann, der auf der Brücke steht,
> grau wie ein Markstein namenloser Reiche,
> er ist vielleicht das Ding, das immer gleiche,

um das von fern die Sternenstunde geht,
und der Gestirne stiller Mittelpunkt.
Denn alles um ihn irrt und rinnt und prunkt.

Er ist der unbewegliche Gerechte,
In viele wirre Wege hingestellt;
der dunkle Eingang in die Unterwelt
bei einem oberflächlichen Geschlechte.

(393)

The blind man who stands on the bridge, grey as the boundary stone of
nameless realms, is perhaps the thing, always the same, around which
from a distance the celestial hour turns, and the still center of the stars.
For everything around him strays and flows and makes a show. He is the
motionless, just man, set among many confused paths; the dark entrance
to the underworld, amidst a superficial race.

The man's characteristics are all key concepts in Rilke's world
view. He is blind and has therefore passed onto a more intense level
of inwardness and sensitivity. He is grey as a boundary stone, that
is, steady and rooted, with a function to perform. He is a "thing,"
possessed, in Rilke's terms, of the simplicity and purity of inanimate
objects. The man is motionless, in contrast to the noisy, pointless
bustle around him. And finally he is a "dark entrance to the underworld"; dark, both because blind and in communion with the
silence and hidden depths of the mind and soul. The realms whose
boundary he precisely marks are nameless—a seeming paradox, yet
also a symbol of his function. For the nameless realms are also the
underworld, they are his natural habitat, rich in unknown wealth
for those who can penetrate there. But clearly only the blind man
can do so, for the people around him are flighty and "superficial."
As the blind woman found within herself riches independent of the
world of light, so the blind man represents a world of profundity
and stability. He is isolated by his condition, but also exalted,
intensified, much like the poet/flag in "Vorgefühl."

Taken together *The Book of Hours* and *The Book of Images* represent
a transition from the somewhat scattered concerns and facile forms
of the early poetry to the mainstream motifs and recognizably Rilkean style of the period of mastery. Rather than working through
these motifs and then going on to other things, in the works that
followed Rilke retained them at the core of his work, developing
ever-more precise and characteristic ways of expressing them.

Chapter Five
Neue Gedichte and the Requiems of 1908

Rilke's next major publications were *Neue Gedichte* (*New Poems*) published in 1907, and *Der Neuen Gedichte Anderer Teil* (*New Poems, Second Part*) published in 1908.[1] *New Poems* contain seventy-nine poems from the years 1905–7 and four from 1903–4. The early ones stem from Rilke's stays in Rome and Sweden, while the later ones were written in Paris, Meudon, and Capri. *New Poems, Second Part* contain 108 pieces written in Paris and on Capri in 1907 and 1908. Each volume begins with a poem about Apollo, the god of music, poetry, and light. Each then moves from groups of poems on ancient subjects through the Old and New Testaments and the Middle Ages, to the present, where the range of topics spreads out like rivulets in all directions (*SW*, 1:479–642).

Whereas the poems in *The Book of Hours* and to a lesser extent those in *The Book of Images* depended in part on the fabric of the whole for their impact—the unifying thought or set of images which bound each together—in the two volumes of *New Poems* different organizing principles are at work. For by this time Rilke was concentrating his energies on writing a different kind of poem. Each was expected to stand on its own. The poems in *New Poems* form a rough circle, for they return, near the end, to a set of poems on ancient subjects, mirroring their beginning, while those in *New Poems, Second Part* remain, in a sense, open. They end with a poem in praise of Buddha that emphasizes his provisory, incomplete nature and his constant growth and change, somewhat like God in *The Book of Hours* or *Geschichten*. Like Buddha, the book itself is subject to expansion and transmutation. While the poems in *New Poems* are placed so that they are mutually illuminating, and by their proximity suggest other levels of meaning, the overall connections in *New Poems, Second Part* are looser and less suggestive.

Subgroups or minicycles exist in both volumes, however. A group of eight poems in *New Poems*, beginning with "L'Ange du meridien"

(The angel of the sundial) and encompassing "Die Kathedrale" (The cathedral), "Das Portal" (The portal [consisting of three poems]), "Die Fensterrose" (The rose window), "Das Kapitäl" (The capital), and "Gott im Mittelalter" (God in the Middle Ages), can be read as a miniature cycle of "cathedral poems." In *New Poems, Second Part* one group of poems is united by their setting in various parts of Italy. Another set of seven, grouped together under the title "Die Parke" (The parks), evokes the decaying splendor of old, neglected parks and formal gardens, while the poems "Der Abenteurer" (The adventurer), "Falken-Beize" (Falconry), "Corrida" (The bullfight), "Don Juans Kindheit" (Don Juan's childhood), "Don Juans Aus-wahl" (Don Juan's selection), and "Sankt Georg" (Saint George— a figure who turns up repeatedly in Rilke's poetry) could be read as a series focusing on unusual men who despite audience, victims, subjects, or supplicants, are ultimately alone with their prominence and their fate. In both volumes we encounter familiar motifs: child-hood, God, nature, history, family lineage, death. We also find, perhaps even more clearly enunciated here, the motifs of art and poetry, and the eternal problem of the poet's situation between the demands of art and life.

In the poems of *New Poems* are mirrored both the horrors of life in Paris and the sense of Rilke's growing comprehension of visual things, aided and shaped by the works of Rodin and Cézanne, Van Gogh, Baudelaire, and Verhaeren. Rilke's vision and his style under-went a marked change and a maturing process during the period between 1903 and 1908. The poems show tighter control, a sharp-ening of focus, and an almost classical sureness of tone. Rilke began to look closely at the material world, a process already noted in *The Book of Images,* and to capture it in precise strokes. The "I" of the earlier poems recedes into the background as a more distant, ob-jective tone takes over. We no longer find Rilke couching his needs and observations in quasi-religious terms. In the words of Eudo Mason, "he appears here no longer as a latter-day St. Francis, but rather as an alert, curious, detached and sometimes almost cynical onlooker on the world. . . . The Russian monk seems almost to have uncannily transformed himself into an aesthete with a perverse hankering after the macabre and revolting."[2]

Although the latter point is considerably overstated, it is true that Rilke, like Baudelaire before him and much of modern painting after him, deemphasizes the distinctions between the "beautiful" and the "ugly." All existing things are deserving of attention and capable of teaching us something. Sometimes the subjects of *New Poems* are surprising, to say the least: dead bodies ("Morgue"), the suppurating wounds of a leprous king ("Der aussätzige König"), large worms that fall from a hermit-saint seated on a column and "reproduce in the velvet" of those who stand below, gazing up at him ("Der Stylit" [The stylite]). I would not call this a "perverse hankering after the macabre and revolting," however, but a logical if sometimes heavy-handed side-effect of Rilke's new determination to look at and portray the physical (and moral) world meaningfully and accurately.

Rilke's new persona, not only as the poet of the disgusting but in general, as the poet of things, caused consternation among those readers who, on the basis of their selective reading of *The Book of Hours* and *The Book of Images,* had chosen to interpret him as a mystic and a believer. He was now criticized for his coldness and lack of concern for his readers. The latter was basically true, for as Rilke himself made clear, he was not a man who wrote to please an audience. But it is not true that the poems in *New Poems* are cold. They offer clearly focused, precise approaches to a great variety of real things: works of art, buildings, persons, plants, animals, fictional and historical characters, all seen through the eyes of a visual artist who was also a thoughtful student of his own inner world.

Rilke referred often to his use of "things" and to his developing conception of man's relation to the visible world.[3] In a letter to Clara written in early 1907, he discussed at length how things had become important for him:

Looking is such a wonderful thing, about which we as yet know so little; with it, we are turned completely outward, but just when we are most outward, things seem to happen inside us which have been yearning for an unobserved moment; and while they take place inside us, intact and strangely anonymous, without us, their meaning grows in the object outside, a strong, convincing name, the only one possible for them, in which we joyfully and respectfully recognize the event within us . . . grasping it only at a distance against the background of a thing that only a moment ago was still alien, and which will be so again the next instant. It often happens to me now, that some face touches me that way . . . that the momentary impression is involuntarily intensified into the symbolic.[4]

One critic compares Rilke's conception of the "thing" in type and intensity, if not in scope, to the "epiphanies" of Joyce's Stephen Daedalus.[5]

The *Dinggedichte* (thing poems) of *New Poems* are neither photographic reproductions, nor do they present random objects which serve as handy illustrations of an abstract idea. As another critic says, "those things appear in a poem only because they are directly meaningful to the poet, and . . . the articulation of his experiences is bound up with the idiosyncratic unfolding of these things, and is comprehensible only through this unfolding."[6] Thus at the same time that Rilke is focusing on a unique object, he endows it with a certain representative quality and gives it a layer of symbolic meaning. Or rather, as he says in the letter to Clara, the impression is intensified to the level of the symbolic in and of itself. Not that a particular swan or rose or church window represents something else in a simplistic one-to-one relationship. But for Rilke, each is always connected with something else, permanently linked in a personal and subterranean way, so that the swan remains a tangible swan, while serving as a cipher for an inner event as well.

Rilke takes his observations, his "unfolding" of the objects, one step further, and it is here that his poems are unique. He rarely describes a thing straightforwardly, stating color, shape, or dimensions. Instead, he uses the methods of a painter, offering isolated details and adding subtle shades. He hints at parallels in other, unrelated realms, until the object stands before us, clearly recognizable as itself; but in the very process of its appearing, it has been linked with other objects or experiences in the material world, as well as with internal events.

One further comment about the *Dinggedichte* is necessary, since the term *Ding* is so central to Rilke's new view of his task as a poet. In earlier generations, the lyric poet drew primarily on his experiences and his subjective responses to them. Rilke was trying to distance himself from this pattern of dependence on emotion and subjectivity, as well as from his particular need for inspiration. He had learned certain practical lessons from watching and listening to Rodin and from studying the works of Cézanne and other artists. Central among these lessons were the need for discipline, a definite daily schedule, and the attitude of a craftsman toward his work, rather than that of a dreamer or mystic. A primary result of these lessons was the concept of the poem itself as a thing—an object among others existing in the world.

An insightful critic of Rilke's works states: "Not the fullness of experience and the subjective mood, not directness of expression or spontaneity of tone concerned him . . . ; he was interested in the writing of poetry as a kind of work, work that is oriented toward the making of art objects, and therefore depends on the observation of things."[7] Thus Rilke's *Dinggedichte* not only focus on things and try to express, to penetrate, and to understand them; these poems *are* things, as new and concrete for Rilke as were Rodin's massive bronzes, and, like them, the justification for his artistic activity.

"Der Panther" (The panther [505]), written at the end of 1902 or in early 1903, is the oldest poem in *New Poems*. Rilke seemed to have sensed that it belonged to a future style. It is very different in subject matter and quality of language from the poems of *The Book of Hours* and *The Book of Images,* many of which were written about the same time. Rilke published the poem in a journal and then included it in *New Poems.* The poem deals with a panther at a zoo (the subtitle is "Im Jardin des Plantes, Paris"), that paces endlessly in his cramped cage, his physical appearance that of a free beast, but his spirit and instincts deadened by long captivity. This poem is placed between several others that reflect and illuminate it by their similar subject matter. Just before it comes the two-part sequence entitled "Der Gefangene" (The prisoner). Here the thoughts of a man in prison are punctuated by the numbing, repetitive drip of water in his cell. In the second of the two, the prisoner tries to portray, for someone outside, the madness and horror of his life. Just after the panther poem is one called "Die Gazelle" (The gazelle). This too portrays an animal in a zoo enclosure. But instead of being ground down by captivity, the gazelle is raised to an image of lightness, self-containment, and beauty. Foliage and a lyre grow from its brow, and its slender legs are loaded rifles—the German word *Lauf* can mean both an animal's legs and a gun barrel—that are held in check only by the animal's tense, inward attitude of listening.

Placed between these poems, the panther represents a particular reaction to imprisonment. The poem portraying the captive cat, a particular animal and yet the type of all captives, at the same time

conveys the poet's feelings of entrapment in his isolation. At the
end of 1902, when "Der Panther" was written, Rilke had finished
the Rodin manuscript and in early 1903 had left Paris, exhausted,
in need of money, and uncertain about his future. His father once
again offered to find him a job in a bureaucracy in Prague, but
Rilke's reaction to this was "I fear this salvation like a dungeon":[8]

> Sein Blick ist vom Vorübergehn der Stäbe
> so müd geworden, dass er nichts mehr hält.
> Ihm ist, als ob es tausend Stäbe gäbe,
> und hinter tausend Stäben keine Welt.
>
> Der weiche Gang geschmeidig starker Schritte,
> der sich im allerkleinsten Kreise dreht,
> ist wie ein Tanz von Kraft um eine Mitte,
> in der betäubt ein grosser Wille steht.
>
> Nur manchmal schiebt der Vorhang der Pupille
> sich lautlos auf—. Dann geht ein Bild hinein,
> geht durch der Glieder angespannte Stille—
> und hört im Herzen auf zu sein.
>
> (505)

"Der Panther" is one of Rilke's best known and most widely discussed poems. It has also attracted a number of translators. All
poetry is difficult to translate; Rilke's is especially so, because of
the multiple layers of meaning and the extent of his integration of
the sounds of the language into the structuring of each poem. The
reader of a translated poem never has the same experience as the
reader of the original. The following is a fairly accurate literal
rendering. The translator does not attempt to rhyme, thus avoiding
some of the pitfalls into which other translators have tended to fall.

> His gaze has from the passing back and forth of bars
> become so tired, that it holds nothing more.
> It seems to him there are a thousand bars
> and behind a thousand bars no world.
>
> The supple pace of powerful soft strides,
> turning in the very smallest circle,
> is like a dance of strength around a center
> in which a mighty will stands numbed.

From time to time the curtain of the pupils
silently parts—. Then an image enters,
goes through the taut stillness of the limbs,
and is extinguished in the heart.[9]

The poem is a masterpiece of suggestion and indirection. Nowhere is a cage ever mentioned, but there is no doubt in our minds as to the whereabouts of the panther. The word *Stäbe* (bars) is repeated three times in the first four lines, and the last word of line three, *gäbe*, rhymes with it. We cannot ignore the sound, which is repeated insistently and underscores the repetitive, inescapable quality of the bars themselves. It seems to the panther that not he but the bars are "passing back and forth," until they have become a dynamic and absolute reality. Nor is the panther himself ever mentioned again, once the title has introduced him. The sound, rhythm, and tactile quality of his pacing are presented through both the meaning and the sound of the words of the second stanza. In the first two lines, which describe the panther's motion, the stressed vowels mainly alternate between high, light sounds *(ei, i)*, and low, dark ones *(a)*. In the first of these lines the consonants alternate between soft, devoiced sibilants *(ch, sch, st)* and hard consonants *(d, g, k)*. The combination makes vividly audible the soft padding of the cat's paws and brings to our mind's eye a vision of his swaying body, as he steps from one weary foot onto another. His motion is characterized as a "Tanz von Kraft"—a dance of strength: he is both graceful and powerful. But this harnessed power has been short-circuited and circles endlessly on itself, devoid of purpose. The "great will" of the cat does not move with the body, which seems animated by some automatic, mechanical force; instead, it "stands numbed" at the center of the circle, incapable of decision.

In the final stanza there is a moment when it seems to the onlooker that the animal's integrity has not been totally destroyed: when his eyes receive a message from beyond the bars. The image passes through the body, which has ceased its pointless circling and seems to await a command. But when the image reaches his heart, it disappears without a trace, leaving the cat to pursue his pacing in the void and the reader with a feeling of sadness at the waste.

Details of diction and structure play a role in creating the overall impression of the poem, by underlining the surface meaning—for example, the large number of actual or implied negatives used.

These include *nichts* (nothing), *keine Welt* (no world), *betäubt* (numbed, without sensation), "silently" (in the original *lautlos,* soundlessly), "extinguished" (in the original it is *hört auf zu sein,* ceases to be). The panther's world is shown to be one of loss and absence. In its form the poem reflects its content. Like the activity of the panther, it is a circle, though this is not evident in the translation. In the original the first word, *sein* (his), and the last, *sein* (to be), are homophones. The poet has brought us back to where we began, just as the panther always must return to the same spot. In addition, lines 6 and 7, describing the small, tight circle of the "dance of strength around a center," fall at the precise center of the poem. Finally, Rilke uses fairly regular iambic feet, with alternating feminine and masculine rhyme, so that a swinging, sinuous rhythm is produced. But the last line, in which the image ceases to exist in the heart of the cat, is short by a foot. The abruptness of this line echoes that of the extinction of the image and, as it were, slams the door on any possibility of renewal.

Many examples could be given of Rilke's instinct for the portrayal of motion and color, his ability to choose precisely the right comparisons. In "Spanische Tänzerin" (Spanish dancer [531–32]), for example, he follows a flamenco dancer from the first tense, tentative gesture of her dance to its explosive finale, using images of fire that go back to the origin of the word flamenco: in *flamear,* to flame. The poem begins:

> Wie in der Hand ein Schwefelzündholz, weiss,
> eh es zur Flamme Kommt, nach allen Seiten
> zuckende Zungen streckt-: beginnt im Kreis
> naher Beschauer hastig, hell und heiss
> ihr runder Tanz sich zuckend auszubreiten.

As in one's hand a sulphur match, whitely, before it bursts into flame, stretches flickering tongues in all directions: so in the circle of nearby watchers, hasty, bright, and hot her round dance begins to flare and spread.

There follows the "bursting into flame" of her dance as her hair ignites. Her arms are compared to startled snakes. As the dance nears its finale the dancer gathers the fire and throws it down, where it "liegt . . . rasend auf der Erde / und flammt noch immer und ergiebt sich nicht" (lies raging on the ground, and goes on flaming, and will not surrender). Finally, she raises her face triumphantly and "stampft es aus mit kleinen festen Füssen" (stamps it out with her small, firm feet). Anyone who has seen a flamenco performance will recognize the familiar sequence of gestures and movements, now provided with a sort of narrative motivation. Through his combination of words, Rilke manages to suggest both visual and aural images. The flickering tongues of the match flame are present in the sharp *t* and *ts* sounds of "*zuckende Zungen streckt*," while the castanets emerge convincingly through the consonants in the lines "wie Schlangen die erschre*ck*en, / die na*ck*ten Arme wa*ch* und *k*lappern*d* stre*ck*en" (like startled snakes, her naked arms stretch, wakeful and aclatter).

"Römische Fontäne" (Roman fountain [529]) demonstrates Rilke's control of the grammatical possibilities of his language in creating an image and a mood.

Römische Fontäne

Borghese

Zwei Becken, eins das andre übersteigend
aus einem alten runden Marmorrand,
und aus dem oberen Wasser leis sich neigend
zum Wasser, welches unten wartend stand,

dem leise redenden entgegenschweigend
und heimlich, gleichsam in der hohlen Hand,
ihm Himmel hinter Grün and Dunkel zeigend
wie einen unbekannten Gegenstand;

sich selber ruhig in der schönen Schale
verbreitend ohne Heimweh, Kreis aus Kreis,
nur manchmal träumerisch und tropfenweis

sich niederlassend an den Moosbehängen
zum letzten Spiegel, der sein Becken leis
von unten lächeln macht mit Übergängen.

Roman Fountain

Borghese

Two basins, one rising from the other
in the circle of an old marble pool,

and from the one above, water gently bending
down to water, which stands waiting below,

meeting the gentle whisper with its silence,
and secretly, as in the hollow of a hand,
showing it sky behind darkness and green
like some unfamiliar object; while it

spreads out peacefully in its lovely shell
without homesickness, circle after circle,
just sometimes dreamily letting itself down

in trickles on the mossy hangings
to the last mirror, which makes its basin
gently smile from underneath with transitions.[10]

The movement of the poem is from top to bottom, from the
uppermost part of the fountain to the second and the third. The
fountain and the water, while not openly personified, have distinctly
human characteristics. Water from the top basin "gently bends"
and "whispers" (actually *leise* here means "quietly") to the water in
the next, which "waited, meeting the gentle whisper with its silence." It shows the sky to its companion in the reflections on its
surface, "as in the hollow of a hand." The water in the second basin
is "without homesickness" and "dreamy" while that in the lowest
basin, by the reflections of light and shadow it casts on the bottom
of the basin above it, makes that basin "smile." We seem to be in
the presence of old friends engaged in a calm, rather stately conversation that has been going on for years.

The mood is produced in part by the large number of words
denoting quietness or calm: *leis* (three times), *schweigend, ruhig,
träumerisch* (gentle, silent, quiet, dreamily). A certain peaceful monotony is produced by the high frequency of *ei* and *äu* sounds and
by alliteration, which together mirror the slow, calm movement of
the water. This motion is reinforced by the judicious use of en-
jambement, particularly from lines 3 to 4 and 11 to 12, where the
water flows, gently in one case and dreamily and in trickles (literally,
"drop by drop") in the other, into the basin below.

Finally, the sense of serenity and continuity, of time in slow
motion, is aided by the fact that the whole sonnet seems to be just
one long sentence, halted only once by a semicolon. On closer

inspection this flow is made even more pronounced by the realization that there is no main verb, and no sentence at all. The only active verbs in the poem appear in relative clauses: in line four, in the "water which *stood* waiting below," and in the last line, in the mirror that "*makes* its basin smile." In the remainder of the poem, the only verbal forms are present participles: *übersteigend, neigend, schweigend, zeigend, verbreitend, sich niederlassend* (rising, bending, being silent, showing, spreading, letting itself down).[11] The effect of this is a double one: the repetitious grammatical rhymes contribute to the sense of calm, and the action is reduced to almost zero, since everything is ongoing, continually present. "Römische Fontäne" is a vivid illustration of Rilke's striving to reproduce in words the characteristic motions and relationships of an object.

Rilke often used an art object—a painting, a building, or a piece of sculpture—as a jumping-off point for a poem. His Saint Sebastian was inspired by a painting by Botticelli, as was his "Geburt der Venus" (Birth of Venus). His knowledge of flamenco came not only from personal experience (he was a guest at a celebration given by the Spanish painter Zuloaga in Paris in 1906, which featured a gypsy dancer),[12] but also from a painting by Goya. Goya was apparently also a primary visual source for "Corrida" (Bullfight), since Rilke had never seen one in person. The poem "Der Berg" (The mountain) praises the subborn persistence of the Japanese artist Hokusai in his attempts, in 136 woodcuts, to portray Mt. Fuji as it really is, "Teilnahmslos und weit und ohne Meinung" (639) (uninvolved and distant and without an opinion). This was an ideal that echoes Rilke's own desire to present things in their integrity and otherness, independent of human interference.

Other poems make use, not of specific works of art, but of generic types, such as the "Damenbildnis aus den Achtziger-Jahren" (Portrait of a lady from the eighties) or "Im Saal" (In the hall), in which the poet walks through a portrait gallery. There he compares the ideal of those long-dead figures—"schön sein" (to be beautiful)—with ours, which is "reifen, / und das heisst dunkel sein und sich bemühn" (521) (to ripen, and that means to be dark, and make an effort). Another, "Der Stifter" (The patron), focuses on the small figure of a donor, typically painted in at one side in a medieval painting that he has commissioned. Here the patron kneels before Christ, while a bishop blesses him. While acknowledging the purely symbolic nature of the scene, Rilke suggests that if the man is humble and quiet enough, and totally concentrates his energies on effacing himself, a miracle might really happen and a wondrous creature might come right up to him, unafraid. The poem was written at a time when Rilke was particularly desperate to achieve a similar kind of patience and openness in his own work. In a letter to Clara written a few weeks before the poem, Rilke speaks of the importance of discipline and of opening himself to the possibility of creation every day: "we'll see what comes of my unconditional decision to lock myself in for such and such a time each day, wherever and under whatever conditions . . . for the sake of my work: whether it really comes or whether I just make the appropriate gestures, unfulfilled. . . . Prayer and its time and its reverent gesture, passed on unabridged, [are] the necessary condition for God and for his return to this person or that one, who hardly expected it any longer, and just knelt down and stood up, and was suddenly full to the brim. . . ."[13] Like the donor in the poem, Rilke hoped that by making the appropriate gestures, he could create the proper atmosphere of humility that would lead to a "miracle."

In another set of poems we find evidence of Rilke's knowledge of the painters' medium; here he utilizes or refers to their methods in the composition of his verbal images. In "Der Balkon" (The balcony [597]) a group of people appear to the poet "angeordnet wie von einem Maler / und gebunden wie zu einem Strauss" (arranged as if by a painter, and bound as if for a bouquet). In the fourth poem of the group called "Die Parke," nature becomes a rococo artist, happy

> . . . um den Tapis-vert
> ihrer Bäume Traum und Übertreibung
> aufzutürmen aus gebauschtem Grün
> und die Abende . . .
> einzumalen mit dem weichen Pinsel.
>   (605)

to pile up, around the greensward of its trees, dream and exaggeration made of puffed-up green, and to paint in the evenings with the soft brush.

In "Blaue Hortensie" (Blue hydrangea [519]) we see Rilke's acute color sense at work.[14] The poem also displays his skill at shifting senses and levels within the same image.

So wie das letzte Grün in Farbentiegeln
sind diese Blätter, trocken, stumpf und rauh,
hinter den Blütendolden, die ein Blau
nicht auf sich tragen, nur von ferne spiegeln.

Sie spiegeln es verweint und ungenau,
als wollten sie es wiederum verlieren,
und wie in alten blauen Briefpapieren
ist Gelb in ihnen, Violett und Grau;

Verwaschnes wie an einer Kinderschürze,
Nichtmehrgetragnes, dem nichts mehr geschieht:
wie fühlt man eines kleinen Lebens Kürze.

Doch plötzlich scheint das Blau sich zu verneuen
in einer von den Dolden, und man sieht
ein rührend Blaues sich vor Grünem freuen.

These leaves are like the last green paint
in the color pans, dry, dull and rough,
behind clustered blooms whose blue is not
their own, only mirrored from far away.

They mirror it tear-stained and vaguely,
as though they wished to lose it once again;
and as with old blue letter paper
there is yellow in them, violet and grey;

washed out as on a child's apron,
the no-longer-worn that nothing more befalls:
how one feels a small life's shortness.

But suddenly the blue seems to revive
in one of the clusters, and you see
a touching blue's rejoicing in green.[15]

Rilke does not describe the flower; instead he focuses on its color. Beginning with the leaves, he declares them to be like the last green in paint pots. This in itself gives us no particular image in terms of color, but the second line provides the connection. The last color in a paint pot is often a blotchy dried-out patch at the bottom, with a cracked surface and rough, curling edges. Just so are the hydrangea's leaves, "dry, dull and rough." The poet has actually compared the leaves' texture, not their color, to that of the old paint. But it is via the idea of green that he was able to use the paint-pot image and arrive at the qualities he wanted.

Going on to the blossoms, Rilke presents their blue in terms of distance in space and time. They are so pale that they do not even have a color of their own, but seem to mirror it from afar; even that is imprecise and fleeting. Theirs is the same blue found in old letter paper—an indeterminate pastel, faded, perhaps from lying forgotten in a drawer for years. It is the blue of a child's castoff pinafore, pale with many washings and no longer needed, since the child is either grown or dead. Both comparisons bring human emotions and fates into the picture. A suggestion of melancholy hangs over the old letters and becomes more specific in the authorial commentary in line eleven. The last tercet gives an optimistic counterweight to what went before, as the observer suddenly discovers a cluster of blooms whose blue is "touching" and "rejoices." There is no overt concluding comment about the human level that was introduced into the poem, but by association with this lucky discovery one has the feeling that for us, too, there is hope.

In "Die Gruppe" (The group [593]), the scene is composed, not by a painter, but with rapid hands and quick decision by a florist creating a bouquet. This image, which appeared in passing in "Der Balkon," is the central one of this poem. Again the flowers are people—in this case, onlookers gathering on a street to watch a weightlifter perform. The fifth *Duino Elegy* treats the same situation in similar images, but in a very different tone. For now, let it stand as another variation on the type of "artist poems" in *New Poems*.

In the context of art, two more poems should be mentioned. These are the two Apollo poems, based on ancient statues, which open the two volumes of *New Poems*. It is surely no accident that each book begins with an invocation of the god of art and music. The first, "Früher Apollo" (Early Apollo [481]), is "early" in several ways. On the most literal level, we can assume that the poem was inspired by an early piece of Greek art. On another level, Apollo is portrayed via images of morning and springtime, thus "early" in the day and the year, fresh and untried, but also bare, not yet blossoming. Finally, Rilke sees in this statue an Apollo early in his career; "zu kühl für Lorbeer sind noch seine Schläfe," (his temples are still too cool for laurel), his mouth is "still . . . niegebraucht und blinkend" (quiet, never-used, and shining). He is not yet experienced and wise enough, as a god, to protect us mortals from the unmitigated power of poetry:

> so ist in seinem Haupte
> nichts was verhindern könnte, dass der Glanz
> aller Gedichte uns fast tödlich träfe.

so there is nothing in his head that prevents the glow of all poems from striking us almost fatally.

Self-contained, he cannot yet act as mediator.

The approach and impact of the second Apollo poem, "Archaïscher Torso Apollos" (Archaic torso of Apollo [557]), are very different:

> Wir kannten nicht sein unerhörtes Haupt,
> darin die Augenäpfel reiften. Aber
> sein Torso glüht noch wie ein Kandelaber,
> in dem sein Schauen, nur zurückgeschraubt,
>
> sich hält und glänzt. Sonst könnte nicht der Bug
> der Brust dich blenden, und im leisen Drehen
> der Lenden könnte nicht ein Lächeln gehen
> zu jener Mitte, die die Zeugung trug.
>
> Sonst stünde dieser Stein enstellt und kurz
> unter der Schultern durchsichtigem Sturz
> und flimmerte nicht so wie Raubtierfelle;
>
> und bräche nicht aus allen seinen Rändern
> aus wie ein Stern: denn da ist keine Stelle,
> die dich nicht sieht. Du musst dein Leben ändern.

We did not know his unheard-of head in which the eyes ripened, but his torso still glows like a gas lamp in which his gaze, just turned down, persists and gleams. Otherwise the bow of the breast could not blind you, and in the slight turning of the loins a smile would not go toward that center that bore generation. Otherwise this stone would stand disfigured and short beneath the transparent plunge of the shoulders, and would not shimmer thus like the hides of beasts of prey; and wouldn't burst all its boundaries like a star: for there is no place that does not see you. You must change your life.

The statue is a torso; that is, it lacks both head and limbs, and this circumstance explains the first two lines and the possibility of clumsy incompleteness alluded to, and rejected, in lines 9 and 10. But despite its fragmentary character, it seems to Rilke to be observant and powerful, its vision merely "turned down" like a kerosene lamp illuminating the torso from within. Fittingly for a god of light, Rilke describes his attraction for us in terms of light: his gaze is like a lamp that "persists and gleams"; the breast's exaggerated curve "blinds" us; and an intense force bursts out "like a star," exploding into being. These images convey a feeling of vitality and aggression not at all in keeping with our expectations—qualities that are underscored by the allusion to the skins of beasts of prey. The image, evoking the light reflexes on the quivering body of an animal tensed to spring, contains, like the others, beauty and vitality, but a sense of threat as well.[16]

Coupled with the images of dangerous power are those that remind us that Apollo was also god of the arts. It is his "Schauen," that conscious gazing that Rilke repeatedly urges on us and that he felt at this time to be the foundation of his own art, which still burns within the figure. Although the genitals, like the head and limbs, have been lost to the ravages of time, Apollo's creative and procreative powers are emphasized, in the "smile" that moves toward the "center which bore generation." The evocation of creativity, aggression, vitality, and light culminates in the surprising statements of lines 13 and 14. We look at Apollo as a work of art and a mythological figure. Both autonomous object and symbol, he looks back insistently and penetratingly at us. The gaze, which was lost with the head and rediscovered in the glowing torso, now permeates the whole figure, and concentrates on us, with the message that we must change our lives.

As the god of artistic inspiration, he urges us to see and to create. One critic suggests that the figure of Apollo has itself undergone this process of change in the course of the poem, from Phoebus Apollo, god of light, to the Delphic Apollo, merged with his prophetic oracle[17] and showing us where our future should lie. I would add that the figure has undergone an even greater transformation from the god of the "Früher Apollo" to his manifestation in the archaic torso. The "early" Apollo was unripe, still learning, unable to protect us from the dangers of poetry. The "archaic" Apollo, distilled to a power beyond physical perfection, throws us the vital challenge of plunging into that world of poetry and danger, and remaking ourselves in the process.

Rilke's negative attitude toward organized religion, and specifically toward Christianity, has been pointed out, yet he often returned to the Bible for his subjects. In the two volumes of *New Poems* there are many poems rooted in the Judaeo-Christian tradition. Twenty-three poems (out of a total of one hundred and eighty-nine) deal directly with material from the Old or New Testaments, and at least twenty-four others utilize figures (nuns, patrons, angels), edifices (cathedrals, a nunnery), or events (resurrection, Last Judgment, a religious procession) clearly connected with religious sources. In addition, there are two poems about Buddha and one about Mohammed.

It is characteristic of Rilke that when, as he so often did, he took a literary, historical, or artistic model as his inspiration, he did not merely relate the traditional story or present the figure as received from literature or legend. Rilke always made creative use of his models and approached them with the self-justifying freedom of the artist, so that under his hands they emerge in a new light, from a different point of view, at times even in conflict with the original. In the case of the religious materials, he almost always reinterprets the idea or figure from which he starts.

The poem "Sankt Sebastian" (Saint Sebastian [507–8]), based on Botticelli's painting, presents the familiar scene of the young man's martyrdom at the hands of a horde of archers. In the legend, Sebastian had left his peaceful home town for hostile Rome, there to find martyrdom for his faith. Rilke's poem ends as Sebastian's eyes "etwas leugnen, wie Geringes, / und als liessen sie verächtlich los / die Vernichter eines schönen Dinges" (deny something, as if it were paltry, and as if they disdainfully dismissed the destroyers of a beautiful thing). For Rilke's Sebastian the damning thing about his murderers is not their hostility, brutality, or violence, but their boorishness in destroying something beautiful—whether his faith or life itself. Even as he dies, his reaction is expressed in purely aesthetic terms.

In "Pietà" (494–95) Mary Magdalene mourns Jesus' death as the woman who loved him, but who was never allowed to be his lover. "Dein Herz steht offen und man kann hinein: / das hätte dürfen nur mein Eingang sein" (Your heart stands open and people can enter; that should have been my entryway alone), she says, in a mixture of accusation and sadness. She goes on, "O Jesus, Jesus, wann war unsre Stunde? / Wie gehn wir beide wunderlich zugrund" (Oh Jesus, Jesus, when was our hour? How strangely we are both perishing). At this point she feels only the loss and the bitter thought that it need not have been that way.

Rilke was becoming increasingly obsessed with the mode of loving he called possessionless love. More and more often he placed upon the women figures in his works (and the women in his life) the burden—he looked upon it as a blessing—of learning to love "intransitively," without need of another person as beloved object. He worked with the idea for many years. It purported to free the woman from the constraints of a mundane and usually disappointing relationship, and released her to love freely. Of course in the process, it also kept her at a safe distance from the beloved, who, if we agree that Rilke was lurking behind this figure, was glad to be freed from responsibility and from any encroachment on his own freedom.[18] In *New Poems* the poem "Der Auferstandene" (The risen one [582]) takes up the relationship of Mary and Jesus again, and continues its development. Rilke raises Mary Magdalene to a new level of consciousness and places her in the pantheon of women who achieve his ideal of possessionless love.

In the poem Mary comes to the tomb to prepare Jesus' body with oils and salves, but she finds him gone. While he lived, she had made a public show of her love, but now, in death, he tells her not to touch him. Only later does she comprehend his refusal:

> um aus ihr die Liebende zu formen
> die sich nicht mehr zum Geliebten neigt,
> weil sie, hingerissen von enormen
> Stürmen, seine Stimme übersteigt.

to make of her the lover who no longer inclines toward the beloved because, wrenched by tremendous storms, she transcends his voice.

"Das jüngste Gericht" (The last judgment [575]) is Rilke's second poem on this subject. The tone is ironic and mocking. The dead,

"oft durchlocht und locker" (often loose and full of holes), "hocken
. . . in dem geborstnen Ocker ihres Ackers" (squat in the burst
ochre of their graveyard). Angels, like God's advance troops, come
to the dead,

> . . . um Öle
> einzuträufeln in die trocknen Pfannen
> und um jedem in die Achselhöhle
>
> das zu legen, was er in dem Lärme
> damals seines Lebens nicht entweihte.

to drip oil into the dry pans, and to put in the armpit of each one whatever
he hadn't desecrated back then, during the noise of his life.

In "Der Ölbaumgarten" (The olive grove [492–94]) Rilke again
takes up a biblical scene: Christ prays alone in the garden while his
disciples are sleeping. Rilke transforms the scene into a statement
of bleakness and despair. The Gospel shows Christ expressing his
fears, but concludes with his submission to God's will: "Father, if
thou be willing, remove this cup from me: nevertheless not my
will, but thine, be done" (Luke 22:42). Rilke's Christ laments that
he feels abandoned to his fate by a God who does not even exist.
The mood is set in the first stanza:

> Er ging hinauf unter dem grauen Laub
> ganz grau und aufgelöst im Ölgelände
> und legte seine Stirne voller Staub
> tief in das Staubigsein der heissen Hände.

He went up under the grey foliage, all grey and dissolved in the olive
grove, and laid his brow, full of dust, deep in the dustiness of his hot
hands.

The repetition of *grey* and *dust* establishes the feeling of weariness
and hopelessness that permeates Christ's thoughts as well. In the
biblical account, an angel appears to Christ at this point; Rilke
challenges the likelihood of this occurrence.

> Warum ein Engel? Ach, es kam die Nacht
> und blätterte gleichgültig in den Bäumen . . .
> Denn Engel kommen nicht zu solchen Betern.

Why an angel? Oh, the night came and leafed indifferently in the trees.
For angels do not come to such worshippers.

We have seen that Rilke had personal reasons for his antipathy
to the Christ figure. But he did not write in a cultural void. By
the turn of the century there was a literary tradition emphasizing
Christ's human, and even vulnerable, side. Rilke's forerunners in
this included David Friedrich Strauss's demythologizing work *Das
Leben Jesu* (*The Life of Christ*, 1835), Ernest Renan's *La vie de Jésus*
(*The Life of Christ*, 1863), and essays by Jean Paul ("Rede des toten
Christus"—The dead Christ's speech, 1796), Alfred de Vigny ("Le
Mont des Oliviers"—The Mount of Olives, 1844), and Gérard de
Nerval ("Le Christ aux Oliviers"—Christ on the Mount of Olives,
1844). In addition, Rilke made use of the work of a nineteenth-
century Russian painter, Ivan Kramskoy, in providing the physical
description of the despairing Christ and the gloomy setting. In
Kramskoy's "Christ in the Desert" one can see the same gray, dusty,
and isolated world, with Christ wrapped in a dusty gray cloak,
huddled on a rock at the center. Finally, there is a good case for
Rilke's use of certain scenes from Dostoyevski's *Brothers Karamazov*
for some aspects of the poem, although here Rilke takes the negative
characteristics of other Dostoevskian figures and applies them to
his Christ.[19]
   Like the child, the artist, the blind person, and the self-sacrificing
woman, a standard figure in Rilke's works is the Prodigal Son. In
Luke 15 we find the story of the young man who abandons his
secure home and family to wander in the world. After leading a life
of luxury and debauchery, he is reduced to serving as a swineherd.
Repentent, he returns home, hoping at most to be allowed to work
for his father as a servant: but his father rejoices at his return and
kills the fatted calf in welcome. Rilke was deeply attached to this
story and used it often, typically changing it to suit his needs. The
first appearance of the motif is in *Geschichten*, where he varies it
subtly from one story to another. In "Wie der alte Timofei singend
starb" the son Yegor leaves home against his father's will to seek
his fortune in the city. When he decides to return home he is
welcomed and receives the knowledge of his father's songs as a reward
and as a duty. Here the Prodigal Son motif is bound up with the
question of art versus life; Yegor must decide between his wife and
child and his role as a singer. In the frame to "Ein Märchen vom

Tod und eine fremde Nachschrift dazu," God himself is seen fleeing
through the back door of heaven. But he will, the narrator implies,
return one day to take up his proper place again, via the darkness
underground.[20]

The motif appears again in *New Poems,* in "Der Auszug des verlorenen Sohnes" (The departure of the Prodigal Son [491–92]). It
is written from the point of view of the son, who contemplates
leaving everything close and familiar, in order to seek his own path
"ins Ungewisse, / weit in ein unverwandtes warmes Land" (into
uncertainty, far into an unrelated, warm country). He realizes that
it will be painful and perhaps futile; but he feels that life at home

> . . . unser ist und uns doch nicht gehört,
> das, wie das Wasser in den alten Bornen,
> uns zitternd spiegelt und das Bild zerstört.

is ours but doesn't belong to us, that like the water in old springs reflects
us, quivering, and destroys the image.

Among his family and their well-known objects he does not exist
as an individual, and his image is distorted in their well-meaning
but unseeing eyes.

Rilke also emphasizes the son's need to gain distance and to learn
to see anew—a familiar motif. In these concerns we recognize Rilke's
belief in the primacy of sight and insight: we also find echos of the
young poet who fled from the confines of provincial Prague and his
traditional, clinging family. The most profound necessity of all,
perhaps, was to escape from the lingering influence of his mother,
a threat and a nightmare to him even in 1906. There is a reference
in the poem to the "Leid . . . von dem die Kindheit voll war bis
zum Rand" (suffering with which childhood was full to the brim).
There is no mention of childhood in the biblical version, but for
Rilke this was an important aspect of the whole fabric of reasons
to leave home, physically and spiritually, and seek himself elsewhere.
The poem ends on a guardedly hopeful note: "Ist das der Eingang
eines neuen Lebens?" (Is this the entrance to a new life?).

Rilke had intended to write a cycle of poems about the Prodigal
Son, but got no further than the *New Poems* poem and one other,
written, like it, in Paris in June 1906. "Vom verlorenen Sohn"
(About the Prodigal Son [*SW*, 2:326–28]) presents a variation on

the basic theme. The speaker is not a youth leaving his family, but a minstrel begging leave of his king and patron to go away, despite his good and privileged life at court. As the motivation in "Der Auszug des verlorenen Sohnes" was to learn to see and to find himself in surroundings that did not know and define him, so here it is the same, but with stronger emphasis on the speaker as artist. "Ich muss allein sein. Mich darf keiner stören" (I must be alone. No one may disturb me), he begs. This clearly echoes the cry so often heard from Rilke, imploring Clara, Benvenuta, Merline, and so many other loving people to leave him in freedom, privacy, and even loneliness, to respect his need for solitude. Like Yegor in the story, the singer in the poem chooses to sacrifice love and companionship for the still unarticulated but pressing inner dictates of his art.

The biblical story is one of Christ's parables; it was intended to illustrate the premise that God rejoices more at the repentance of one sinner than at the unobjectionable lives of ninety-nine good people. Rilke was far more interested in why the son leaves in the first place.[21] When it came to the return part of the story, Rilke shifted the emphasis from repentance and forgiveness to the inner necessities of the son himself. As we shall see in *Malte Laurids Brigge,* where the motif serves as a metaphor for the protagonists's dilemma, even when the son comes home, a permanent rift remains between him and the people who welcome him but still do not really comprehend him.

Rilke returned to the subject one last time; in 1913 he translated André Gide's "Return of the Prodigal Son," a narrative that examines the motivations that led to both his departure and his weakened, demoralized, and exhausted return. Here the son, now that he has returned, will do his best to negate himself and take on the mask of his family, living by their beliefs. But hope lives on in the younger brother: instead of dissuading him as he is supposed to do, the older brother encourages the younger to leave and never to return.[23] It goes without saying that Rilke found this version congenial, for it resembles closely the values expressed in his own treatments of the legend.

A number of poems in *New Poems* deal with the familiar constellation of poetry, the poet, possessionless love, and the tension between art and life. A succinct statement of Rilke's position is the poem "Der Dichter" (The poet [511]):

> Ich habe keine Geliebte, kein Haus,
> keine Stelle auf der ich lebe.
> Alle Dinge, an die ich mich gebe,
> werden reich und geben mich aus.

I have no beloved, no house, no place where I live. All things to which
I give myself become rich, and squander me.

Expressed in these few lines is the state that Rilke consciously chose
and in which he increasingly found himself. Cut off from "normal"
life, he devoted himself to writing instead: he became his work.
He felt that for himself as a poet, and indeed for all artists, art and
life represented an either/or. The men he most respected, Rodin
and Cézanne, lived among people, but essentially alone, engrossed
in their inner lives and their creations. More and more Rilke came
to focus on the figure of the poet in his works. *Malte Laurids Brigge*
is the diary of a struggling writer, and twelve years later the *Sonette
an Orpheus* are dedicated to and permeated by the figure of Orpheus,
paragon of poets.

In "Orpheus. Eurydike. Hermes." written in 1904, we find an
interesting merging of many Rilkean motifs. It is also one of Rilke's
earliest treatments of Orpheus. As he does with biblical material,
Rilke makes fairly free use of classical myths and legends, as in the
stories of Alcestis or Leda. In the case of Orpheus, a strong tension
is created as he develops in an unprecedented direction the story of
the mortal poet who defied the gods.

Ovid's *Metamorphoses* tells the story: Orpheus, a poet and singer,
marries Eurydice, but she dies the next day. His sense of loss is so
great that he advances to the very throne of Hades to sing his lament.
The gods of the underworld are so moved that they are willing to
make an exception and allow Eurydice to return to earth, on the
condition that Orpheus go first and not turn back until he has
reached the upper world again. He looks back and loses Eurydice
permanently. Orpheus then remains chaste and wanders through
the world singing and charming nature with his songs. He is torn
limb from limb by jealous and insulted Bacchantes, who resent his
chastity; his head and lyre are washed up on the shores of Lesbos,
and he is avenged by Bacchus (Dionysus).

Rilke based his poem both on the traditional tale and on an
ancient relief showing the three figures whom he includes. He leaves

out the events of the wedding, Eurydice's death, and Orpheus's trip
to Hades to plead for her return. The poem starts in the murky
landscape of the underworld, as the three are already on their way
up, Orpheus leading, Eurydice following on the arm of Hermes,
the messenger of the gods. Rilke sets the scene in a way that is
both painterly and reminiscent of a set of stage directions. He takes
great care to place things in the eery landscape, building it up detail
by detail and making emotionally charged use of color:

> Das war der Seelen wunderliches Bergwerk.
> Wie stille Silbererze gingen sie
> als Adern durch sein Dunkel. Zwischen Wurzeln
> entsprang das Blut, das fortgeht zu den Menschen,
> und schwer wie Porphyr sah es aus im Dunkel.
> Sonst war nichts Rotes.
>
> (542)

That was the strange mine of souls. They moved like silent silver ore in
veins through its darkness. Among roots the blood arose that goes forth
to the world of men, and dense as porphyry it seemed in the darkness.
There was nothing else red.

This world is both a mine, with veins of ore and with roots pro-
truding from above, and a living organism, source of man's life-
blood, which moves in other sorts of veins and makes the only spot
of color in a gray, formless world. Rilke sketches in the outlines of
the place, with cliffs, meadows, shapeless forests, bridges over nothing, and a "grosse graue blinde Teich / der über seinem fernen
Grunde hing / wie Regenhimmel über einer Landschaft" (a great
gray blind pond, that hung above its distant bottom like a rainy
sky over a landscape). The image of the pond hanging like a sky is
disconcerting and vivid; we are not certain from what perspective
it is seen, but the general inversion and indeterminacy of the place
is made more intense by the image.

Into this world, on a path that he has just put in place, Rilke
then introduces his actors. First comes Orpheus, a spot of earthly
brightness in his blue cloak. We learn that he is impatient and that
his lyre, the thing that brought him success in his daring mission,
hangs forgotten in his hand, yet an inseparable part of him, "in die
Linke eingewachsen . . . / wie Rosenranken in den Ast des Öl-
baums" (grown into his left hand, like rose vines into the branch

of an olive tree). We know only from the title that this is Orpheus; thus we know, too, what he is doing here, though we are not yet informed directly. We are aware only from our previous familiarity with the story how much rides on his ability to trust the gods and to control his understandable fears until he reaches daylight. His growing tension is portrayed through references to his gait, his painfully strained senses, and the dialogue with which he tries to persuade himself that they are really following him. Rilke's images here are striking, fresh, and apt. "Ohne zu kauen frass sein Schritt den Weg / in grossen Bissen" (543) (Without chewing his stride devoured the path in giant bites). His senses are divided and at war; his eyes eagerly reach ahead seeking daylight:

> indes der Blick ihm wie ein Hund vorauslief,
> umkehrte, kam und immer wieder weit
> und wartend an der nächsten Wendung stand.
>
> (543)

while his glance ran ahead of him like a dog, turned, came back and ever again stood waiting far off at the next turning.

Meanwhile, his hearing strains backward to catch a reassuring sound from the two behind him on the path.

Rilke then moves his focus to the other actors: Hermes, divine messenger, and Eurydice. The importance attached to her in the legend and in the poem is indicated by the way she is introduced, led by Hermes: "und seiner linken Hand gegeben: *sie*" (and entrusted to his left hand: *her*), with a colon and italics for emphasis. The next stanza, which recapitulates Orpheus's reaction to her death and his powerful lament for her sake, begins and ends with the phrase "die so-geliebte" (the so-beloved). The strength of his love is, after all, the background and motivation for the present situation and what is always emphasized in traditional versions of the tale.

The next lines give the first indication that something is wrong; and with them begins Rilke's actual deviation from the original story:

> Sie aber ging an jenes Gottes Hand,
> den Schritt beschränkt von langen Leichenbändern,
> unsicher, sanft und ohne Ungeduld.

Sie war in sich, wie Eine hoher Hoffnung,
und dachte nicht des Mannes, der voranging,
und nicht des Weges, der ins Leben aufstieg.
Sie war in sich. Und ihr Gestorbensein
erfüllte sie wie Fülle.
Wie eine Frucht von Süssigkeit und Dunkel,
so war sie voll von ihrem grossen Tode,
der also neu war, dass sie nichts begriff.

                                                    (544)

But she went at that god's hand, her step hindered by long winding-
sheets, uncertain, gentle and without impatience. She was in herself, like
an expectant woman, and didn't think of the man who walked ahead, nor
of the path which led up into life. She was in herself. And her having
died filled her like abundance. She was as full of her own great death,
which was so new that she comprehended nothing, as a fruit is of sweetness
and darkness.

Eurydice, we discover, is not involved in the passionate adventure
that means everything to Orpheus. Her lack of impatience would
be like a slap in the face to Orpheus, if he knew of it. She is pregnant
with death, and there is no sense of fear or sadness. Rather, she is
numbed by the new experience, and all her attention goes toward
coming to terms with it. The next stanza reinforces the sense of her
separateness, from both the present undertaking and her own past.
Rilke speaks of her "neue[s] Mädchentum," her new virginity, and
says that she is so far removed from marriage that even the light
touch of Hermes, her guide, is offensive. This does not bode well
for Orpheus, who in his grief had braved the very underworld to
regain her. Hammering home the fact of distance, Rilke names the
roles which she has cast off. She is no longer the blond woman who
appeared in his songs, the scent and island of his bed, nor "that
man's property." There follow four lines that replace these with her
new characteristics:

Sie war schon aufgelöst wie langes Haar
und hingegeben wie gefallner Regen
und ausgeteilt wie hundertfacher Vorrat.

Sie war schon Wurzel.

                                                    (545)

She was already loosened like long hair, and dispersed like fallen rain, and distributed like a hundredfold surplus. She was already root.

She is no longer limited to existence within a predetermined and circumscribed world, subservient to another person, even to one who loves her as no mortal ever loved. She has become like a natural force, a root among roots. In her dispersal, however, she has paradoxically become more herself, as is clear from the repetition of "she was in herself," and from the whole inward-turning nature of her state of mind.

We do not see Orpheus turn, but only hear the sorrow of Hermes, who in his regret and pity is now closer to the world of human emotion than is Eurydice:

> Und als plötzlich jäh
> der Gott sie anhielt und mit Schmerz im Ausruf
> die Worte sprach: Er hat sich umgewendet—,
> begriff sie nichts und sagte leise: *Wer?*
>
> Fern aber, dunkel vor dem klaren Ausgang,
> stand irgend jemand, dessen Angesicht
> nicht zu erkennen war. Er stand und sah,
> wie auf dem Streifen eines Wiesenpfades
> mit trauervollem Blick der Gott der Botschaft
> sich schweigend wandte, der Gestalt zu folgen,
> die schon zurückging dieses selben Weges,
> den Schritt beschränkt von langen Leichenbändern,
> unsicher, sanft und ohne Ungeduld.
>
> (545)

And as abruptly the god held her back and with pain in his exclamation spoke the words, "He has turned around," she understood nothing, and said softly, "Who?" But far off, dark before the bright exit, stood someone or other, whose face couldn't be made out. He stood and saw how on the strip of meadow path the god of messages turned silently, with sorrowful glance, to follow the figure who was already going back down the same path, her steps hindered by long winding-sheets, uncertain, gentle and without impatience.

In the final lines Rilke allows the point of view to shift and hover in a strange way. First we are with Hermes, pained at Orpheus's failure, and Eurydice, who by her question shows the extent of her self-absorption and her distance from Orpheus and his hopes. It is from her point of view that we see him only as a faceless silhouette against the doorway which he had almost reached. Then without transition we find ourselves standing with him, as he looks back down the path and watches them turn away. Rilke underscores one final time Eurydice's indifference: Hermes need not lead her away, for she has already started back on her own, and the god can only hurry to catch up with her.

This is an easy poem to love, a hard poem to like. The dramatic situation is captured with great insight and skill, the setting and characters gracefully depicted, the language rich and precise. But the reader feels that violence has been done to his expectations, to the primacy of his traditional understanding of the tale. We knew Orpheus was going to fail and lose his beloved forever. But we feel with him, and expect that naturally Eurydice would share in the sense, first of hope, and then of tragedy. Rilke has inserted a new element into the story that requires some effort on the part of the reader. What had we assumed? That Eurydice would be glad and grateful to leave Hades and be with her husband again. But she has already forgotten him, forgotten his great love and her own life on earth. She is oblivious to the risk he has taken for her and his unprecedented success. If she were made aware of it, she would probably say that that is *his* life and he must deal with it: *she* has entered a new stage of existence which she already accepts and struggles to understand. That this should be incomprehensible to the living seems natural.

But in Rilke's view, for her to return to life, or to wish to do so, would represent a relapse, a setback. Again and again he preaches the equal value of life and death, the importance of our accepting death as the other side of existence rather than fearing or denying it. Eurydice has advanced beyond Orpheus, and his impatience and insistent passion must now seem to her childish, as incomprehensible to her as her abstraction and coldness are to Hermes. (We can only assume that Orpheus did not know of the change in her until that final disconcerting vision of her preceding Hermes back down the path.) Finally, Eurydice has achieved another goal that bears a positive value in Rilke's world: she has outgrown the beloved, gone beyond him to a reality where, like Mary Magdalene in "Der Au-

ferstandene" and many other female figures, she no longer needs
him.

But what of Orpheus, the poet? The emphasis in the poem seems
to have been on Eurydice, but we know how important the poet
was for Rilke. Orpheus of course is devastated; the legend and
common sense tell us that, though Rilke does not. He had come
so near to conquering death, to regaining his beloved. But in Rilke's
world precisely that success would have been bad. The artist may
not participate in normal domestic joys, for that would mean the
destruction of his creativity. If Orpheus had succeeded in restoring
his marriage, who knows what might have become of him? One
imagines him, grown fat and contented, playing his lyre occasionally
at feasts and smiling across the room at a graying and dissatisfied
Eurydice, who tells everyone how well her husband used to sing.
As it is, Orpheus must lead another sort of life. Alone, purified by
sorrow, he becomes the chaste singer of woods and fields, the symbol
of poetry itself. Here, I believe, lies the key to Rilke's intentions.
The woman/lover is raised to a purer level, fulfilled in herself,
seemingly glorified, but also gotten safely out of the way. The male/
poet is freed in spite of himself from earthly longings and attach-
ments, and lives only for his art.

Two other important poems from this period unite the motifs of
death and the artist. These are the requiems that Rilke wrote in
the autumn of 1908 for two artists: Paula Modersohn Becker, and
a young poet who had committed suicide. "Requiem für eine Freundin" (Requiem for a friend [*SW*, 1:647–56]) was written between
31 October and 2 November 1908, not quite a year after Paula's
death. Her name is never mentioned, but it is clear that she is the
subject—a young painter who dies shortly after giving birth.

Rilke addresses the woman who alone of all his dead—friends,
and figures from his poems—does not rest easy but returns to haunt
him. It upsets him that she should still be "homesick" for life. He
had thought of her as an artist, further along in her relation to
things, more like Eurydice in her willingness to let go of the world.
And he preceives that she comes with some request, whose nature
he tries to guess. He offers to travel to some far-off land where she
has never been, but which is spiritually part of her. There he will
see and learn for her sake as much as possible. About one third of

the way into this long (nine-page) poem, Rilke introduces the first
crucial fact about Paula: that she was a painter whose insight, skill,
and objectivity he praises:

> Denn das verstandest du: die vollen Früchte.
> Die legtest du auf Schalen vor dich hin
> und wogst mit Farben ihre Schwere auf.
> Und so wie Früchte sahst du auch die Fraun
> und sahst die Kinder so, von innen her
> getrieben in die Formen ihres Daseins.
> Und sahst dich selbst zuletzt wie eine Frucht,
> nahmst dich heraus aus deinen Kleidern, trugst
> dich vor den Spiegel, liessest dich hinein
> bis auf dein Schauen; das blieb gross davor
> und sagte nicht: das bin ich; nein: dies ist.
> So ohne Neugier war zuletzt dein Schaun
> und so besitzlos, von so wahrer Armut,
> dass es dich selbst nicht mehr begehrte: heilig.
>
> (649)

For that you understood: the ripe fruits. You laid them on dishes in front
of you and balanced their weight with colors. And like fruits, too, you
saw women, and you saw the children so, driven from inside into the
shapes of their existence. And at the end you saw yourself like a fruit,
took yourself out of your clothes, carried yourself before a mirror, let
yourself in except for your gaze. That remained, large, out in front, and
didn't say: this is me; no: this exists. So without curiosity was your gaze
at last, so without possession, of such true poverty, that it didn't even
desire yourself: sacred.

Much personal detail is condensed in these lines. Among the best
of Paula's works were a number of still lifes with fruit. She also
painted many pictures of the farm women and village children at
Worpswede, each face uniquely itself, separate and uninvolved as a
piece of fruit, or a watchful animal. The phrase "you balanced their
weight with colors" serves as a kind of code word, introducing into
the poem an important facet of Rilke's and Paula's relationship. In
a letter to Clara about the Cézanne exhibition in Paris in 1907, he
quotes a painter with whom he had attended the exhibition. Speaking of Cézanne's art, she observed, "It's as if it were laid on a scale:
the thing here, and there the color, never more, never less than the
balance requires. That can be a lot or a little, depending, but it's

precisely what corresponds to the object."[23] In another letter written the following day, Rilke speaks of the necessity of overcoming even love in a work of art, so that one does not judge or take sides, and the object is presented in its own integrity. To Cézanne's "colossal reality" he contrasts the lesser art of "Stimmungsmalerei," atmospheric or mood painting. "They painted: I love this thing here; instead of painting: here it is"[24]—the opposite of the praise he has for Paula's art. It was Paula who first made Rilke aware of Cézanne, and by weaving ideas about Cézanne into his discussion of her art, he is both acknowledging a debt to her and according her high praise.

The section where Paula steps naked before her mirror refers to her nude self-portraits and one late one in particular, in which she stands clothed only in an amber necklace, gazing out at the viewer as perfect and detached as the fruits in her other paintings. Several other key phrases occur here. Her gaze is "without possession," an echo of Rilke's conception of love; it is full of "true poverty," an echo of the virtue propounded in the figure of Saint Francis in *The Book of Hours*. Here the terms are applied in a new context, to looking. The artist should be so detached that he or she possesses and desires nothing, but only sees and portrays. The highest degree of such creative renunciation Rilke finds in the fact that Paula's gaze did not even desire herself. That is, in her own eyes she had become a pure thing, an object among objects. The poem goes on,

> So will ich dich behalten, wie du dich
> hinstelltest in den Spiegel, tief hinein
> und fort von allem. Warum kommst du anders?
>   (649)

That's how I want to keep you, as you placed yourself in the mirror, deep and distant from everything. Why are you coming differently?

After gently remonstrating with her because of her apparent recantation, he comes to the second crucial fact of her life, and gradually realizes that this is the key to her presence now. He suggests: "Lass uns zusammen klagen, dass dich einer / aus deinem Spiegel nahm" (650) (Let us lament together that someone took you out of your mirror). As an artist she had been in the process of turning all her powers into seeing and creating, but then chance had ripped

her back into the world, where she succumbed bit by bit to its
biological demands. The words Rilke uses to describe this transformation are brutal and culminate in the image of Paula digging
up the unripe seeds of her own death and eating them before it was
time. He describes how she did violence to her blood by diverting
it toward the new life within her, meanwhile trying to persuade
herself that her actions were not permanent or irrevocable. He laments the great waste:

>   Du . . .
>   zogst den schönen Einschlag aus dem Webstuhl
>   und brauchtest alle deine Fäden anders.
>
>   (652)

You pulled the lovely weft out of the loom, and used all your threads for
something else.

After the birth Paula steps in front of her mirror once more, as
a reward, but it is full of deception. The mirror of truth becomes
a distorting mirror. The death that follows is not her own, cannot
be, since she has eaten its seeds prematurely by abandoning her
calling and her true nature, and returning to the world. It is an
unfitting death, as inauthentic and alien to her as her life had become
at the end:

>   So starbst du, wie die Frauen früher starben,
>   altmodisch starbst du in dem warmen Hause
>   den Tod der Wöchnerinnen, welche wieder
>   sich schliessen wollen und es nicht mehr können,
>   weil jenes Dunkel, das sie mitgebaren,
>   noch einmal wiederkommt und drängt und eintritt.
>
>   (653)

And thus you died, as women used to die, you died old-fashionedly in
the warm house, the death of women after childbirth, who want to close
themselves again and cannot do it, because the darkness which they also
bore returns and insists and enters.

In the next section Rilke mourns Paula (*his* Paula, the woman
who had sacrificed herself in vain) but then moves from mourning
(*klagen*) to accusation (*anklagen*). He does not blame directly "the

one . . . who pulled you back out of yourself," that is, Modersohn, who had talked her into returning from Paris and had fathered her child. Rather he accuses all men, himself included, who are infected with the insistence of possessive love. His words, angry now, echo closely the ethos of "Orpheus. Eurydike. Hermes," as he demands, "Wo ist ein Mann, der Recht hat auf Besitz?" (Where is a man who has a right to possession? [654]). The section closes with one of Rilke's strongest statements of his credo of possessionless love and respect for the other.

> Denn *das* ist Schuld, wenn irgendeines Schuld ist:
> die Freiheit eines Lieben nicht vermehren
> um alle Freiheit, die man in sich aufbringt.
>
> (654)

For *that* is guilt, if anything is: not to increase the freedom of a loved one by all the freedom that one has at one's disposal.

Despite the scope of his accusation and his attempt to make it universal, it is important to make some distinctions between its application to the situations in the two poems. Orpheus is a poet. He had tried, selfishly, to keep Eurydice as his personal possession, but was thwarted, to his ultimate benefit, as I have suggested. By her death, he is freed to make his poems, without the distractions and mundane demands of human love. By her death, Eurydice is supposedly freed to be herself, although exactly what this means is never verbalized. Certainly it is not to create or to develop, except in Rilke's highly abstract and idiosyncratic use of the word. In fact, it is Orpheus who goes on to realize himself as a poet. In the other poem, the dead woman is at the same time the artist. (Modersohn was an artist too, but no attention is paid to this fact in the poem. He and all men are seen merely as selfish oppressors, possessors who refuse to grant maximal freedom to their partners.) Death does not liberate Paula, as it did Eurydice. On the contrary, it seems the inevitable outcome of a decision that had already imprisoned her in life and that came about under pressure from her selfish lover.

Despite the great beauty and emotional intensity of Rilke's position in the "Requiem," the larger view suggests that universal generosity and concern for the freedom of the loved one are not alone at the core of Rilke's insistence on possessionless love. Also inextricably involved was a desire to ensure the freedom of the artist, first and foremost. Orpheus lives to sing, but Eurydice is dead. Paula, not allowed to paint, dies, leaving Modersohn alone and guilty. The message: an artist cannot live a normal life with other people. If he tries, either he must die or they must.

In the "Requiem" Rilke is obviously expressing genuine sorrow at Paula's loss. But that he was also thinking of himself becomes evident in the last section. Here the roles are reversed: at the beginning Paula, an uneasy ghost, comes to the poet with a plea; now Rilke turns to her, as one artist to another, to beg for help. He fears giving in as she had:

> So hör mich: Hilf mir. Sieh, wir gleiten so,
> nicht wissend wann, zurück aus unserm Fortschritt
> in irgendwas, was wir nicht meinen; drin
> wir uns verfangen wie in einem Traum
> und drin wir sterben, ohne zu erwachen.
> Keiner ist weiter. Jedem, der sein Blut
> hinaufhob in ein Werk, das lange wird,
> kann es geschehen, dass ers nicht mehr hochhält
> und dass es geht nach seiner Schwere, wertlos.
> Denn irgendwo ist eine alte Feindschaft
> zwischen dem Leben und der grossen Arbeit.
>
> (655–56)

So hear me: help me. See, we glide thus, not knowing when, back out of our progress into something that we don't intend; where we get caught as in a dream, and where we die without waking. It can happen to everyone who has lifted up his blood to a task which drags on, that he doesn't hold it up any longer, and that it sinks with gravity, worthless. For somewhere there is an old enmity between life and a great task.

He recognizes the danger that threatens him constantly. That it was not an idle fear we know, from the many abortive attempts at love, companionship, and community into which he "glided" over the years, and from which he always fled. He links himself here specifically with the creative people, those "who lifted up their blood to a task." The others, whose life task does not demand such sacrifices, or who have no such high goals, are not threatened in the same way. It was not that he was categorically against love or marriage. He had many married friends whose happiness was evident to him, and he was capable of love on a very profound level. Perhaps it was just this capability that posed such a threat; this, plus the overgreat need, stemming from his childhood, for the security of love, made him wary. He knew that he could become engulfed and he therefore tried to protect himself and the solitude that was crucial to his writing by developing a severe and ascetic sounding creed to which he could cling.

"Requiem für Wolf Graf von Kalckreuth" (*SW*, 1:659–64) was written in early November 1908, two days after the "Requiem für eine Freundin." It is addressed to a young poet whom Rilke never met, but whom he had learned of from his publisher, Kippenberg. As in the poem to Paula, Rilke here uses the occasion of an artist's death to propose and develop his ideas about the relation of the artist to life and to his craft. While there was surprise, guilt, and anger in the words spoken to Paula, here Rilke mainly expresses gentle regret that the young man has thrown away everything, while still showing understanding for the state of mind that drove him to do so.

What Rilke accuses Wolf of are sins against himself and his chosen art: impatience, lack of confidence, lack of insight into the messages and promises that existed for him in the world. The first criticism is launched against the act of suicide itself. Perhaps, says Rilke, the great insight was about to arrive, was standing in front of your door when you slammed it shut. Rilke suggests the destructive effects of a suicide on the entire fabric of nature:

> O dieser Schlag, wie geht er durch das Weltall,
> wenn irgendwo vom harten scharfen Zugwind
> der Ungeduld ein Offenes ins Schloss fällt.
> Wer kann beschwören, dass nicht in der Erde
> ein Sprung sich hinzieht durch gesunde Samen;
> wer hat erforscht, ob in gezähmten Tieren
> nicht eine Lust zu töten geilig aufzuckt,
> wenn dieser Ruck ein Blitzlicht in ihr Hirn wirft.
>
> (660)

Oh this concussion, how it goes through space, when anywhere the hard, sharp wind of impatience blows shut something which was open. Who can swear that in the earth a crack doesn't spread through healthy seeds; who has investigated whether in tame animals an urge to kill doesn't lustfully spring up, when this jolt throws a flashing light into their brain?

Though death is a positive value in Rilke's world, he never advocated a self-chosen one. This seemed to him as much a betrayal of the concept of one's own death, ripening within, as Paula's premature death had been. He blames Wolf for having destroyed—a serious accusation from one creator to another. He wishes Wolf could have encountered a gentle love, the calm example of a man deeply involved in life, a busy workshop, or even the sight of a struggling beetle: any of these could have saved him by giving meaning to a seemingly senseless muddle.

But most important from the standpoint of Rilke's philosophy of the artist are the three gifts that he tells Wolf were already his. These are "Raum um dein Gefühl" (space around your feelings), that is, distance from himself; "das Anschaun / das nichts begehrt" (the gaze that desires nothing), the same that he praised in Paula; and "ein Tod von guter Arbeit / vertieft gebildet, jener eigne Tod, / der uns so nötig hat, weil wir ihn leben" (662) (a death more profoundly formed by good work, that personal death that needs us so, because we live it). These are expressed in images from the realm of sculpture, as if each of them were the finished bronze within a hollow casting mold. Wolf had prematurely broken the mold of the third gift, death, and its emptiness confused him. The idea of the hollow form that must be filled with the final reality was a favorite of Rilke's, inspired, no doubt, by his observation of Rodin at work.

Rilke then focuses anew on the error of impatience. In his own life he strove for its opposite, for humility and strength to wait for ripeness and insight. We saw one example in "Der Stifter." Impatience also meant the too early use of ideas or images, in immature verses or unpolished, clumsy forms. Here he lashes out against this shortcoming that dogs the path of poets:

> . . . O alter Fluch der Dichter,
> die sich beklagen, wo sie sagen sollten,
> die immer urteiln über ihr Gefühl,
> statt es zu bilden.
>
> (663)

Oh ancient curse of poets, who lament instead of saying, who always make judgments about their feelings, instead of forming them.

What is necessary is not the fresh emotion itself, but the hard work of beating it into shape and making a poem of it. This fits the ideal of the objective, observing artist, the one who says not, I love this, but: here it is. Wolf could have been saved, Rilke states, if he had

> . . . nur *ein* Mal
> gesehn, wie Schicksal in die Verse eingeht
> und nicht zurückkommt, wie es drinnen Bild wird
> und nichts als Bild. . . .
>
> (663)

seen just *once* how fate goes into verses and does not return, how it becomes image inside, nothing but image.

But at the end Rilke pulls back, realizing that such criticism is futile now. He tries to comfort the newly dead youth with a phrase which, like all the advice and warnings which he has just been giving him, is intended equally for himself: "Wer spricht von Siegen? Überstehn ist alles" (664) (Who speaks of victory? Survival is everything). In this outcry lies condensed the experience and suffering, the insight and hope of a man whose whole life was spent trying to live by a difficult creed. This creed is given its most succinct and eloquent expression up to this time in the two requiems.

Chapter Six
Malte Laurids Brigge

Rilke's acquaintance with Paris began in August 1902 when he arrived from Worpswede to begin work on the Rodin monograph. He was charmed and impressed by the grand old man, but appalled by the city itself. A letter from July 1903 to Lou Andreas is typical of his first impressions: "I want to tell you, dear Lou, that Paris was for me an experience similar to the military school. As then a great anxious amazement seized me, so now once again horror seized me. . . ."[1] He describes the oppressive heat of summer in the long, gray streets, together with the noise, haste, and anonymity. Above all he was struck by the poor, ill, old, and misshapen people he saw there. We have already seen some fruits of these impressions in the second and third parts of *The Book of Hours*. The city seemed to him a hellish chaos: "Oh, what kind of world is this? Pieces, pieces of people, parts of animals, remains of former things and everything still in motion, as if mingling in an uncanny wind, borne and bearing, falling and passing one another in mid-fall."[2]

Many figures and anecdotes in this and other letters find their way into the pages of his novel, *Die Aufzeichnungen des Malte Laurids Brigge (The Notebooks of Malte Laurids Brigge* [SW, 6:707–946]). Rilke consciously began work on the novel in Rome in February 1904; but the experiences and insights, and the actual formulation of his reactions to them had begun as early as 1902. Rilke worked on the book off and on, simultaneously with other major projects, from 1904, with most of the novel being written in 1908–9. The book appeared in two volumes in 1910. While writing the novel, Rilke lived mostly in Paris or at Rodin's in nearby Meudon. In the early years there were long gaps when he was traveling or living in Rome or Capri. But he spent large portions of 1906, 1907, and from May 1908 through December 1910 in Paris. Despite continuing financial and medical problems, his attitudes toward the city changed drastically over the years, so that in a letter written in January 1908, during a visit to Clara's family at Oberneuland, he could express his longing to be back in Paris: "for far from Paris I feel as if exiled from my cherished solitude."[3] But Malte's Paris remained the Paris of Rilke's early days there, the impersonal, destructive, and terrifying city in which a young stranger could become disoriented or lose himself entirely.

Throughout 1908 and 1909 the novel is mentioned in Rilke's letters, particularly those to his publisher, Anton Kippenberg. Usually he refers to things that have prevented him from finishing the book and to his hopes of soon having a manuscript to send. Nevertheless, during this time he continued to collect impressions and make notes—on his travels to Avignon, Orange, and Les Beaux, for example—which would take their places in the novel. In October 1909 the still uncompleted manuscript was in such a state of disarray that Rilke asked Kippenberg to provide him with a secretary for a few days to make a fair copy for him; at this time, he was still referring to it as half-finished. It was also about this time that Rilke first met the Princess Marie von Thurn und Taxis. Important forces were gathering that were to act as transition and foundation for the next phase of his life. Finally, in December 1909, he felt himself in gear again, engrossed and productive. From 12 to 31 January he lived at the Kippenbergs' in Leipzig, where he dictated the finished text of the novel to a typist.

His comments in various letters indicate the importance of his work for Rilke. In January 1909 he had written to Kippenberg of the "joys and progress" he was experiencing in his work on it: "Sometimes it seems to me that I could die when it is done: with such finality do gravity and sweetness converge in these pages, so conclusively does everything stand there and yet so limitless in its innate transformation, that I have the feeling that I'm propagating myself with this book, far and with sureness, beyond all danger of death."[4] He felt he was creating for himself "a massive, lasting prose, with which almost anything can be done."[5] In March 1910 he wrote to Kippenberg in a euphoric mood about *Malte Laurids Brigge*. He was pleased with Clara's reactions as she read her way into the book; and he himself felt that the work constituted "something like a basis" for his new prose: "Now everything can actually begin. . . . Poor Malte starts so deep in misery and reaches, if you take it precisely, eternal joy: he is a heart that spans a whole octave; after him almost all songs are possible."[6]

One important question that has often been raised and that is important to an understanding of the novel is the extent to which

Malte and his creator are identical. That the novel is strongly autobiographical is obvious and was readily admitted by Rilke. But
it is also obvious that Malte, though he experiences many of the
concerns and fears of Rilke, indeed "expresses" them in the same
terms as had Rilke in his own letters from Paris, is also a carefully
drawn fictional character with a life and fate of his own. In a letter
he wrote to Clara in 1908 Rilke comments on his own hesitant
reaction to the writings of Buddha that she had sent him and
attempts to explain his reluctance to involve himself in them. He
suggests that it is because of Malte that he cannot open himself to
this new experience: "I am at one with him insofar as I have to be,
in order to feel the necessity of him and concur in his decline. I
may not go too far beyond his sufferings, otherwise I won't comprehend him any more. . . . I don't want to limit *my* insights,
but his, whose cycle and direction I still must be able to believe
in."[7] This is the reasonable caution of an author who feels himself
threatened with growing beyond his character before the latter's
whole story has been told. In 1911, some time after the completion
of the book, Rilke wrote to Lou, asking her opinion of it: "The
good Ellen Key promptly confused me with Malte and gave me up;
but no one but you, dear Lou, can make the distinction and detect
if and how much he resembles me."[8]

The "notebooks" of the title reveal the basic structural principle
of the novel. It is conceived as the diary of a Danish poet who has
just arrived in Paris and is attempting to deal with his reactions.
There are seventy-one "entries," covering a period of roughly a half
year,[9] during which the young man experiences a physical and
mental crisis. Although written in diary form, the text is not limited
to the present, but contains an abundance of references to Malte's
childhood and youth, to the books he has read, and to figures and
events in European history. The locale of the most recent scenes is
Paris—much the same sections and aspects of the city that Rilke
knew intimately. Earlier events from his life, told in flashbacks,
occur in Copenhagen, Venice, and St. Petersburg, as well as in the
family seats of his grandparents, Ulsgaard and Urnekloster. These
scenes from his present and past are smoothly integrated with the
others, which deal with fictional or historical characters.[10] All are
equally real and valid for Malte, since all serve him as material
through which to work out his own pressing problems.

The novel has no plot in the traditional sense. It focuses instead on Malte's observations and confrontations, and on his crisis, which develops on parallel levels as an increasing feeling of fear and threat, and a growing sense of purpose as a writer. Malte's is the story of an outsider. He is already isolated by the fact that he is a foreigner, and his identity as a poet sets him doubly apart from the everyday world. The focus of the novel is Malte's crisis of identity. Confronted with the ugly and seemingly absurd world of the city, Malte gradually realizes that as a poet he has lived dishonestly, closing his eyes to large portions of reality and trying to invent a world instead of really looking at the existing one. Thus his crisis is one of vision and leads to a process of learning to see, the same process that Rilke had emphasized in the poems discussed in chapter 5. At the same time, Malte finds his view of himself changing under pressure from his new surroundings. He feels mysteriously drawn to the poor outcasts of Paris, the beggars and wanderers, the sick and dying in the many clinics and hospitals, but is simultaneously repelled by them, and tries to flee their ever-watchful gaze. Gradually he learns that he must not only learn to see, but must also allow this ruthless process of change to pass over him. He must be stripped of preconceptions and definitions so that, passive, an open vessel, he can become the writer he wants to be.

The novel is divided into two sections. In the first, the dual process of learning to see and of losing himself begins, against a background of urban misery and strangeness. Malte's attention is repeatedly drawn to his own past, and in flashbacks we see the two families that have contributed to his personality and thus to his current dilemma. His father's family, the Brigges, are rational, practical people; they fear death, and regard the supernatural with distaste. For them past, present, and future are distinct entities that should not overlap or interfere with one another. The Brahes, his mother's family, are very different. Dreamy, vague, nervous, they regard both death and spirits as natural parts of existence. Time for them is fluid, our place in it not fixed or limited. The mixed heritage of these two families lives and wars for dominance within Malte.

In the first part of the novel Malte comes to the conclusion that he has a duty toward life and reality, and that the way for him to fulfill himself as a poet lies in his reevaluating and reliving his childhood. In this section, too, Malte fights against his growing sense of kinship with the outcasts. He insists on his difference from them, and to symbolize this fact emphasizes his access to the national library. There he, with his clean cuffs and his library card, can escape from them to sit and read "a poet," while they must remain outside. But bit by bit he is overcome by their presence and at last falls ill with an undiagnosed and untreatable nervous disease. In part 2, the problems of the first section are continued and intensified. To memories of childhood and daily events are added recollections of books and historical anecdotes. The section presents examples of failed and successful attempts at possessionless love. Malte is torn between his feelings of homelessness, nostalgia, and loneliness, and his realization of his need, as a poet, for solitude and selflessness. Here, as on many levels in *Malte Laurids Brigge* and elsewhere, Rilke creates a tension between opposing needs and warring urges.

One of the dominant motifs is death. Seventeen deaths occur in this short book, ranging from the flies in autumn and the numerous anonymous deaths in Paris, to those that directly affect Malte (his parents, other relatives, his dog), to those he invokes from literature and history. The first sentence of the diary introduces this theme that dominates the whole book: "So this is where people come to live—I'd say, rather, it was a place for dying" (709). The emphasis is on the concept of an individual, personal death. The examples present contrasting possibilities for dying: unprepared, full of fear and denial, or accepting the process as both natural and unique. An authentic death can occur peacefully or violently, the main thing being that the person's death somehow suits his life and personality, and is not regarded by him as an aberration.

Examples of two approaches to death are those of Malte's father and his grandfather, Christoph Detlev Brigge. Paradoxically, Christoph Detlev, though a Brigge, accepts his death, though physically he fights it every inch of the way. Christoph Detlev, a Chamberlain, is dying of dropsy. In his last weeks he orders the servants to carry his swollen body from one room to another at Ulsgaard, but he rarely finds relief, except in the small, delicate room where his mother had died. His screams take on mythic proportions, penetrating beyond the walls of the estate, keeping the villagers awake and causing cows to miscarry. His death tyrannizes the lives of everyone around; personified as a summer guest who refuses to leave ahead of schedule, "it had come for ten weeks, and it stayed the full time." Most important, this noisy, protracted, and recalcitrant death is seen as intrinsically belonging to the Chamberlain. It was "the angry, princely death which the Chamberlain has borne and nourished within him all his life." Despite his pain, the old man accepts the state of things as right and fitting: "How would Chamberlain Brigge have looked at anyone who had required of him to die a different death from this one. He died his difficult death" (720).[11]

Malte's father, on the other hand, has always dreaded death like something in bad taste. More important, he regards it as something separate and final, not a part of life but another entity entirely. This is shown in his last request, which is duly carried out after his death: that his heart be pierced by a doctor, to assure that he is really dead. Malte, in Copenhagen for the funeral, is present at this bizarre ceremony. Without being told, he understands his father's desire; his father had wanted no accidental, appalling confusion of life and death. "And then I knew," Malte says, "that he wanted assurances. Basically, he had always wanted them. And now he would get them" (853). The event takes on an added dimension for Malte, who realizes that with it the line of the Brigges is ended. Himself he excepts from that group, just as he excepts his own heart from those that might be subject to such a final act of assurance: "It was an individual heart. It was already starting over again, from the beginning" (855). As life and death must be tidily separated for his father, one succeeding and canceling the other, the past and the future become, in a certain sense, separated for Malte, who is "starting over," learning to see anew, becoming a new man. The book is full of images of beginnings, which echo Malte's process of renewal.

Among the many deaths in the novel the most significant for Malte is that of a stranger in a café, an old man whom he watches dying at the next table. The encounter comes at a moment when Malte is particularly vulnerable. He has been driven out of his shabby room by a smoking stove; rowdy carnival crowds on the street offend and frighten him; and he has just had an experience that shook him profoundly. Wandering around the streets, he had come upon an apartment building whose end wall, in the stains, paint patterns, dangling pipes, and truncated stairways, showed the scar of an adjoining house which had been demolished. Malte, always hypersensitive to change and decay, is overwhelmed by the scene, which he reads as a record of human lives. He flees to a café and orders supper, but soon perceives that the man seated near him is in the grip of death. Malte first pictures in his mind each step of the

process; when he forces himself to look, he sees that for once reality
and his imagination coincide. As with the outcasts and the poor,
Malte feels a kinship with the old man, and is horrified that the
latter accepts passively what is happening to him: "Thus he sat there
and waited until it should have happened. And no longer resisted.
And I'm still resisting. . . . I was able to understand that man
only because in me, too, something is happening which is beginning
to distance and isolate me from everything" (755). Malte is aware
that the process within him, which one critic calls "Ent-Ichung,"
the "devolution of self,"[12] is drastic and merciless. He also recognizes
that it is something he must go through if he is to achieve honesty
and lucidity. But one part of him clings to the false comforts of his
old self, reassuring and familiar even if outgrown. Thus it is that
he equates *his* process with that of death, with which he has *also*
not yet come to terms.

All crises, all terrors are for Malte ultimately connected with his
growth as a poet. So it is with the episode of the old man, for it
leads into a diary entry in which Malte expresses both his fears and
his frustration at himself for being afraid: "If my fears weren't so
great, I would be able to console myself with the thought that it
is not impossible to see everything differently and still to live. But
I am afraid, I am namelessly afraid of this change. I'm not yet at
all at home in this world, which seems good to me. What should
I do in a different one?" (755–56). From the elemental level of his
fear, he goes on to the actual core of his problem. He will, he says,
be able to write about these things in this way for a little while
longer, but then his hand will begin to write things he had not
intended; words will go out of control, and his very world will lose
its meaning. He is able to feel a positive excitement in all of this:
"With all my fear I am, after all, like someone who stands before
something great, and I recall that it was often like this within me,
before I began to write. But this time I will be written. I am the
impression which will be transformed. Oh, it lacks only a little,
and I could comprehend and approve of all this. Just one step, and
my misery would become joy. But I can't take that step . . ."
(756). Like all of Malte's diary entries, this one is tentative and
unsatisfying for him. Each records his struggles, his new insights,
or his despair at backsliding. The whole is a record of his difficult
maturation and of his changing conception of art. The passage just
cited culminates in two quotations that Malte writes down in his

diary for courage and support; these are a prayer by Baudelaire, in which he begs God to allow him "the grace of producing a few beautiful lines which prove to myself that I am not the lowliest of men," and a passage from the lamentations of Job (757).

There are numerous examples of Malte's struggle to learn to see. The most difficult problem he faces is his habit of imagining the world instead of dealing with the one that actually exists, and having the courage to portray it as it is. He is constantly surprised by the intensity and uniqueness of reality, which he had shunned and underestimated. He had chosen to stay in the room with his father while the doctors performed the heart procedure, for example, with the cool assertion that it seemed a shame to let such an unusual opportunity go by, and anyway, he no longer believed in disappointments. But then the experience is so much more than, and so different from, what he thought: "No, no, you cannot imagine anything in the world, not the slightest thing. Everything is put together out of so many single details, which can't be predicted" (854). Elsewhere he willfully creates a life history for his neighbor whom he never sees, or for people on the street. In one episode we follow Malte from his habitual conceit of invention, unrooted in truth, through the shock of recognition and the grateful humility that follows. He had been aware of a blind newspaper vendor who walked up and down a certain stretch of wall, calling out his papers. Malte admits that he was trying to create this man out of his imagination: "I was busy trying to picture him to myself. . . . For I had to make him, as one makes a dead person, for whom there are no longer any proofs, no components. . . ." (900). He utilizes all sorts of outside referents, as well as preconceptions of how a blind man looks, to create the image. But eventually the difficulty of the process, and his own uneasy awareness of the falseness of what he is trying to do, force Malte to test himself: "In my cowardice in not looking I went so far that finally the image of this man often without any reason would so strongly and painfully contract within me, to such dense misery, that, oppressed by it, I decided to intimidate the increasing skill of my imagination and to annul it by means of the external fact" (901). He decides to stroll past the man one evening and look at him closely. Once again reality comes as a shock: "I knew immediately that my conception was worthless" (902). He enumerates all the subtleties and the essential things that he had neither known nor been able to capture. The encounter turns into a crucial one for Malte, a kind of turning point, in which he comes one step nearer to his goal of humble objectivity: "My God, it occurred to me impetuously, that's how you *are*. There are proofs for your existence. . . . This is your taste, this is what pleases you" (903). Malte is so overwhelmed by the uniqueness, the un- touchability, and the thinglike quality of the blind man that he regards it, for the moment at least, and metaphorically, as a proof of God! For whom else could the man be wearing his garishly patterned tie, his green hatband, the colors that he cannot see but which for Malte were "like the greatest softness on the underside of a bird" (902). The gain for Malte in this experience is expressed in his desire, "that we could only learn, above all, to endure and not to judge" (903). The man's otherness is absolute; he is a thing among things, and neither Malte nor anyone else has the right to judge him, that is, to impose himself or his assumptions on him.

It is significant that the thing about the blind man that most moves Malte, and that is most convincing of the man's reality, is the colors. Rilke's native sensitivity to color had grown since his electrifying encounters with Cézanne's art at the Salon d'Automne in 1907. In letter after letter he speaks to Clara of the character and effect of Cézanne's colors, and links them to the painter's power to capture objects precisely and finally. The fruits in his still lifes are "materially real . . . simply indestructible in their stubborn existence."[13] Cézanne's art reconfirmed Rilke in his struggle for poetic objectivity. Rilke also perceived him as important in the creation of the figure of Malte. In one of the letters he reflects on the rightness of finding truth in ugliness as well as in beauty. He is impressed by the fact that Cézanne could recite Baudelaire's fa- mous and shocking poem "Une Charogne" (Carrion) from memory. In this context he suddenly feels that he understands Malte's fate: that Malte had failed his test in reality, although he had honestly tried to pass it. A little later in the same letter, however, Rilke goes on, "but perhaps he passed it," but was exhausted by the effort and "like Raskolnikov he remained behind, used up by the act."[14]

A year later, in another letter to Clara Rilke makes clear the connection he felt between what he valued in Cézanne and the writing of *Malte Laurids Brigge:* "Actually I should have written [Malte] last year, I now feel; after the Cézanne letters, which made such close, hard contact with his figure: for Cézanne is nothing but the first primitive, dry success at that which in Malte had not yet succeeded. Brigge's death; that was Cézanne's life. . . ."[15] Cézanne's last thirty years were devoted wholly and uncompromisingly to his work, and Rilke's admiration and wonder at the man's singleness of purpose shine through his letters. He had lived as Chamberlain Brigge had died: self-contained, concentrated, and consistent with himself. And Cézanne's accomplishment, for Rilke, had been the unsentimental and concrete portrayal of real things based on thirty years of merciless observation. It was this kind of containment and energy that Rilke had dreamed of for his struggling young poet. Occasionally, in his feeling for color or his unsentimental portrayal of life and death, Malte is allowed to approach this goal.

As we have seen, Rilke continually concerns himself with the nature and role of art. At times the making of art, broadly defined, is seen as the only viable human activity. In *The Book of Hours* the monk by his actions creates an ongoing, ever-new deity. In *Duino Elegies* we find it posited as man's duty to name, praise, and thereby immortalize the world. In *Malte Laurids Brigge* Rilke presents art on one level as an ordering force, a way of regarding, structuring, and creating, by means of which the world is made comprehensible and accessible. But in keeping with his habit of presenting opposites and creating tensions between different possibilities, Rilke also allows the idea of "art as ordering principle" to appear in an extreme, comic light. We have seen that Malte's transfiguration depends in part on his ability to relinquish the habit of fantasizing an unreal world. He will become a poet only after he has first learned to perceive and portray reality. In one of the novel's few comic characters (as opposed to humorous moments, of which there are quite a few), Rilke shows a man clinging tenaciously to art and forcing it to fulfill the function of his only contact with reality.

Nikolai Kusmitsch is a neighbor of Malte's in St. Petersburg. His character owes a lot to the Russian literary tradition of the downtrodden petty bureaucrat; his ancestors can be found in the pages of Pushkin, Gogol, and Dostoevsky. After a series of misadventures in which Nikolai Kusmitsch "changes" his spare time into "small change" of minutes and seconds, is cheated by his double, becomes aware of the passage of time as it whistles by his face, recalls that the earth's axis is on a tilt, and finally becomes nauseous from the movements of the earth underfoot, the poor man takes to his bed in despair. He is overwhelmed by the proliferation of reminders of motion and change. The one thing to which he can cling and which brings some calm and order into his ruined life is the recitation of poetry. He lies clutching his bed, seeking a still point amid the cosmic bustle, and "recited long poems. . . . by Pushkin and Nekrasov, in the tone of voice in which children say poems when we require it of them" (865); "If someone slowly recited such a poem, with regular stress of the end rhymes, then there was to a certain extent something stable there, at which one could gaze, internally, of course. What luck that he knew all those poems" (870). There is no doubt that Nikolai Kusmitsch's conception of art as a provider of stability amid chaos is meant to show in humorous form the dangers of art divorced from life and experience.

Malte too regards his poetic activity as a defense against the chaos of life. Early in the diary he declares, "I have done something against fear. I sat and wrote all night . . ." (721). Creativity, willed and conscious, works against the amorphous terrors that he encounters everywhere in Paris, and that, he begins to realize, are typical, not just of Paris, but of human life. But unlike Nikolai Kusmitsch, Malte is not a passive consumer of poetry, nor does he use it mechanically to create a false order. A little further on he propounds his theory of poetry, involving a personal, almost physiological process of internalization: "Verses are not, as people think, feelings (you have those soon enough)—they are experiences. For the sake of one line one must see many cities, people, and things, must know the animals. . . . and it's not enough, either, to have memories. You must be able to forget them . . . and have great patience to wait until they return. . . . Only when they become blood in us, gaze and gesture, nameless and no longer distinguishable from ourselves, only then can it sometimes happen that in a very rare hour the first word of a line stands up in their midst, and emerges from them" (724–25).

An important variant on the theme of art is the subject of storytelling. We have seen the importance Rilke attached to the role of the bard and the storyteller. The structure of *Geschichten* and the narrator's insistence that the stories be passed on to the children bear this out. In addition, several of the tales in that collection deal directly with the telling of stories or the singing of tales: Yegor and his father Timofei, the blind bard Ostap, Ewald with his questions about the medieval skazki. In *Malte Laurids Brigge* the motif resurfaces; here storytelling serves to communicate a sense of order, continuity, and hope. Malte's mother was a good storyteller, able to make him "see" the people she tells about. But Malte learns that the art is difficult, rare, and perhaps endangered. When he asks people to tell him about a particular woman, for example, they "listed all sorts of other things that they knew; but in the process she became once more quite imprecise, and I no longer could picture anything" (786). He discovers for himself the difficulty of telling an event. Recalling a mysterious and terrifying scene in his childhood, he also recalls his inability to relate it to anyone. He had wanted so badly to tell about it, but encountered two difficulties simultaneously: "I pulled myself together indescribably, but it couldn't be expressed so that anyone understood it. . . . And suddenly the fear seized me that [the words] could all at once be there after all, . . . and it seemed to me the worst thing of all, to have to say them" (796). Malte sees this moment in his life as the beginning of his awareness of his solitude and uniqueness. He feels that the moment when he discovered the unsayable is the moment when he began to grow up.

Elsewhere the desire for a real storyteller surfaces overtly. "That people narrated, really told stories, must have been before my time. I never heard anyone telling stories" (844). That Malte is either contradicting himself (which certainly does happen, in the course of the diary) or referring to a specific kind of talent is clear, since he has already said that his mother could tell stories well. Malte must go back into the past, through a series of intermediaries, before he finds such a storyteller. His mother's sister Abelone "couldn't tell stories," but she relates to Malte how as a young girl she had been commanded by her reclusive father, the old Graf Brahe, to write down his memoirs as he dictated them. Her father in turn recalls meeting, as a child, a famous eighteenth-century adventurer and charlatan, the brilliant Count Saint-Germain, "Marquis of Belmare." This Marquis was a natural storyteller—the only real kind, according to the Graf: "Books are empty . . . the blood, that's what is important, that's where we must be able to read. He had remarkable tales . . . in his blood . . . he could open up wherever he wanted, something was always described there" (848). The Marquis had told tales so vivid that the old Graf sometimes feels "that my hands still smell of them" (848). In Malte's demand that poetry "become blood in us" lies a bridge to the archstoryteller, with tales in his blood. Graf Brahe becomes more and more excited as he describes the talents, grace, and peculiar honesty of that man whose entire life was a series of elaborate lies, but who never betrayed his own inner, secret truth. At the end of his passionate outburst, the Graf thrusts a lighted candlestick into Abelone's face and demands, " 'Do you see him?' . . . Abelone recalled that she had seen him" (850). Malte's grandfather, like the bogus Marquis, had been a true storyteller, concerned with the realization of his subject, not with superficial or accidental details. Malte takes after his grandfather in several ways. Both feel that recapturing the days of their childhood is a vital task: and both value the ability to communicate the essence of their subject, so that it can be "seen."

Malte, in the throes of change and growth, often questions his own ability to write a thing the way it ought to be written. Describing the pregnant silence that arose as he sensed that something momentous was about to happen to a neighbor beyond the wall, he says "and now (well, how shall I describe it?) . . ." (875). Or after portraying in sympathetic and intense language the brief career of the False Dmitry, pretender to the Russian throne, Malte loses heart. "Up to this point the thing goes by itself, but now, please, a storyteller, a storyteller: for the few lines that remain must exude a power beyond all contradiction" (884). At many levels *Malte Laurids Brigge* is about the limits and possibilities of language, and the difficulty of communicating. It is itself an attempt to create a new kind of prose, as we know from Rilke's comments about the work in progress.

The now familiar motif of the Prodigal Son can also be viewed as a problem of communication—the conveying in adequate terms of each person's needs in the matter of loving and being loved. Throughout the novel runs the theme of "possessionless love." Rilke praises a number of "great lovers"—all women—who have achieved this rarefied state. In the parable of the Prodigal Son, with which the novel breaks off, the focus is on the beloved rather than the lover—an unwilling beloved, who flees from affection. The diary entry begins, "People will have a hard time convincing me that the story of the Prodigal Son isn't the legend about the man who didn't want to be loved" (938). Malte develops his version of the biblical story from this point of view. The youth so dreads being loved that he does not even want his dogs to follow him into the fields, because "not even before them could one do anything without causing joy or pain" (938). The key to this aversion to being loved lies in Malte's definition and experience of love as a habit that limits and defines the beloved. The youth's greatest pleasure is wandering alone in the countryside, playing whatever role appeals to him at the moment. His greatest unhappiness is having to go home at the end of the day. He had only to enter the house, and "one was already the one who they considered him to be; the one for whom they had long ago created a life out of his little bit of a past and their own wishes" (940).

This fear of limitation, and the desire for absolute freedom of choice about one's own identity, appear several times earlier in the novel, building up to the final parable. They are present in the story of the False Dmitry, who was happy as an imposter until he was accepted, and thus imprisoned, in the role. They were present in the vivid and frightening anecdote from Malte's childhood, where after many afternoons spent creating new selves before a mirror with the help of odd bits of cloth, masks, feathers, and finery found in an attic, Malte suddenly finds himself trapped in one of the costumes. No longer able to choose, identified against his will and cut short in his freedom to create himself, he is so upset that he faints and afterwards falls seriously ill.

In the parable Malte tries once again to express his horror at being limited by an external definition. Here he tries to create a way out for the Prodigal Son, his alter ego. Like the biblical figure, the youth leaves home, but this time because he wishes to escape from the stultifying love of his family. He vows, in vain, never to love, so as not to inflict the same pain on anyone else. Typically Malte, like Rilke, assumes that others feel as he does about being loved. This is a blind spot that Rilke was never able to overcome in his own life, despite the frustrated attempts of various people to convince him that being loved need not mean being subsumed and destroyed.

The Prodigal Son's greatest wish is to be loved as he loves: with a "penetrating, radiant love" (943) that will go right through him without changing him. He finally realizes that the only person capable of a cosmic X ray of this sort is God. Throwing himself into his efforts to love and be loved by God, he discovers how difficult a task this is. At this stage he enters into a sort of tenacious humility that resembles the state of mind of the monk in *The Book of Hours,* or the willed patience that Rilke so often urged upon himself. Not the goal, but the process was all-important: "He nearly forgot God in the hard work of approaching him, and all he hoped

in time to achieve from him was 'his patience in enduring a soul' "
(944).

In the process, he learns to know himself better and decides that
he cannot leave anything in his life undone. His childhood especially
seems to him unfinished, and "to take all of this upon himself again
and truly this time, was the reason that the alienated man returned
home" (945). Believing in himself, he is able to return to his
beginnings. But in the intensity of concentrating on himself, he
had forgotten the love that had driven him away, and is appalled
to find it still flourishing when he returns. His automatic reaction
is to fall to his knees with a gesture of supplication. What he means
is "please don't love me!" What they see is "forgive me"—and they
do, taking him back into the family and smugly picking up their
roles where they had left off. But because they do not really "mean"
him, as the young man now realizes, but some other, nonexistent
person, he is able to remain in their midst, unscathed by their love.
The entry, and the novel, end with the statement, "What did they
know about who he was. He was now fearfully difficult to love, and
he felt that only One was capable of it. But he didn't yet want to"
(946).   ·

The Prodigal Son is, transparently, Malte himself; and in his
intense interest in the parable and his interpretation of the story,
Malte in turn is very close to *his* creator. Many of the problems that
had occupied Malte throughout the novel—communication, the
power of language, authenticity, the importance of reliving childhood, the necessity of change (an echo, in greater detail, of the
straightforward message of the second Apollo poem, "You must
change your life")—come together in the final anecdote. These
strands become ever more tightly interwoven in the works of Rilke's
last years. But first came years of silence and the growing fear that
he had already reached the end.

Chapter Seven

Poems, 1912–26

In chapter 1 I discussed in some detail Rilke's life in the years following the publication of *Malte Laurids Brigge* in 1910: his physical exhaustion, his complex reactions to the outbreak of the war, the reduction of his productivity to a mere trickle. In reading Rilke's letters from this period and looking at the relatively small number of poems published in journals, one gets the impression of a nearly total artistic drought. Yet as Michael Hamburger points out,[1] the uncollected poems from the years after 1908 take up hundreds of pages in volume 2 of the collected works. Many of the poems grew out of the multiple crises of those years. Most important among Rilke's worries was his obsessive concentration on finishing the *Elegies,* begun in 1912, compared to which everything else seemed insignificant to him. In addition, the changes in his attitude toward writing, expressed in *New Poems* and *Malte Laurids Brigge,* had continued to grow and become contradictory, contributing to his paralysis. For these reasons Rilke tended to ignore and underestimate the productions of the years between 1910 and 1922. But some excellent and very revealing poems emerge during this time. It is worth examining a few of the uncollected poems more closely before going on to *Elegies* and *Sonnets.*

By uncollected I mean those poems that were not combined by Rilke into a book or cycle. There had been, of course, individual poems written simultaneously with the great cycles—*The Book of Hours, The Book of Images,* and parts 1–2 of *New Poems.* During the crisis years Rilke wrote almost exclusively such isolated, individual poems; many remained unpublished during his lifetime. He produced no major collections between 1908 and 1922, though he did publish two smaller cycles, the fifteen-poem cycle "Das Marienleben" (The life of Mary, 1913) and "Fünf Gesänge" (Five songs, 1915), a group of hymns to the god of war. Many of the poems from these years were meant as inscriptions and dedications in books that Rilke sent his friends. Of the rest, a number are marked "beginnings and fragments from the realm of the Elegies." Rilke was preoccupied with the great project that he felt he had left unfinished. Certain poems or fragments of poems he felt to be intrinsically related to the *Elegies,* by tone, topic, rhythm, or a combination of these elements; he made notes to that effect in the manuscripts. Others, such as "An den Engel" (To the Angel), obviously arose from the same set of images and concerns.

Familiar Rilkean themes appear in these poems. Some are interpretations of biblical subjects that probe traditional events or figures for new meanings. Others reflect Rilke's ambivalent feelings about an ideal love, related to the one for which Malte had longed— neither with much hope of success. In a poem from June 1914 the poet addresses "You beloved / Lost in advance, you who never arrived" (2:79). In another from July of the same year he warns that it is fitting for a youth to sing about women, "deadly, . . . unreachable . . . strange" (2:85), but that a grown man should be silent about his experiences, as an "older seaman" is silent about his "terrors withstood" (2:85). A bitter poem from 1915 complains, "Alas, my mother tears me down" (2:101). The forty-year-old man still chafed at the obtuseness and egotism of his mother; implied is frustration at himself as well, for still caring so deeply about her opinion of him.

Another subject that still preoccupies the poet is death. Among the poems of this period we find "Der Tod Moses" (Moses' death [2:102]), "Zu der Zeichnung, John Keats im Tode darstellend" (On the drawing showing John Keats in death [2:75]), and "Auferweckung des Lazarus" (Awakening of Lazarus [2:49–50]). In the latter, an angry Christ, his patience at an end, raises the dead just to prove he can do so, but is overcome by horror at his own action. "Requiem auf den Tod eines Knaben" (Requiem on the death of a boy [2:104–7]) presents the thoughts of a newly dead child who had long harbored doubts about the dependability of the adult world, in contrast to his stable, simple, beloved objects: a sugarbowl, an apple, a wooden horse.

The most interesting of these poems about death is the one called simply "Der Tod" (Death) from 1915:

> Da steht der Tod, ein bläulicher Absud
> in einer Tasse ohne Untersatz.
> Ein wunderlicher Platz für eine Tasse:
> steht auf dem Rücken einer Hand. Ganz gut

erkennt man noch an dem glasierten Schwung
den Bruch des Henkels. Staubig. Und: *'Hoff-nung'*
an ihrem Bug in aufgebrauchter Schrift.

Das hat der Trinker, den der Trank betrifft,
bei einem fernen Frühstück ab-gelesen.
   Was sind denn das für Wesen,
die man zuletzt wegschrecken muss mit Gift?

Blieben sie sonst? Sind sie denn hier vernarrt
in dieses Essen voller Hindernis?
Man muss ihnen die harte Gegenwart
ausnehmen, wie ein künstliches Gebiss.
Dann lallen sie. Gelall, Gelall. . . .
. . . .
O Sternenfall,
von einer Brücke einmal eingesehn—:
Dich nicht vergessen. Stehn!

               (2:103–4)

Here you have death, a bluish decoction in a cup without a saucer. A very strange place for a cup: it stands on the back of a hand. Quite easily you can make out on the glazed roundness where the handle broke off. Dusty. And "ho-pe" inscribed on its curve in faded letters. The word the drinker whom the drink concerns read off at a breakfast that's remote. What sort of creatures are these, whom in the end one has to scare off with poison? Would they stay else? Here, are they so infatuated with this meal full of hitches? You have to take hard reality out of them, like a set of false teeth. Then they begin to babble: babba, lalla. . . . O fall of stars, seen from a footbridge once, and scanned: Never may I forget you. Stand![2]

This is not the dignified, intrinsic, and authentic death of the individual which Rilke so often praises. Here death is an unappetizing fluid in a broken cup, dirty, shabby, and incongruous ("on the back of a hand").[3] The poet asks with distaste about these human beings who have to be scared away ignominiously when they cling too long to life. His disgust is expressed in the vivid image of the removal of reality like a set of false teeth. Humans must be forcibly separated from life, and even then they keep on talking incomprehensibly. Mankind is in the habit of regarding death and life as mutually hostile entities, mutually exclusive. We saw this attitude in the Brigge side of Malte's family. Rilke's own view of death is

expressed obliquely in the final three lines. He wrote to Princess
Marie about a meteor he had seen in Toledo; it flamed across the
sky and plunged into darkness at the horizon, beautiful and final.[4]
For him the image represented the union of sky and earth, light
and darkness, that mirrored, in turn, his view of life and death as
a harmonious and mutually necessary whole.

As always, many poems from this period concentrate on the nature
of poetry. Several address or concern other poets—Keats, Shake-
speare (via the "Spirit Ariel" from the *Tempest*), Hölderlin. Rilke
emphasizes in his fellow poets those aspects that occupy himself:
the poet's pain, his relation to inspiration, his risks, and the lesson
his triumphs ought, by rights, to present to us readers: "Why, since
such an eternal one existed, do we / still mistrust the earthly?"
(2:94). Several focus on the poetic crisis in which Rilke found
himself. The most direct and merciless are two from June 1914,
which in their original form were parts of a single poem: "Waldteich" (Forest pond [2:79–82]) and "Wendung" (Turning point
[2:82–84]). In both Rilke looks critically at his former method of
writing and his ideology of impersonal looking—"Anschaun." He
has come to the conclusion that this approach to the world, which
he had worked so hard to achieve and perfect, was in fact cold,
loveless, and therefore doomed to ultimate failure. In "Waldteich"
the poet, speaking in the first person, describes his former method:

> Wenn ich innig mich zusammenfasste
> vor die unvereinlichsten Kontraste:
> weiter kam ich nicht: ich schaute an;
> blieb das Angeschaute sich entziehend,
> schaut ich unbedingter, schaute knieend,
> bis ich es in mich gewann.
>
> (2:81)

When I pulled myself together inwardly before the most incompatible
contrasts, I got no further: I looked on. If the observed thing remained
aloof, I looked more absolutely, looked kneeling, until I won it over into
myself.

He is suddenly worried about how he had treated all those captured
objects:

> Fand es in mir Liebe vor?
> Tröstung für das aufgegebne Freie,

> wenn es sich aus seiner Weltenreihe
> wie mit unterdrücktem Schreie
> in den unbekannten Geist verlor?
>   (2:81)

Did it find love in me? Consolation for relinquished freedom, when out of its world order, as if with a suppressed scream, it lost itself in the unknown spirit?

"Wendung," narrated in the third person, seems at once more distanced and more damning. Like "Waldteich" it first describes the methods of the poet, then passes judgment. The first stanza is a list of supposed successes, as the poet applied his powerful gaze to stars, towers, birds, beasts, and women, willing them into place in his poetic universe. But there came a time when the world took his heart to task and decided "dass er der Liebe nicht habe. / (Und verwehrte ihm weitere Weihen)" (that it was lacking in love, and forebade him further communions [2:83]).[5] For, he goes on,

> . . . des Anschauns, siehe, ist eine Grenze.
> Und die geschautere Welt
> Will in der Liebe gedeihn.
>   (2:83)

Looking, you see, has a limit. And the more looked-at world wants to be nourished by love.[6]

Then follow the lines that form both the turning point of the title and that of the poem—a turning point in the poet's view of himself in relation to the world: "Werk des Gesichts ist getan, / tue nun Herz-Werk" (Work of seeing is done, now practise heart-work [2:83]).[7] The last lines of the poem propose the task before him: to approach once again the "imprisoned images" and get to know them, treat them with respect and kindness. He calls upon himself to turn to the "inward maiden" within him, both the more loving feminine side of his personality, and the conquered maiden who stands for all his loveless poetic conquests. She is

> dieses errungene aus
> tausend Naturen, dieses

erst nur errungene, nie
noch geliebte Geschöpf.
(2:84)

her the laboriously won from a thousand natures, her the being till now
only won, never yet loved.[8]

He readily admits the necessity of this change but knows it will
not be easy. This is implied in the epigraph to the poem, a slightly
altered quotation from his friend, the philosopher Rudolf Kassner:
"Der Weg von der Innigkeit zur Grösse geht durch das Opfer" (The
way from intense inwardness to greatness leads through sacrifice).[9]
What Rilke would have to sacrifice was the hard-won aesthetic
insights and beliefs of many years, on which he had built his best
and most intensely personal works. He would have to turn aside
from a position he had regarded as philosophical and artistic truth,
to approach his subjects in a far humbler, yet more difficult, way.
It is probable that for Rilke this also meant taking a different attitude
toward people. But that would be even more of a challenge.

The year of the "Wendung," 1914, was still relatively fruitful,
producing at least twenty-seven completed poems,[10] twenty-one
dedications[11] (many of them for Loulou Albert-Lazard), and a number of unfinished or rejected sketches for poems. The year 1915
brought only nine finished poems and three dedications, while 1916
saw only seven dedications and no new poems at all. In 1917 and
1918 Rilke wrote one poem and one dedication each. It was only
after the war, in 1919, when he traveled to Switzerland on his
reading tour and began to make new friends, that the number of
dedications rises steeply again, to eighteen. In 1920 at Berg am
Irchel, as we have seen, the icy silence seemed about to thaw, as
Rilke wrote down the twenty-one mysteriously "dictated" poems
"From the Posthumous Papers of Count C. W." Then followed
more silence, travels, the search for a home. Finally, in February
1922, at Muzot, the great project was completed.

Ever since the first poems came to him at Castle Duino in 1912,
Rilke had regarded the completion of the *Elegies* as his principal
poetic task. These poems also came to dominate his personal life,
coloring his moods and influencing his decisions, as much by their
stubborn refusal to be written once and for all, as by their tantalizing

presence. We have seen the difficulties and hesitations that preceded
his finally moving into the tower at Muzot in July 1921. Even then
there were delays, as he addressed himself first to settling in, then
to the huge stack of letters waiting to be answered, and finally, as
a kind of limbering-up exercise, to his translations of Petrarch.

The dam suddenly broke on 2 February in quite an unexpected
way. In three days he produced a group of sonnets, dedicated to
the figure of Orpheus and forming a memorial to a young girl whose
death he had recently heard about. Wera Knoop, the daughter of
a couple Rilke had known in Munich and Paris, had been a gifted
dancer. After contracting a mysterious glandular disease, she ceased
dancing and turned, first to music and then to drawing, moving
gradually from an active art to one that was subtler, quieter, and
less demanding of her physically. Rilke had learned the details of
her illness and death in a letter from her mother on New Year's
Day, 1922, just a few weeks before he wrote the sonnets. Now her
fate as artist and woman merged with his longtime fascination with
the poet Orpheus and burst from him in twenty-five poems that he
had never intended to write.

It was only after this surprising poetic explosion that the actual
work he had hoped for and planned for so long could be accomplished. On 7 February he wrote what would become the seventh
and eighth *Elegies,* and on the next day two more, the completion
of the sixth and ninth. On 11 February he rewrote most of the tenth
and thought he was done. In a letter to Princess Marie, owner of
Duino and supportive friend through the hard years, he wrote:
"Finally, Princess, finally the blessed, how blessed day, when I can
send you the completion—as far as I can see—of the Elegies: ten!
. . . Everything in a few days, it was an inexpressible storm, a
hurricane in the spirit . . . all the fibres and tissues in me groaned—
there was no thinking about food, God knows who fed me."[12]
Interspersed among the larger works of these days were additional
sonnets. And on 14 February in a rush came a final *Elegy,* which
Rilke placed at the center of the cycle as the fifth, replacing another,
"Antistrophes," which he felt fitted less well.

Finally, between 15 and 23 February he wrote another twenty-
nine poems in sonnet form. Not only had the long years of waiting
for the *Elegies* come to a glorious end, the stubborn insistence on
patience and solitude had been vindicated. There now existed a cycle
of fifty-five *Sonnets to Orpheus* as well. Rilke soon recognized that

the two cycles, so different in form and conception, had grown out of the same impulses. Several years later, in a revealing letter to his Polish translator Witold von Hulewicz, Rilke described the work of those long years and concentrated days thus: "I see an endless blessing in the fact that I was able with the same breath to fill these two sails: the little rust-colored sail of the Sonnets and the giant white canvas of the Elegies."[13]

"Elegy" was first used as a formal term for poems in distichs— paired lines, usually in dactylic hexameter, and capable of treating a variety of subjects. Later the term was applied specifically to poems expressing lamentation, renunciation, or melancholy; the early German theorist Martin Opitz in 1624 recommends the elegiac form for "sad matters." *Duino Elegies,* a cycle of ten long poems, continues both of these traditions. The lines, though irregular, rest on a framework of dactylic feet; and the underlying tone, at least of the first five and the eighth elegy, is that of a lament, while the tenth raises "lament" to the level of allegory, with stately figures inhabiting their own melancholy land.

The central concerns of the cycle are the structure of human fate and the mission of the poet to praise, and thereby to help give purpose and significance to, human life. Man is portrayed somewhere between the realm of animals, who live harmoniously and by instinct, and the absolute, represented here not by God but by angels. The poet tries to establish a dignified and acceptable relationship with these aloof figures. Man is at home neither in earthly life nor in the permanent world of the spirit. He has continually botched his chances and has made a lie of his relationship to death. In the *Elegies* the poet takes a long, critical, and at times almost despairing look at mankind, and attempts to discover a niche for which we alone are suited in the grand scheme of existence.

One of the most striking images in the *Elegies,* and one that unites the various poems, is the figure of the angel. This figure dominates the first two poems and hovers in the background of the others, acting as sounding board and standard by which to judge our success as human beings. The Rilkean angel departs from the biblical tradition, opposing the familiar angelic figure and discouraging attempts to read the *Elegies* as a Christian work. The traditional angels were active, serving as messengers of God and executors of his commands. They communicated directly with man, wrestling with

Jacob, announcing her fate to Mary, visiting Tobias in the guise of a traveler. (The latter tale is referred to in the second *Elegy* as an example precisely of the way men were once able to relate to the angels.) Rilke's angels, however, exist beyond the world of men, pursuing their own mysterious purposes, oblivious to time and space.

The angels have occasioned a great deal of debate among Rilke critics, with varied and often opposing results. For the critics Kretschmar and Dehn, the angels are "a substitute creation, an eschatological beloved."[14] For Mason and Günther, they are the "symbol of a demonic artistic calling," while Holthusen sees them as an ideal to be striven for, a "projection of human possibilities." For Angelloz they are the "absolute existing angel," and to Guardini they seem "newly arisen gods." Two of the best-known translators of Rilke's works, J. B. Leishman and Stephen Spender, in their commentary to the *Elegies,* provide a far-reaching and thoughtful appraisal of the angels: "a perfect consciousness . . . a being in whom the limitations and contradictions of present human nature have been transcended, a being in whom thought and action, insight and achievement, will and capability, the actual and the ideal, are one. He is both an inspiration and a rebuke, a source of consolation and also a source of terror; for, while he guarantees the validity of Man's highest aspirations and gives what Rilke would call a 'direction' to his heart, he is at the same time a perpetual reminder of Man's immeasurable remoteness from his goal."[15] Rilke himself addressed the problem of interpreting his angels in a letter he wrote to Hulewicz in 1925. In the course of his work on the Polish translation, Hulewicz had asked a number of questions about problematic lines. In reply Rilke calls the angels "those beings who surpass us," and goes on:

The "Angel" of the Elegies has nothing to do with the angel of the Christian heaven (rather with the angelic figures of Islam).[16] . . . . The angel of the Elegies is that creature in which the transformation of the visible into the invisible, which we are performing, appears already accomplished. . . . The angel of the Elegies is that being which stands for the recognition of the invisible as a higher level of reality. Therefore "terrible" for us, since we, its lovers and transformers, still cling to the visible.[17]

The dichotomy of visible/invisible that Rilke stresses in the letter, and whose unifying transformation we and the angels are engaged in, is a central image in the *Elegies*. Positing man's lostness in the universe and his failure to discover his true role, the poet searches for and gradually arrives at an answer. Our task is to sing, to praise the world, and thereby immortalize it, by transforming the visible things into "invisible" objects of language, the imagination, and the spirit. The *Elegies* follow a zigzag course of lament and hope, sometimes regressing as the poet is struck by another proof of our insufficiency, then rallying again as the concept of praise takes shape and begins to seem possible.

In the very first lines of the first *Elegy* the poet demands,

> Wer, wenn ich schriee, hörte mich denn aus der Engel
> Ordnungen? und gesetzt selbst, es nähme
> einer mich plötzlich ans Herz: ich verginge von seinem
> stärkeren Dasein.
>
> (1:685)[18]

Who, if I cried out, would hear me in the ranks of the angels? And even assuming that one suddenly took me to his heart, I would expire from his stronger existence.

The angels are aloof, unaware of our inferior presence, and even if one were to notice us, the experience would kill us. The abyss between our natures is too great. Rilke goes on in the first poem to describe some aspects of man's sorry state; we are not at home here and have no genuine connection to the rest of creation. He asks whether lovers might not be mankind's hope, existing on a different level of consciousness; but this idea is rejected as mutual- and self-delusion. If anything, hope might lie in *abandoned* lovers, familiar from earlier works, who have managed to free themselves from the need for reward or permanence. The youthful dead have been initiated into the true relation of life and death, but those who are alive "machen / alle den Fehler, dass sie zu stark unterscheiden" (all make the mistake of making too sharp a distinction [688]) between the two realms. Angels, on the other hand, are at home in both; in fact, they "[wissen] oft nicht, ob sie unter / Lebenden gehn oder Toten" (often don't know if they walk among the living or the dead [688]).

A further question posed here, and pursued through the succeeding *Elegies,* is, who or what on earth needs us? The dead no longer do, and at those times when some object has offered itself to us—a star, a violin which desired our attention—we failed to do what was hoped for:

> Das alles war Auftrag.
> Aber bewältigtest du's? Warst du nicht immer
> noch von Erwartung zerstreut, als kündigte alles
> eine Geliebte dir an?
>
> (686)

That was all an assignment. But were you able to master it? Weren't you always distracted by expectation, as if everything were announcing a lover for you?

In the second *Elegy* the idea of the angels' vast superiority to us is reiterated: "Jeder Engel ist schrecklich. Und dennoch, weh mir, / ansing ich euch, fast tödliche Vögel der Seele . . ." (689) (Every angel is terrible, and yet, alas, I greet you, nearly fatal birds of the soul). But as frightening as they are, the poet has no choice but to address them, since they are our only possible audience. He apostrophizes them by many names, eliciting their glorious, bright nature. The rest of the *Elegy* presents by contrast our feeble essence and fading emanations, in a world where everything nonhuman seems stable and solid:

> Wie Tau von dem Frühgras
> hebt sich das Unsre von uns, wie die Hitze von einem
> heissen Gericht. O Lächeln, wohin?
>
> (690)

Like dew from the early grass, that which is ours rises from us, like the heat from a hot dish. Oh smile, where to?

Once again Rilke considers the lovers as a possible salvation, since they might be capable of an exalted exchange of love, something peculiarly human. But love, too, is fleeting, and human emotions change. At the end of the poem the poet expresses his yearning for a place for us:

Fänden auch wir ein reines, verhaltenes, schmales
Menschliches, einen unseren Streifen Fruchtlands
zwischen Strom und Gestein.

(692)

If only we too could find a pure, reserved, narrow humanity, our own
strip of fertile land between stream and stone.

The desire for permanence is a troubling and ambivalent question
that persists throughout the cycle. The lovers desire but cannot
achieve permanence, for "Bleiben ist nirgends" (abiding is nowhere
[687]). The second *Elegy* laments the temporary, insubstantial nature
of man and ends with a cry for a place, no matter how humble,
which mankind could call its own. But later the desirability of
permanence is called into question. And throughout the cycle it is
implied that not permanence in the realm of life but the unification
of life and death, of the visible and the invisible, is the desired
goal.

No angels appear in the third *Elegy*, which is devoted wholly to
earthly things, to the dark, sexual, subconscious portion of our
lives. The protective love of mother and bride is overshadowed by
the subterranean forces of anonymous lust. "Eines ist, die Geliebte
zu singen. Ein anderes, wehe, / jenen verborgenen schuldigen Fluss-
Gott des Bluts" (693) (It's one thing to sing the beloved. It's another,
alas, to sing that hidden guilty river god of the blood). The poet
invokes a mother figure who, like Malte's mother, was gentle and
loving, but who, unlike either Malte's or Rilke's own, represented
safety and peace, was always there to fend off the shadows and noises
of the night. But even she could never defend him against human
nature:

. . . Aber *innen:* wer wehrte,
hinderte innen in ihm die Fluten der Herkunft?
. . . Liebend
stieg er hinab in das ältere Blut, in die Schluchten,
wo das Furchtbare lag. . . .

(695)

But within: who prevented, hindered inside him the floods of origin?
Loving, he descended into the elder blood, into the ravines where terror
lay.

The ages of human experience and biological urges that are stored within him resent the presence of the girl who loves him. The poet begs her to protect the youth from them and from himself, to take over the role, transformed and still precarious, of the mother whose aid had failed him long before.

The fourth *Elegy* returns to the themes of alienation and once again compares our clumsy, inept behavior to the harmony thought to exist in nature:

> Wir sind nicht einig. Sind nicht wie die Zug-
> vögel verständigt. Überholt und spät,
> so drängen wir uns plötzlich Winden auf
> und fallen ein auf teilnahmslosen Teich.
>
> (697)

We are not at one. Are not in agreement like the birds of passage. Overtaken and delayed, we force ourselves suddenly on the winds and fall onto an indifferent pond.

Rilke points out our propensity for strife and, echoing his familiar conviction, declares that lovers, instead of bringing mutual liberation, limit one another's horizons. This idea leads into a vivid metaphor, that of the theater of the heart. The poet sits before the "heart's curtain" and waits for the show to begin. He rejects the dancer who appears on stage, as merely an actor in disguise, a bourgeois wearing a mask. Even the soulless doll would be preferable, he says, for at least it is "full": identical with itself, it has its own peculiar integrity.

The poet digresses to address his dead father and others who had once loved him. Like Malte and the Prodigal Son, he had escaped from the misdirected love of people who did not understand him. All that remains to him, seated before the empty stage, is *"Zuschaun"* (watching [698]). In earlier works Rilke had often emphasized the importance of the engaged onlooker; here too he invokes this paradoxical activity. The lyric "I" declares that he will watch so intensely that an angel will be forced to appear on the stage. This spiritual creature, all-knowing and at home in the realms of life and death, will join with the doll, which is completely artificial and without a soul, to create the play: "Dann kommt zusammen, was wir immerfort / entzwein, indem wir da sind" (699) (Then is re-

joined that which we continually separate by our very existence).
The poet then passes from the theater metaphor to a vision of a
child. The child has the potential for wholeness; he is unaware of
past or present, life or death as separate entities, and is content with
what he knows of the world and his own place in it. But adults in
their false consciousness cannot grasp this harmony and purity, and
force him into their bifurcated mold. For

> . . . den Tod,
> den ganzen Tod, noch *vor* dem Leben so
> sanft zu enthalten und nicht bös zu sein,
> ist unbeschreiblich.
>
> (699–700)

to contain death so gently, the whole of death, even *before* life, and not
to be angry, is indescribable.

The fifth *Elegy,* the last to be written, focuses on a troupe of
traveling acrobats about to perform. It takes its visual imagery from
two principal sources: Père Rollin, a French acrobat whose troupe
Rilke had seen in Paris, and the Picasso painting *Les Saltimbanques*
(The acrobats), which hung in an apartment in Munich in which
Rilke had lived for several months during the summer of 1914.[19]
The emphasis of the poem is once again on man's temporary and
unintegrated existence, exemplified here by the lives of the performers who, shabby and passive, are wrung, tossed, and bent like
toys by a "never-satisfied will" outside themselves. The pace and
intensity of this poem are immense. It leaps from one set of images
to another by unpredictable but apt transitions. First the acrobats
perform on a threadbare carpet, "Aufgelegt wie ein Pflaster, als
hätte der Vorstadt - / Himmel der Erde dort wehe getan" (701)
(laid on like a bandage, as if the suburban sky had wounded the
earth at that spot). Standing there, ready for their next act, they
form "des Dastehns grosser Anfangsbuchstab" (the great initial letter
of Duration). This image reflects the distribution of the figures in
Picasso's painting; in the poem it represents for a fleeting instant
that elusive state of permanence that haunts the poet. But then they
are tossed again by the playful and merciless hand, and the poem
moves on to another image, that of an ever-blossoming, ever-de-
foliating rose of spectators.

The focus then shifts to the separate performers. Rilke captures salient features while denying them real individuality: a shriveled man whose skin looks as if it once held two; an innocent and burly simpleton, "als wär er der Sohn eines Nackens / und einer Nonne" (as if he were the son of a neck and a nun [702]). Rilke dwells with affection on the two children in the troupe—a little boy whose shy smile the poet would like to place in a vase with the inscription *"subrisio saltat."*—acrobat's smile—because of its courage in existing in spite of everything, and the young girl whom he describes, unripe and vulnerable, as a "market fruit of resignation" (703–4).

Rilke envisions the process by which the performers, practicing a new act, are transformed suddenly from something ungainly, all effort and clumsy intensity, into its opposite, "Jenes leere Zuviel, / wo die vielstellige Rechnung / zahlenlos aufgeht" (that empty surfeit where the long column of figures adds up to zero [704]). In this state, their perfected motions are smooth, accurate, and lifeless. The process reminds him of the movement of all of us toward death and leads into the image of a square in Paris where "die Modistin, *Madame Lamort"* (the hat maker, Madame Death [704]) plies her trade, creating cheap, shabby hats out of artificial materials. Our life, like that of the wandering acrobats, is a series of new beginnings and subsequent disappointments. Our death is false, like the hats of Madame Lamort. This insight brings Rilke to the climax of the poem, in which he cries out to the angel, as perhaps the only one who can understand him, his wish for a place on some ineffable carpet somewhere in the universe. There the lovers—he returns here to the figures in whom, in spite of everything, he places most hope—could perform like cosmic acrobats, achieving rare feats of unity and completion before grateful audiences of the dead.

A southern image, that of the fig tree, opens the sixth *Elegy,* which was begun in Spain in 1912 and finished in Muzot. The fig tree bears almost no blossoms; it seems instead to concentrate all its energy in the fruit. Unlike the tree, most humans linger in life at the blooming stage, focusing on the exterior, and squander their essence in "show." Only the hero and those destined to die young can fairly be compared with the fig tree. Like it, they concentrate their forces early, within, and are soon ready for action. Rilke briefly maintains the comparison with the fig tree, whose branches are bent and trained to grow in a certain direction, by his use of the image of "der gärtnernde Tod" (the gardening death [706]). In the case

of the hero he "anders die Adern verbiegt" (twists the veins differently [706]) to produce a special fruit. Rilke then drops the garden
metaphor and goes on to the character of the hero. Like the youthful
dead, he is not tempted by permanence. The hero's whole life
consists of being, will, and choice. Even in his mother's womb he
exercised his will, deciding who to be. At the end of the poem,
Rilke returns to the figures emphasized in the third *Elegy*, the mother
and the lover, who create, nourish, and sacrifice for the hero. The
last lines echo Rilke's belief both in the importance of love in forming
another person and in its ultimate powerlessness to hold him back:

> Denn hinstürmte der Held durch Aufenthalte der Liebe,
> jeder hob ihn hinaus, jeder ihn meinende Herzschlag,
> abgewendet schon, stand er am Ende der Lächeln,—anders.
>
> (708)

For the hero stormed through lodgings of love, every heartbeat aimed at
him lifted him up; already turned away, he stood at the end of the smiles,
transformed.

Rilke adds to the doctrine of possessionless love the idea of the
strongly intentioned man, focused on daring and change and, above
all, not distracted by externals or concerned with permanence—
which, it seems, human beings can never achieve. A life like the
season of the fig tree, short, intense, and productive, is perhaps the
best we can hope for.

The seventh *Elegy* continues the upswing of mood felt in the
tentative hopefulness of the sixth. The poem begins with a joyful
comparison of the poet's voice and his search to the cry and flight
of a bird in spring. The bird song is portrayed in stages that show
Rilke's fine ear and careful observation. Contained within this series
of rising, spreading notes, however, is the concept of falling; for
bird and man, a return to earth is seen as natural and inevitable.
The lines singling out the wonders of nature—summer mornings,
pathways, meadows, the freshness after a storm, the stars of summer—are the most positive and hopeful in the *Elegies* up to this
point, and the reader senses the shift immediately.

The next section focuses on young girls, living and dead, who
love life and would come in answer to the poet's call. Here Rilke
begins to sound a new theme that will expand and gain in contour

until it represents both the poet's solution to the search, so near despair in the earlier parts of the cycle, for man's unique purpose, and the final message of the *Elegies*. He begins with a strong, unequivocal statement: "Hiersein ist herrlich" (Being here is glorious [710]). Even those who died early or led miserable lives in filthy cities (an echo of the *The Books of Hours* and *Malte Laurids Brigge*) experienced, at one time or another, a moment of true Being, were authentic and intensely alive.

The problem is that the greatest joys exist fully only after we have internalized them and made them invisible: "Nirgends, Geliebte, wird Welt sein, als innen. Unser / Leben geht hin mit Verwandlung" (711) (Nowhere, Beloved, will world exist but within. Our life passes in transformation). He refers obliquely and disparagingly to the modern world of electricity and power plants, of indifference to the old and the sacred. His advice is to cling to the things we know, the man-made forms that have withstood change. The next stage in Rilke's contemplation brings him closer to the answer he had sought; he addresses the angel once more, but this time with the feeling that he has something worth saying and showing. Referring to the soaring monuments of architecture, he asks,

> War es nicht Wunder? O staune, Engel, denn *wir* sinds,
> wir, o du Grosser, erzähls, dass wir solches vermochten, mein Atem
> reicht für die Rühmung nicht aus. So haben wir dennoch
> nicht die Räume versäumt, diese gewährenden, diese
> *unseren* Räume. (Was müssen sie fürchterlich gross sein,
> da sie Jahrtausende nicht unseres Fühlns überfülln.)
> Aber ein Turm war gross, nicht wahr? O Engel, er war es,—
> gross, auch noch neben dir? Chartres war gross—, und Musik
> reichte noch weiter hinan und überstieg uns. Doch selbst nur
> eine Liebende—, oh, allein am nächtlichen Fenster . . .
> reichte sie dir nicht ans Knie—?
>   Glaub *nicht*, dass ich werbe.
> Engel, und würb ich dich auch! Du kommst nicht. Denn mein
> Anruf ist immer voll Hinweg; wider so starke
> Strömung kannst du nicht schreiten. Wie ein gestreckter
> Arm ist mein Rufen. Und seine zum Greifen
> oben offene Hand bleibt vor dir
> offen, wie Abwehr und Warnung,
> Unfasslicher, weitauf.
>   (712–13)

Wasn't it a miracle? Oh marvel, angel, for it is *we,* we oh you great one; tell how we were capable of such a thing, my breath doesn't suffice for the praising. So after all we didn't neglect the spaces, these generous spaces of ours. (How fearfully large they must be, since thousands of years of our feelings haven't overfilled them.) But a tower was tall, wasn't it? Oh angel, it was,—tall even next to you? Chartres was great, and music stretched up even further and outstripped us. But even a lover, alone at the window at night . . . didn't she reach up to your knee? *Don't* think I'm wooing. Angel, and even if I did, you won't come. For my call is always full of distance: you cannot stride against such a strong current. Like a stiffened arm is my call. And its hand, open up there, for grasping, remains open before you like resistance and warning, Incomprehensible One, up there.

Here is the proud cry of man, small but brave, who discovers that he has made a gesture in eternity after all. The seventh *Elegy* began "Werbung nicht mehr, nicht Werbung" (wooing no longer, not wooing [709]); this intention is picked up and reinforced in the passage quoted. The angel remains our audience, the boundary of our existence. But he is no longer to be courted and sought after like a coy and superior lover. The poet, as spokesman for our race, announces to the angel that we too have our valuable achievements, things that even an angel must notice and acknowledge. As we become aware of our own worth, we grow in dignity and independence, so that the appeal to the angel for his attention and praise is at the same time a warning to him to keep his distance.

Upon this expression of joy and pride at being human, the eighth *Elegy* comes as a shock. In the questions it asks, it echoes the fourth *Elegy*; in its tone it represents a sudden plunge back to the edge of despair. Once again Rilke compares the animals, which live in equanimity because they are unaware of death, with human beings, who are aware *only* of death. We even turn our children around so that they gaze backward at creation, rather than ahead into openness, totality, and freedom from fear. Again Rilke suggests that lovers have the most potential for such real vision. But then he reminds himself that they get in each other's way and block the view.

This poem goes further than the fourth *Elegy* in one sense, for here Rilke suggests that even other mammals share our sense of loss (an idea that does not entirely surprise, recalling the dog poems of earlier years):

> Denn ihm auch haftet immer an, was uns
> oft überwältigt,—die Erinnerung,

als sei schon einmal das, wonach man drängt,
näher gewesen, treuer und sein Anschluss
unendlich zärtlich.
(715)

For he too is tinged with that which often overpowers us—with memory,
as if that for which we strive had once been nearer, more innocent, and
its connection endlessly tender.

He goes on, "Nach der ersten Heimat / ist ihm die zweite zwitterig
und windig" (after the first home, the second seems to him hybrid
and drafty [715]). The origins of this Neoplatonic yearning seem
to lie in the fact of birth itself. For, Rilke goes on, the little creatures
not born of a womb lead a different kind of life, secure and un-
troubled by loss:

O Seligkeit der *kleinen* Kreatur,
die immer *bleibt* im Schoosse, der sie austrug;
O Glück der Mücke, die noch *innen* hüpft,
selbst wenn sie Hochzeit hat: denn Schooss ist alles.
(715–16)

Oh blessedness of the little creature who always remains within the womb
that bore it. Oh joy of the gnat, which still hops within, even when it
celebrates its wedding: for womb is all.

The passage continues with the striking image of a bat, a creature
born of a womb but doomed to fly:

. . . Wie vor sich selbst
erschreckt, durchzuckts die Luft, wie wenn ein Sprung
durch eine Tasse geht. So reisst die Spur
der Fledermaus durchs Porzellan des Abends.
(716)

as if shocked at itself, it zigzags through the air like a crack through a
cup. Thus the trail of the bat cleaves through the porcelain of evening.

This is one of Rilke's most vivid images of disorientation and dis-
harmony; the harsh sounds of the words "wie vor sich selbst er-

schreckt, du*rchzuckts* die Luft" reflect the visual image of the darting
bat and Rilke's conception of it as quintessentially not at home.

Rilke then turns to the plight of alienated man, the eternal
spectator. By implication, our attempts at ordering the world are
like the seemingly pointless, frenetic movements of the bat. Rilke
asks, Who turned us around so that we always appear to be taking
leave? The imagery of the eighth *Elegy* repeats many details from
the fourth: the initial comparison of the sovereign animals and
alienated man, the emphasis on parting (in the theater of the fourth
Elegy, "die Szenerie war Abschied," the stage-set was parting [697]),
the child that has potential for wholeness but is perverted by adults,
the failure of lovers to transcend. It is as if Rilke in 1922 were
summoning all the fears he had expressed in 1915, when the earlier
poem was written, to confront and exorcize them.

One important difference exists between the two poems: this is
the shift in emphasis toward *Schauen.* In the fourth *Elegy,* there
seems to be little for the human being to do but watch; even after
the actors have left the theater of the heart, he remains stubbornly
sitting on: "Ich bleibe dennoch. Es gibt immer Zuschaun" (I'll stay
regardless. There's always watching [698]). In the eighth, watching
is no longer the only alternative. In fact, it is seen as negative, a
sign of our nonintegration into life: "Und wir: Zuschauer, immer,
überall, / dem allen zugewandt und nie hinaus!" (and we: onlookers,
always and everywhere turned toward everything, and never out-
wards [716]). We are passive and awry, our sight turned away from
the one thing worth watching.

The poem is gloomy, like the fourth, but in the back of our
minds remains the germ of renewal and liberation that we found in
the intervening sixth and seventh *Elegies.* In fact, the ninth reopens
the brighter registers of these poems and surges forward with the
message of joy at our newly discovered power and purpose. Returning to the idea of the goodness of existence, Rilke emphasizes
the finiteness and uniqueness of our lives, repeating the phrase "ein
Mal"—"once"—six times in four lines, and incidentally remainding
us of his non-Christian orientation. The new element in the ninth
Elegy is the realization that the world needs us—us, of all creation
"die Schwindendsten" (the most transient [717]).

Little that is concrete can we take with us into death. Rilke
presents as a metaphor for this fact the wanderer, who, upon his
return from the mountaintops to the valley, brings back, not a

handful of earth, but "ein erworbenes Wort, reines, den gelben und blaun / Enzian" (a word he's acquired, pure, the blue and yellow gentian [718]). Our new task will resemble his: to take words on our journey as the symbol and container of our experiences. At this juncture Rilke asks what amounts to a rhetorical question, for it is clear that he is already swept away by the idea:

> . . . Sind wir vielleicht *hier,* um zu sagen: Haus
> Brücke, Brunnen, Tor, Krug, Obstbaum, Fenster,—
> höchstens: Säule, Turm . . . aber zu *sagen,* verstehs,
> oh zu sagen *so,* wie selber die Dinge niemals
> innig meinten zu sein.
>
> (718)

Are we perhaps *here* in order to say: house, bridge, fountain, gate, pitcher, fruit tree, window,—at most: column, tower . . . but to *say* it, understand, to say it in such an inward way as even the objects never imagined for themselves.

He goes on to answer his own question firmly, combining a declaration and a command: "*Hier* ist des *Säglichen* Zeit, *hier* seine Heimat. / Sprich und bekenn" (*Here* is the time for the *tellable, here* is its home. Speak and acknowledge it [718]). The emphasis is on earth, the present, our human realm. Referring once again in passing to the empty and impersonal things and actions of modern life, Rilke arrives here at the heart of the *Elegy,* and articulates the task that is possible for us humans alone: "Preise dem Engel die Welt" (Praise the world to the angel [719]). We are warned not to get fancy, not to try to show him things at which he can always beat us. Rather we should show him the simple, everyday things like music or handicrafts, which are permeated by our human essence.

The path to this act of praise passes through the act of transformation, as suggested in the seventh *Elegy.* We fulfill ourselves as human beings, the speaking animal, descended from Adam the namer, at the same time that we fulfill the longing of all visible creation to become invisible—that is, absorbed by us, turned into words and images and thus immortalized.

> Erde, ist es nicht dies, was du willst: *unsichtbar*
> in uns erstehn?—Ist es dein Traum nicht

einmal unsichtbar zu sein?—Erde! unsichtbar!
Was, wenn Verwandlung nicht, ist dein drängender Auftrag?
Erde, du liebe, ich will.

(720)

Earth, isn't this what you want: to arise in us *invisible?* Isn't it your dream
once to be invisible? Earth! invisible! What, if not transformation, are
your urgent instructions? Earth, dear one, I will.

Nor should we assume that this is a purely aesthetic solution, intended for poets alone—though it certainly is a personal solution
and a vindication of his own life in the poet's eyes. But Rilke is
careful to include all people in the task. Objects, he says, want us
to transform them in our invisible hearts, "wer wir am Ende auch
seien" (whoever we are [719]). What we as human beings all share
is language and the ability to transform the world into words that
cannot decay. Anyone can do it; and in a tone reminiscent of the
1908 Apollo, "you must change your life," Rilke urges us all to
begin.

In reading the tenth *Elegy* one has the feeling that Rilke has
mounted to a different plane of consciousness. The poem focuses on
lamentation, but the mood is sure, firm, calmly triumphant. The
poem opens with a series of wishes on the part of the poet. Sorrow
should not be shunned or despised, but greeted as "unser winter-
währiges Laub, unser dunkeles Sinngrün, / *eine* der Zeiten des heim-
lichen Jahres" (our hardy winter foliage, our dark sensual evergreen,
one of the seasons of the secret year [721]). The dark side of existence,
always important for Rilke, is raised to new prominence as the
concluding statement for the entire *Elegy* cycle.

The first set of images after this introductory section creates a
marvelously scathing allegory of modern life in the form of the Leid-
Stadt, the City of Pain, and its surrounding suburbs and fairgrounds.
Here he pillories false piety, institutional religion, games of chance,
peddlers of moral values of all kinds, and, for adults only, true
pornography: "wie das Geld sich vermehrt, anatomisch" (how money
reproduces, anatomically [722]). The images contain a brilliant
evocation of the tawdry world of the carnival, filled with sharp
observations of modern man as a social animal. The ready-made
church (presumably one that was not built from the ground up on
faith and community, but bought, as it were, off the rack) is "rein-

lich und zu und enttäuscht wie ein Postamt am Sonntag" (clean and closed and disappointed like a post office on Sunday [722]). Onomatopoeic passages evoke the sound of the shills and the shooting galleries.

But just beyond the fence enclosing this pandemonium, reality begins. Here we find children, dogs, and lovers—three of Rilke's positive types concentrated as a contrast to the noisy falseness of the city and the fair. We follow a youth who "loves a Lament," but he turns back; he cannot go with her. But the youthful dead can, and do, follow her into a second allegorical landscape, the Land of the Laments. The mood and diction of this section are reminiscent of those in "Orpheus. Eurydike. Hermes." Here, too, the young dead are led gently along a path through a silent meadow, during the "ersten Zustand / zeitlosen Gleichmuts" (the first state of timeless serenity [723]). An older Lament guides a dead youth through the countryside, pointing out the monuments, ruins, and crops in the land of the dead. Here we find images arising from Rilke's trip to Egypt. The serenity and mystery of the Sphinx form an important part of the mythological landscape and of Rilke's conception of an afterlife.

In a spectacular series of synaesthetic images, Rilke portrays the heightened and transformed senses of the dead youth. The Lament gazes at the face of the Sphinx, and

> hinter dem Pschent-Rand hervor, scheucht es die Eule. Und sie,
> streifend im langsamen Abstrich die Wange entlang,
> jene der reifesten Rundung,
> zeichnet weich in das neue
> Totengehör, über ein doppelt
> aufgeschlagenes Blatt, den unbeschreiblichen Umriss.
>
> (724–25)

from behind the edge of the double crown it [her gaze] flushes an owl. And in a slow downward stroke along the cheek, that ripest roundness, softly it sketches on the new hearing of the dead, across a doubly opened page, the indescribable outline.

The owl's flight, described in visual terms of surface and contour, is recorded in the dead youth's hearing, a spatial occurrence made audible. This is possible only in the land beyond death's threshold. Other new experiences await the youth there, including a new set

of stars. One constellation is "das klar erglänzende *'M,'* / das die
Mütter bedeutet" (the clearly glowing *"M"* that stands for the Mothers [725]). This double reference not only evokes the ambiguous
figure who has represented both love and security and threatening
dependence through Rilke's works. It also echoes the land of the
Mothers in the second part of Goethe's *Faust*—those mysterious
chthonic figures who control the archetypes, the forms of all future
life. Thus in the night sky over this land of death we find a source
of life, Rilke's desired union made manifest.

The dead boy climbs away from us into the mountains of primeval
pain. His last discovery, or rather, the sign he would give us if he
could, is the drooping catkins of the hazel bush, which symbolize
the paradox of life in death:

> Und wir, die an *steigendes* Glück
> denken, empfänden die Rührung,
> die uns beinah bestürzt,
> wenn ein Glückliches *fällt*.
>
> (726)

And we, who think of *mounting* happiness, would feel the emotion that
almost fills us with consternation when something fortunate *falls*.

The youth is dead to our world, yet experiences new, touching, and
inspiring things in death. He accepts the burden of lamentation
and enters the mountains alone. The hazel buds hang down, just
as the spring rains fall downward, both seemingly images of death
and despair. Yet the catkins will turn to blossoms and leaves, and
the rains will urge new life from the earth. We must, Rilke implies,
unlearn our stock responses to the world, and specifically to the
downward-pulling images of sorrow and death. He reiterates the
view he has held and developed over the years, that death itself is
fruitful, the key to wholeness.

After the intense, painful grappling of the *Elegies* and their grand
conclusion, the two sequences of the *Sonette an Orpheus*, fifty-five
poems in all, come as a sense of relief.[20] It is as if we were reading
a miniature, warmer, more intimate version of the same process;
they are indeed a "small rust-colored sail" to the *Elegies'* "giant white
canvas." Formally there is great variety in these poems. Many of

them are sonnets only by the broadest definition of the term. All do have fourteen lines, and all are divided, in the manner of the Petrarchan sonnet, into an octave (two quartets) and a sestet (two tercets). But the variety of rhyme scheme and line length is astonishing. In addition to iambic pentameter, "Ein Gótt vermágs. Wie áber, ság mir, sóll . . .", (732), we find trochaic lines, "Stíller Fréund der viélen Férnen, fúhle" (770), and two-foot dactyls, "Wír sind die Tréibenden / Áber den Schrítt der Zéit" (745). Elsewhere Rilke experiments with an extremely long line: six-foot dactyls, "Sínge die Gärten, mein Hérz, dié du nicht kénnst; wie im Glás" (765) or even seven-foot lines, "Wó, in wélchen ímmer sélig bewässerten Gärten, an wélchen" (762).

Some lines seem purposely constructed to forestall scansion, to make the reader halt and stumble. Such a poem is the first of the second sequence, which begins,

> Atmen, du unsichtbares Gedicht!
> Immerfort um das eigne
> Sein rein eingetauschter Weltraum. Gegengewicht
> in dem ich mich rhythmisch ereigne.
>
> (751)

breathing, you invisible poem! Worldspace, constantly, purely exchanged for our own existence. Counterweight, in which I rhythmically occur.

The uneven stresses, the abrupt *g, d, t* and intermittent *m* sounds, and the staccato internal rhyme of *sein, rein, ein-,* combine to make a great boulder of a strophe, strongly at odds with its message, which is a paean to the continuous, effortless "poem" of the act of breathing.

The first sequence of sonnets is more tightly structured than the second, its strophic forms and subject matter internally more consistent. The second sequence contains more formal experimentation. The two sets of poems are held together by the figures of Orpheus and the young dancer Wera Knoop. They also share with each other and with the *Elegies* an emphasis on praise and lamentation and on the positive interpenetration of life and death. The themes of poetry and the poet permeate the sonnets, evoked by the figure of Orpheus.

In the third poem of the first set, Rilke asks how a mere human being can achieve the clarity and distance of real poetry, as the gods know it:

Ein Gott vermags. Wie aber, sag mir, soll
ein Mann ihm folgen durch die schmale Leier?
Sein Sinn ist Zwiespalt. An der Kreuzung zweier
Herzwege steht kein Tempel für Apoll.

Gesang, wie du ihn lehrst, ist nicht Begehr,
nicht Werbung um ein endlich noch Erreichtes;
Gesang ist Dasein. Für den Gott ein Leichtes.
Wann aber *sind* wir? Und wann wendet *er*

an unser Sein die Erde und die Sterne?
Dies *ists* nicht, Jüngling, dass du liebst, wenn auch
die Stimme dann den Mund dir aufstösst,—lerne

vergessen, dass du aufsangst. Das verrinnt.
In Wahrheit singen, ist ein andrer Hauch.
Ein Hauch um nichts. Ein Wehn im Gott. Ein Wind.
                                                  (732)

A god can do it. But how, tell me, is a man supposed to follow him
through the narrow lyre? His mind's dichotomy. At the crossroads of two
heart-paths no temple to Apollo stands. Song, as you teach it, is not desire;
not the pursuit of something that's finally achieved. Song is Being. Easy,
for the god. But when will we *be?* And when will *he* turn the earth and
stars toward our existence? This *isn't it,* Youth, the fact that you love,
even though your voice then wrenches your mouth open—learn to forget
that you began to sing. That will pass. To sing truly is a different breath.
A breath about nothing. A breeze in the god. A wind.

We find here once again the underlying complaint of the *Elegies:*
man's ambivalence, his ineptness, his inability to reach the essential
core of things. Man appears here in his Faustian guise. Like Faust,
"two souls" tear at him—in this case, the opposing forces of art
and life. In the second quartet Rilke states simply the ethos that is
implied in the conduct of his own life: song is Being. It is not
something linear or practical, partial or temporary. It is essential
and whole. But how to achieve this wholeness? The suggestion made
by Malte is reiterated here more compactly. Poetry is not mere
experience, mere emotion; these are only the first steps. The difficult
part is to suppress them, "forget" and assimilate them, renounce
one's personality and the urge to express it. Experience must first
ferment within us before it can reemerge as truth or as poetry.

Orpheus exercises his symbolic function in various guises in the *Sonnets*. He charms the beasts out of the forest with his singing, presents the possibility of praising "in spite of," and stands for the longed-for union of life and death. Orpheus is familiar with death from his descent into Hades to retrieve Eurydice, and from his own death at the hands of the jealous maenads and his subsequent resurrection and repeated death. Here Rilke mixes the Orphic legend with that of Dionysus, the god of the vine, ever dying and reborn. As in "Orpheus. Eurydike. Hermes," Orpheus is equated with the poet per se. By alluding to his special role as a singer of both realms, Rilke restates the need to unite life and death via song and praise. In the sixth sonnet Rilke asks of Orpheus, "Ist er ein Hiesiger? Nein, aus beiden / Reichen wuchs seine weite Natur" (Is he from here? No, his ample nature grew out of both realms [734]). And in the ninth poem he states unequivocally,

> Nur wer die Leier schon hob
> auch unter Schatten,
> darf das unendliche Lob
> ahnend erstatten.
>
> Nur wer mit Toten vom Mohn
> ass, von dem ihren,
> wird nicht den leisesten Ton
> wieder verlieren.
>
> (736)

Only he who has already raised his lyre among the shades may carry out the endless praise, with foreboding. Only he who has eaten of the poppies of the dead will not lose the slightest tone.

Orpheus has literally sung among the dead. The mortal poet is to do the same, by means of experience and willing suffering. He is urged to forget—to eat the poppies of the dead, their lulling opium—in order to remember ultimately and permanently. As in the third poem, a kind of apprenticeship of suffering and humility is called for.

Related to the figure of Orpheus and the ideals of praise and death is the motif of transformation that appears in the first set of sonnets and dominates the second. Some of the most graceful and convincing poems of the cycle are those dealing with transformation and growth. Several deal with the change of a piece of fruit into the fibers and feelings of the person eating it. In one of these Rilke also suggests that the essence of dance is transformation—the same idea that appeared in "Spanische Tänzerin." Young girls are urged to "dance the orange" they have just eaten. The fruit becomes one with the girls, who in turn transform its sweetness and the residue of southern climes latent in it, into their dance. The dance poems in the cycle are a tacit memorial to Wera Knoop, the dancer who was transformed against her will.

In another poem a sort of family tree of mankind grows up out of a crowd of pugnacious, jostling ancestors. The twigs and branches are tangled, until one at the very top "biegt sich zur Leier" (takes shape as a lyre [742]), undergoing a change into a higher form of human life, by becoming an instrument for song. In the first poem of the second set Rilke stresses the very act of breathing, which absorbs pure space into human life and in turn fills space itself with the speaker's essence. The sestet expresses a warm feeling of kinship between man and the rest of the universe:

> Wieviele von diesen Stellen der Räume waren schon
> innen in mir. Manche Winde
> sind wie mein Sohn.
>
> Erkennst du mich, Luft, du, voll noch einst meiniger Orte?
> Du, einmal glatte Rinde,
> Rundung und Blatt meiner Worte.
>
> (751)

How many places in space were once within me! Many a wind is like my own son. Do you recognize me, Air, full of places that used to be mine? You, once smooth rind, the curve and leaf of my words.

More important, perhaps, than the sense of kinship is the fact that here, as in the later *Elegies,* man is not only on the receiving end of the gift, but he also has something to offer and rejoices that the air is full of exhalations still bearing traces of him, the "curve of his words."

A number of other poems affirm the need for and rightness of transformation. Sonnet 12 of the second series begins with a command: "Wolle die Wandlung. O sei für die Flamme begeistert, /

drin sich ein Ding dir entzieht, das mit Verwandlungen prunkt"
(Will the transformation. Oh, be charmed by the flame in which
a thing which flaunts metamorphoses retreats from you [758]). It
is not enough to accept change passively; we must desire it and seek
it out. The poem contains references to all four of the basic elements—earth, air, water, and fire—thus symbolically embracing
all the possibilities for physical transformation. The sonnet also
reiterates the warning, contained at various points in the *Elegies,*
that in life, duration and stasis are ephemeral.

Rilke's personal favorite among the *Sonnets* was the thirteenth of
the second group, a poem permeated by the same urgency as the
one just before it. In March 1922 he sent a copy of it to Frau
Oukama Knoop, Wera's mother, with the message, "Today I'm
sending you just one sonnet, since . . . it's the closest to me and
ultimately, the most valid."[21] It begins,

> Sei allem Abschied voran, als wäre er hinter
> dir, wie der Winter, der eben geht.
> Denn unter Wintern ist einer so endlos Winter,
> dass, überwinternd, dein Herz überhaupt übersteht.
>
> (759)

Be ahead of all parting, as if it were behind you, like the winter that's
just on its way out. For among winters, one is so endlessly winter that,
having made it through the winter, your heart survives after all.

That is, do not wait for events to catch up with you, for life to
move you. Exercise your human will and the ability to desire and
to act. Do not be overcome by partings, but seek them, severing
ties before they are severed for you by circumstance. Do not fear
growth, or solitude, or death. This statement of values is obviously
significant, coming from a man whose whole life was a series of
partings, from people he loved or who loved him, from situations
that offered warmth and protection. But Rilke always felt the call
to break away for the sake of his work; here he urges the reader to
do the same, while reassuring us that after the deepest of winters,
the dark night of the soul, we will in fact survive. The power of
this quartet lies in the audacious use of repetition. Words based on
"winter" appear four times in three lines, and the perceptible up-
surge in the last line comes via three words beginning with *über*

(over, upward), and reaching their finale in the triumphant *übersteht* (survives, comes through).

The second quartet begins with an invitation to imitate Orpheus, "Sei immer tot in Eurydike" (Be ever dead in Eurydice [759]), and ends, "sei ein klingendes Glas, das sich im Klang schon zerschlug" (be a ringing glass which already burst in the ringing [759]). The poet urges us to take risks, and sing out even if the act of singing is your destruction. Holthusen calls this image a typically Orphic transformation of the visible (the glass) into the invisible (the glass shatters, leaving pure sound).[22] It is also a concrete example of the ideal act suggested in the *Elegies*. In the tercet the poet reminds us of the simultaneous and equal demands of life and death. "Sei— und wisse zugleich des Nicht-Seins Bedingung" (be, and know, at the same time, the requirements of Non-being [759]). The poem ends with a command to merge with the totality of nature, to achieve annihilation in a celebration of wholeness.

The final poem in the cycle seems an intensification and sharpening of the message of previous poems, as well as a reprise of their images and a summation of their tendencies. It opens with an image reminiscent of the earlier sonnet in praise of the transformational act of breathing. In this poem the reader is reminded how his breath fills and expands space itself; he has become air and resounds through it like a tolling bell. He is then urged:

> Geh in der Verwandlung aus und ein.
> Was ist deine leidendste Erfahrung?
> Ist dir Trinken bitter, werde Wein.
> (770)

Go in and out amidst transformations. What is your worst experience? If drinking is bitter for you, become the wine.

One should will not only change, but contradiction. We are told to seek out precisely what pains us, and learn to know it intimately, embracing our antiselves. The poem ends with the lines

> Und wenn dich das Irdische vergass,
> zu der stillen Erde sag: Ich rinne.
> Zu dem raschen Wasser sprich: Ich bin.
> (771)

And though earthly things forgot you, say to the quiet earth: I'm flowing,
to the rapid water speak: I am.

In this paradoxical self-affirmation lies the whole ethos of poetry-
making. Man must exert his will and imagination over the accidents
of existence, and make art out of chaos. In the *Elegies* Rilke's ultimate
solution was to declare to the angels man's one talent and purpose,
that of making the world immortal through the language of praise.
Here, too, man is portrayed as the creature who imposes order. By
laying his identity on the line and himself on the scales, he creates
a tension between himself and the world; out of the one-sidedness
of nature comes a balance of opposites. A creature of protean flex-
ibility and watchful perceptiveness, man has finally found his niche
in creation.

The years between the completion of the *Elegies* and Rilke's death
in 1926 were shadowed by illness and foreboding. But many of the
poems from this period reflect the warm afterglow of the events of
February 1922, focusing on the regenerative powers of nature. Many
deal with the delicate subtleties of spring. In one the aging poet
urges the young to enjoy their youth:

> was war ich jung!
> Und nun seid ihrs. Oh seids, oh seids!
> Ohne Bedenken, ohne Geiz.
>
> (2:265)

How young I was! And now you are young. Oh, be it, be it! Without
qualms, without stinginess.

But he goes on, and this makes the poem more than just the
sentimental nostalgia of a man past his prime, casting a melancholy
look at the young: "Ich bin es *noch*. Und bin sogar noch Kind. /
Fühlende *bleiben,* was sie fühlend *sind*" (2:265) (I am still young.
And am even still a child. Feeling ones remain, what they are
through feeling). After all that he has experienced, and already filled
with the final disease, Rilke places himself in the ranks of the
eternally young, by virtue of his essential sensitivity to life. In "Die
Weide von Salenegg" (The willow of Salenegg [2:274]), written in
August 1926, four months before his death, Rilke praises the te-

nacity of the life force within an ancient willow tree that, apparently
dead, suddenly put forth new shoots within the rotten trunk.

Familiar motifs recur in other poems between 1922 and 1926.
The dead still wander among us, purifying our actions or testing
their own new state. Falling reappears as a value, echoing the *Elegies'*
vision of a "fallendes Glück." Roses and mirrors abound, and we
are reminded that there is no permanence for mankind. Several of
the late poems are remarkable for their tightness and economy, such
as the cryptic "Idol," or "Gong," which presents paradoxical transformations at a new level, inverting and convoluting the relationship
between sound and source, hearing and silence.

Rilke's last poem was written in his diary in mid-December 1926.
Aware of his approaching death, he bids the last, greatest pain to
come to him, "du letzter, den ich anerkenne, / heilloser Schmerz
im leiblichen Geweb" (you final one whom I acknowledge, hopeless
pain in the corporeal fabric [2:511]). Images of fire occur seven
times; the poet speaks of having "climbed onto the confused pyre
of suffering" and compares his former spiritual fire with that which
now devours his body. Toward the end of the poem he approaches
a problem that had always been a source of dread for him: the loss
of self:

> Bin ich es noch, der da unkenntlich brennt?
> Erinnerungen reiss ich nicht herein.
> O Leben, Leben: Draussensein.
> Und ich in Lohe. Niemand der mich kennt.
>   (2:511)

Is it still I who burn there unrecognizably? I do not drag in memories.
Oh life, life: to be outside. And I in flames. No one who knows me.

He had always feared the time when he might no longer be in
control of his body or his mind. It was this thought most of all
that depressed him during his progressing illness. Even at the end
he refused painkillers, because of their side effect of dulling his
perceptions and his clarity of mind.

Now he is a prisoner within the flames of his body and realizes
fully the truth of each person's ultimate isolation. Like the old man
in the Crémerie, he is filled with "horror at something that was
happening within him," and "he knew now that he was retreating

from everything" (6:754). He recognizes that what he is experiencing is unique in his life. It cannot and ought not be compared to other illnesses, which always contained the hope of recovery:

> Verzicht. Das ist nicht so wie Krankheit war
> einst in der Kindheit. Aufschub. Vorwand um
> grösser zu werden. Alles rief und raunte.
> Misch nicht in dieses was dich früh erstaunte.
>   (2:511)

Renunciation. This is not how sickness once was, in childhood. Postponement. An excuse to get bigger. Everything called and murmured. Do not mix with this, what once astonished you.

With this poem Rilke acknowledged the imminent event that he had long feared, yet which had been the praised subject of his writing for many years. Few have faced the knowledge of death so calmly or lucidly, or with such poignant control.

Chapter Eight
Conclusion

In the preceding pages we have followed Rilke's career from his somewhat uncertain beginnings in the provinces, through experimentation and an increasing firmness and delicacy of style, to his achievements as a poet of world magnitude. We have seen how indelibly certain experiences in childhood and youth impressed themselves on his psyche, and how he pursued certain topics with consistency and fortitude through a career of over thirty years. Living when he did, Rilke witnessed the demise of an era and a way of life. He was born into a Europe of aging empires, of tradition, culture, and, for those who could manage it by birth or by luck, of mobility and grace. When he died he left a world sobered by war, revolution, and famine, a world of new boundaries and new technologies.

Like all members of his generation, Rilke had to come to terms with these things, and they are reflected in his works. Above all, however, he remained drawn to questions which do not disappear through mass disasters or with the redrawing of lines on a map, but are only intensified and made more urgent by being of an essentially individual nature. I have tried to show how his attitude toward religion, art, love, death, and the writing of poetry took shape over the years. I have also tried to show the essentially open, cosmopolitan nature of this man whose interests, travels, and friendships were in the entire European world. Despite the ambiguities present in his personality and his works, Rilke was a large man, expansive in his concern for the fate of human beings in a difficult world.

His reputation has had it ups and downs, often for reasons extraneous to the quality of his writing. Attitudes have ranged from that of an early biographer who claimed to have seen an aureole around Rilke's head the first time she saw him, to Georg Lukacs's assertion that in at least one work by Rilke there is an affinity to Hermann Goering. Critics have tended to take extreme positions, thus alienating both the readers in the other camp and those who, initially full of goodwill and in search of new literary experience, are put off by the irrational furor surrounding this author. The 1970s have seen a healthy resurgence of interest in Rilke, spurred in part by the hundredth anniversary of his birth in 1975 and the fiftieth anniversary of his death in 1976. We now have a large choice of recent translations and biographies, while scholars continue to produce specialized studies and new editions of letters. Those readers who insisted on Rilke's place as a religious poet have fallen silent, as have those for whom the poet was damned either as the suspect favorite of a militaristic generation of Germans, or the spokesman for a decadent aristocratic world. It is to be hoped that the future will bring more balanced studies, with a renewed emphasis on the works produced by this often unhappy, always contradictory man. This will be aided as more information becomes available from archival sources and from hitherto unpublished (or expurgated) letters and diaries. The Rilke legend—or legends—are in the process of being laid to rest. It is time for Rilke to take center stage once more as citizen of modern Europe and a world-class poet.

Notes and References

Chapter One

1. *Briefe aus den Jahren 1914 bis 1921* (Leipzig: Insel, 1938), 351 (*GB,* vol. 4).

2. Hans Egon Holthusen, *Rainer Maria Rilke in Selbstzeugnissen und Bilddokumenten* (Hamburg: Rowohlt, 1958), 26.

3. Unlike most of his later patronesses, lovers, and friends, Valerie left in her memoirs a rather spiteful account of her relationship with Rilke, who appears there as a pimply, clinging adolescent who took advantage of her love and goodwill.

4. For more on Lou, see H. F. Peters, *Lou: Das Leben der Lou Andreas-Salomé* (Munich: Kindler, 1962), and Rainer Maria Rilke and Lou Andreas Salomé, *Briefwechsel* (Zurich: Max Niehans & Insel, 1952).

5. For Rilke's Russian connections see Patricia Pollock Brodsky, *Russia in the Works of Rainer Maria Rilke* (Detroit: Wayne State University Press, 1984); Sophie Brutzer, *Rilkes russische Reisen* (Königsberg, 1934; reprint, Darmstadt: Wissenschaftliche Buchgesellschaft, 1969); Leonid Chertkov, *Rilke in Russland: Auf Grund neuer Materialien* (Vienna: Verlag der Österreichischen Akademie der Wissenschaften, 1975); and *Rilke und Russland: Briefe, Erinnerungen, Gedichte,* ed. Konstantin Asadowski (Frankfurt: Insel, 1986).

6. For more about Rilke and landscape, as well as about his Worpswede period, see J. Sandford, *Landscape and Landscape Imagery in R. M. Rilke* (London: University of London, Institute of Germanic Studies, 1980); Richard Pettit, *Rainer Maria Rilke in und nach Worpswede* (Bremen: Worpsweder Verlag, 1983); and H. W. Petzet, *Das Bildnis des Dichters* (Frankfurt: Insel, 1976).

7. Pettit, *Worpswede,* 44–45.

8. *Tagebücher aus der Frühzeit* (Frankfurt: Insel, 1942), 217–18.

9. Pettit, *Worpswede,* 120.

10. For more on Paula Becker, see Pettit, *Worpswede;* Petzet, *Bildnis;* and Paula Modersohn-Becker, *In Briefen und Tagebüchern,* ed. Günter Busch and Liselotte von Reinken (Frankfurt: S. Fischer, 1979).

11. William Weaver, *Duse* (London: Thames & Hudson, 1984).

12. Wolfgang Leppmann, *Rilke: Leben und Werk* (Bern: Scherz, 1981), 328.

13. Ibid., 330.

14. Magda von Graedener-Hattingberg, *Rilke und Benvenuta: Ein Buch des Dankes* (Vienna: Wilhelm Andermann, 1943).

15. Pettit, *Worpswede*, 255.

16. Leppmann, *Rilke*, 370.

17. Ibid., 386.

18. For a detailed discussion, see J. R. von Salis, *Rainer Maria Rilke: The Years in Switzerland* (Berkeley: University of California Press, 1966), and *Schweizer Vortragsreise, 1919*, ed. Rätus Luck (Frankfurt: Insel, 1986).

19. Von Salis, *Years in Switzerland*, 60–61.

20. *Briefe an Nanny Wunderly-Volkart*, vol. 1 (Frankfurt: Insel, 1978), 496.

21. Rilke often preferred nicknames for his women friends. Thus Baladine was Merline, Magda von Hattingberg was Benvenuta, and Nanny Wunderly-Volkart was Nike.

22. Paul Valéry, foreword to "Les Roses," quoted in Von Salis, *Years in Switzerland*, 195–96.

23. For an account of these meetings see Maurice Betz, *Rilke Vivant: Souvenirs, lettres, entretiens* (Paris: Editions Emile-Paul Frères, 1937), or the German version, *Rilke in Frankreich: Erinnerungen, Briefe, Dokumente* (Vienna: Herbert Reichner Verlag, 1938).

24. Von Salis, *Years in Switzerland*, 257.

25. For information about Rilke's friendship with Cvetaeva and the literary effects on both writers, see Patricia Pollock Brodsky, "On Daring to be a Poet: Rilke and Marina Cvetaeva," *Germano-Slavica* 3, no. 5 (Fall 1980); and Rainer Maria Rilke, Marina Zwetajewa, and Boris Pasternak, *Briefwechsel*, ed. Jewgenij Pasternak, Jelena Pasternak, and Konstantin M. Asadowskij (Frankfurt: Insel, 1983).

26. Patricia Pollock Brodsky, "Objects, Poverty and the Poet in Rilke and Cvetaeva," *Comparative Literature Studies* 20, no. 4 (Winter 1983):388–401, presents a detailed study of Rilke's influence on Cvetaeva's long poem "Lestnica" (The staircase).

27. For descriptions of his last days, see Von Salis, *Years in Switzerland*, and George C. Schoolfield, *Rilke's Last Year* (Lawrence: University of Kansas Libraries Series no. 30, 1969).

Chapter Two

1. See Sandford, *Landscape*.

2. Leppmann, *Rilke*, 252.

3. Ibid.

4. Andrea Pagni, in *Rilke um 1900: Ästhetik und Selbstverständnis im lyrischen Werk* (Nürnberg: Verlag Hans Carl, 1984), devotes a chapter to the works of Rilke's early period (1:7–36).

5. Ibid., 19.

6. For an extended comparison, see Karl Webb, *Rainer Maria Rilke and Jugendstil: Affinities, Influences, and Adaptations* (Chapel Hill: University of North Carolina Press, 1978).

7. A valuable article is Ursula Münchow's "Das 'tägliche Leben: Die dramatischen Experimente des jungen Rilke," in *Rilke-Studien: Zu Werk und Wirkungsgeschichte* (Berlin: Aufbau Verlag, 1976), 9–52. See also Howard Roman, "Rilke's Psychodramas," *Journal of English and Germanic Philology* 43 (1944):402–10; Frank H. Wood, "Rilke and the Theater," *Monatshefte* 43 (1951):15–26: and Pettit, *Worpswede,* 170–79.

8. For a detailed comparison, see Brodsky, *Russia,* 36–42.

9. Leppmann, *Rilke,* 159.

10. Pettit, *Worpswede,* 172.

11. Leppmann, *Rilke,* 31.

12. Eudo Mason, *Rilke, Europe and the English-Speaking World* (Cambridge: Cambridge University Press, 1961), 19ff.

13. Ernst Zinn, afterword to *Übertragungen,* ed. Karin Wais (Frankfurt: Insel, 1975), 320.

14. He wrote eight poems in Russian between November 1900 and April 1901. They are published, together with German translations, in *SW,* 4:947–71. For a discussion see Brodsky, *Russia,* 44–55.

15. Génia Tschernositow, "Les Derniers mois de Rainer Maria Rilke," *Les Lettres* (Paris), 1952, 218 (special Rilke issue).

16. *Das Igor-Lied: Eine Heldendichtung* (Leipzig: Insel, 1960).

17. For a detailed discussion see André von Gronicka, "Rainer Maria Rilke's Translation of the 'Igor Song' (Slovo)," in *Russian Epic Studies,* ed. Roman Jakobson and Ernest J. Simmons (Philadelphia: American Folklore Society, 1949), 179–202: Caryl Emerson, "Rilke, Russia and the Igor-Tale," *German Life and Letters* 33, no. 3 (April 1980):220–33: and Brodsky, *Russia,* 31–35.

18. *Übertragungen,* 329.

19. Quoted in *Rilkes Leben und Werk im Bild,* ed. Ingeborg Schnack (Wiesbaden: Insel, 1956), 13.

Chapter Three

1. Leppmann, *Rilke,* 32.

2. By 1969, more than 1,077,000 copies had been sold.

3. The Insel Publishing House, founded by Anton Kippenberg in 1902, published most of Rilke's major works, and is today still the major publisher of works on and by Rilke. The Insel-Bücherei was a series of books published by the house beginning in 1912. Each volume consisted of a single work or several short works by a single author. They were slender volumes with interesting type faces and handsomely designed covers, and included both the best new writers, and authors from the previous century. These little books were a milestone in quality publishing.

4. August Stahl, *Rilke Kommentar: Zu den Aufzeichnungen des Malte Laurids Brigge, zur erzählerischen Prosa, zu den essayistischen Schriften und zum dramatischen Werk* (Munich: Winckler, 1979), 107.

5. *Cornet,* 7.

6. Rainer Maria Rilke and Marie von Thurn und Taxis, *Briefwechsel,* vol. 2 (Zurich: Niehans & Rokitansky, 1951), 543.

7. Mason, *Rilke, Europe,* chap. 10.

8. Walter Seifert, *Das epische Werk Rainer Maria Rilkes* (Bonn: Bouvier, 1969), 73.

9. Rilke and Lou Salomé, *Briefwechsel,* 143.

10. For discussions see Brigitte Bradley, "Rilke's *Geschichten vom lieben Gott:* The Narrator's Stance toward the Bourgeoisie," *Modern Austrian Literature* 15, nos. 3–4 (1982):1–24; Thomas Elwood Hart, "Simile by Structure in Rilke's *Geschichten vom lieben Gott,, Modern Austrian Literature* 15, nos. 3–4 (1982):25–70; Walter Seifert, *Das epische Werk,* 88–109; and Brodsky, *Russia,* 96–131.

11. Seifert, *Das epische Werk.*

12. The *bylina* (plural *byliny*) was the oral epic of early medieval Russia. The historical songs served a similar function in the later medieval period. It is important to note that the Middle Ages lasted well into the seventeenth century in Russia. *Byliny* usually occurred in cycles, similar to the *Chansons de Gestes* or the Arthurian tales in the West. The largest had as its setting the court of Prince Vladimir of Kiev (978–1015); it focuses on semilegendary heroes. The historical songs focus on real people; many of them deal with the exploits of Czar Ivan IV (the Terrible).

13. Kobzars were the traditional folk singers of the Ukraine, so called because of the stringed instruments they played, called a kobza or a bandura.

Chapter Four

1. Many readers have seen in these lines an echo of the early German mystics, particularly some verses of the seventeenth-century writer Angelus Silesius. However, as E. C. Mason convicingly argues, Rilke had little to do with the asceticism, surrender, and emphasis on faith of traditional mystics. ("Zur Entehung und Deutung von Rilkes Stunden-Buch," in *Exzentrische Bahnen: Studien zum Dichterbewusstsein der Neuzeit* [Göttingen: Vandenhoeck & Ruprecht, 1963], 191–92). Rather, Rilke's concept takes us in the opposite direction, to an affirmation of the creative self.

2. The monastery referred to in the poem about the monks, as well as in the list of God's "inheritance," is the Pecherskaya Lavra, a monastery founded in caves near Kiev in the eleventh century by a community of ascetic monks. Gradually they retreated further and further from the distractions of ordinary life, until they lived in dark individual cells in total silence. When they died, their bodies were preserved by a quirk of the air and climate underground, and Rilke saw them there when, with hundreds of Russian pilgrims, he visited the monastery in 1900. Rilke's point is that in their zeal they became totally useless for themselves or for God.

3. See, for example, the short drama *Waisenkinder* (Orphans [*SW*, 4:919]); the stories "Albrecht Ostermann" (*SW*, 4:663–71), "Frau Blahas Magd" (Mrs. Blaha's maid [*SW*, 4:623–29]), and "Der Drachentöter" (The Dragonslayer [*SW*, 4:672–88]); the poetic cycle "Aus einer Sturm-nacht" (From a stormy night [*SW*, 1:460–64]), later incorporated into *The Book of Images;* and the last two Russian poems (*SW*, 4:959, 964).

4. Mason, "Zur Entstehung," 202.

5. Wolfgang Bittner, quoted in Reinhold Grimm, *Von der Armut und vom Regen: Rilkes Antwort auf die soziale Frage* (Königstein: Athenäum, 1981), 78.

6. The lines in the girl's books will close over as did her eyes. But the word *verwachsen* contains a wealth of nuances, including to become overgrown like a neglected garden, to grow wild, and, as an adjective, to be crooked or deformed; all shadings are implied in Rilke's image.

7. T. S. Eliot, "Four Quartets," in *The Complete Poems and Plays, 1909–1950* (New York: Harcourt, Brace & World, 1962), 121.

Chapter Five

1. Several critics have attempted to analyze *New Poems* from the point of view of structure. The most helpful studies are two by Brigitte Bradley on the two parts of the cycle. Brigitte Bradley, *Rainer Maria Rilkes Neue Gedichte: Ihr zyklisches Gefüge* (Bern: Francke, 1967), and *Rainer Maria Rilkes 'Der Neuen Gedichte Anderer Teil': Entwicklungsstufen seiner Pariser Lyrik* (Bern: Francke, 1976).

2. Eudo C. Mason, *Rilke* (Edinburgh: Oliver & Boyd, 1963), 53.

3. Among the most fruitful sources, for the reader, of Rilke's ideas on these subjects, and on how art ought to be made, are the *Rodin* monograph (*SW*, 5:139–280), and the letters written to Clara from Paris in October 1907, in which he discusses his confrontation with Cézanne's art (*Briefe aus den Jahren 1904 bis 1907* [Leipzig: Insel, 1939]—*GB*, vol. 2).

4. Ibid., 279–80.

5. Bradley, *Der Neuen Gedichte Anderer Teil*, 9.

6. Hans-Henrik Krummacher, review of *Rainer Maria Rilkes Neue Gedichte: Versuch einer Deutung*, by Hans Berendt, *Euphorion* 53 (1959):478.

7. Paul Böckmann, "Der Strukturwandel der modernen Lyrik in Rilkes 'Neuen Gedichten,' " *Wirkendes Wort* 12 (1962):341.

8. Ingeborg Schnack, *Rainer Maria Rilke: Chronik seines Lebens und seines Werkes*, vol. 1 (Frankfurt: Insel, 1975), 160.

9. *New Poems*, trans. Edward Snow (San Francisco: North Point Press, 1984), 73.

10. Ibid., 41.

11. Snow in his translation has transformed one of the participles, *sich . . . verbreitend*, "spreading itself," into an active verb, "spreads out."

12. August Stahl, *Rilke Kommentar zum lyrischen Werk* (Munich: Winckler, 1978), 206.

13. *Briefe aus den Jahren 1906 bis 1907* (Leipzig: Insel, 1930), 41.

14. A year later, on 21 October 1907, Rilke remarks in a letter to Clara that from Cézanne he had learned "to what extent painting takes place among the colors, how one has to leave them alone, so that they come to terms with one another. Their interaction among themselves: that is the whole of painting" (*Briefe 1904–1907*, 442–43). His comprehension of Cézanne's message was obviously based on his own feelings for color and composition.

15. Snow, *New Poems*, 113.

16. Bradley, *Der Neuen Gedichte Anderer Teil*, 10, suggests that this may also refer to the panther skins associated with Dionysus and be intended as a reminder of Apollo's ancient connection with this figure.

17. Ibid., 25. For a detailed analysis of the poem, see ibid., 19–26. For a discussion of the poem in relation to Dionysus, Nietzsche, and Dostoevsky, see Brodsky, *Russia*, 186–92.

18. Eudo Mason, "Merline und die besitzlose Liebe," in *Exzentrische Bahnen*, 265ff.

19. See Brodsky, *Russia*, 182–86, for a discussion of these motifs.

20. On the Prodigal Son in *Geschichten*, see Brodsky, *Russia*, 96–131. For an analysis of the theme in Rilke's works in general, see Byong-Ock Kim, *Rilkes Militärschulerlebnis und das Problem des verlorenen Sohnes* (Bonn: Bouvier, 1973).

21. The inspiration for the two poems from 1906 may also have included a statue by Rodin entitled "Prière" (Supplication), which portrays the Prodigal Son, and a medieval tapestry in a church in Marburg. See Jennifer Liebnitz, "The Image of the Prodigal Son in Rilke's Poetry," in *Rilke and the Visual Arts*, ed. Frank Baron, (Lawrence: Coronado Press, 1982), 11–17.

22. *Übertragungen*, 125–48.

23. *Briefe, 1904–1907*, 418.

24. Ibid., 421.

Chapter Six

1. Rilke and Lou Salomé, *Briefwechsel*, 53.

2. Ibid., 56.

3. Rilke to Emile Verhaeren, 4 January 1908, in Schnack, *Chronik*, 1:297.

4. *Briefe an seinen Verleger, 1906 bis 1926* (Leipzig: Insel, 1936), 52 (*GB*, vol. 6).

5. Ibid., 53.

6. Ibid.

7. *Briefe aus den Jahren 1907 bis 1914* (Leipzig: Insel, 1933), 53–54.

8. Rilke and Lou Salomé, *Briefwechsel,* 246.

9. Stahl, *Kommentar . . . Zu den Aufzeichnungen,* 154.

10. Because of the obscurity of many of the references in *Malte Laurids Brigge,* it can be difficult to read the novel without some outside help—although Rilke maintained that it should not be necessary and might interfere with a real understanding of the book. Several works exist that aim to decipher some of the historical and other references for the modern reader. These include *Materialien zu Rainer Maria Rilke "Die Aufzeichnungen des Malte Laurids Brigge,"* ed. Hartmut Engelhardt (Frankfurt: Suhrkamp, 1974), especially the article in that volume by Brigitte von Witzleben, "Zu den historischen Quellen von Rilkes 'Die Aufzeichnungen des Malte Laurids Brigge,' " 280–304; and Stahl, *Kommentar . . . Zu den Aufzeichnungen,* 152–252.

11. The episode of Christoph Detlev's death was strongly influenced by Tolstoy's "Death of Ivan Ilich." For a discussion see Brodsky, *Russia,* 132–76.

12. Walter H. Sokel, "Zwischen Existenz und Weltinnenraum: Zum Prozess der Ent-Ichung in *Malte Laurids Brigge,"* in *Rilke Heute: Beziehungen und Wirkungen,* ed. Ingeborg H. Solbrig and Joachim W. Storck (Frankfurt: Suhrkamp, 1975), 105–29.

13. *Briefe, 1904–1907,* 406.

14. Ibid., 434.

15. *Briefe, 1907–1914,* 54.

Chapter Seven

1. *An Unofficial Rilke,* trans. Michael Hamburger (London: Anvil Press Poetry, 1981), 18.

2. Ibid., 63.

3. Rilke described to Princess Marie in detail how this image, reminiscent of a surrealistic painting, came to him while he was walking through a park. See Stahl, *Kommentar zum lyrischen Werk,* 284.

4. Ibid.

5. Hamburger, *An Unofficial Rilke,* 49.

6. Ibid.

7. Ibid.

8. Ibid.

9. Ibid., 47.

10. The term comes from *SW,* vol. 2, where "completed poems" are those which Rilke himself considered finished.

11. Rilke's dedications and personal verses covered a wide range in terms of length, tone, and quality. Some were only three or four lines

long, while between 1924 and 1926 Rilke engaged in a full-fledged correspondence in verse with a young poet, Erika Mitterer. This exchange fills forty pages in *SW*, vol. 2.

12. *Briefe aus Muzot, 1921 bis 1926* (Leipzig: Insel, 1940), 114–15 (*GB*, vol. 5).

13. Ibid., 377.

14. These summaries are taken from the discussion of the angels in Ludwin Langenfeld, "Rainer Maria Rilke," in *Deutsche Literatur im zwanzigsten Jahrhundert*, ed. Hermann Friedmann and Otto Mann (Heidelberg: W. Rothe, 1961), 2:47–48.

15. *Duino Elegies*, trans. J. B. Leishman and Stephen Spender (New York: Norton, 1939), 87–88.

16. In Islam the angels fulfill the same function as in the Judaeo-Christian tradition; there are guardians, messengers, chroniclers, and recorders, as well as avenging angels and the angel of death. The angels are pure heavenly spirits made of light, whose main activity is to praise God. Unlike the Judaeo-Christian angels, they are wholly good; Islam has no concept of a "fallen angel." Instead, Satan and his minions sprang from a separate class of creatures, the fiery "Jinn," who, like men, have free will and can therefore be corrupted. It may be this important distinction that Rilke had in mind in his letter to Hulewicz. His angels are pure, lofty, and of a totally different nature from mankind. For information on the Islamic angels, I am indebted to Dr. Iman Khalil.

17. *Briefe aus Muzot*, 376. In their emphasis on the praising and transforming word as the key to a meaningful human existence, the *Elegies* can be regarded as metapoetry. In this context the angels, those beings who have already achieved "the transformation of the visible into the invisible," symbolize the perfect poet. They contain, perhaps, Rilke's predecessors, models, those he wished to emulate or surpass. The angels, like the great poets of the past or the symbols of the poetic ideal, have already solved the problems of "transformation," while the mortal poet still struggles toward insight. My thanks go to David A. Brodsky for first pointing out this reading.

18. All citations are from *SW*, vol. 1.

19. The painting now hangs in the National Gallery in Washington, D.C. The poem is dedicated to Hertha Koenig, the woman who owned it at that time.

20. Citations from the Sonetten are from *SW*, vol. 1.

21. *Briefe aus Muzot*, 133.

22. Hans Egon Holthusen, "Sei allem Abschied voran," in *Wege zum Gedicht*, vol. 1 (Munich, 1965), 294.

Selected Bibliography

PRIMARY SOURCES

1. Books

Auguste Rodin. Frankfurt: Insel, 1984. Contains ninety-six illustrations of Rodin's works discussed in the essay.

Rilke und die bildende Kunst: Insel-Almanach auf das Jahr 1986. Edited by Gottfried Boehm. Frankfurt: Insel, 1985. Contains many of Rilke's essays, poems, and letters about art, with twenty-seven illustrations.

Sämtliche Werke. Edited by Ruth Sieber-Rilke and Ernst Zinn. 6 vols. Frankfurt: Insel, 1955–66. The standard collected works, edited by Rilke's daughter. Brief editorial notes in volume 1, more extensive notes in volumes 2–4. Notes to volumes 5–6 in volume 6.

Tagebücher aus der Frühzeit. Frankfurt: Insel, 1942. Contains the Florence, Schmargendorf (Berlin), and Worpswede diaries.

Das Testament. Edited by Ernst Zinn. Frankfurt: Insel, 1975. Written at Schloss Berg in 1921, it reaffirms Rilke's need for solitude.

Übertragungen. 1927. Reprint. Edited by Ernst Zinn and Karin Wais. Frankfurt: Insel, 1975. Contains Rilke's translations from English, French, and Italian.

Worpswede. Künstler-Mongraphien, no. 64. 3d ed. 1903. Reprint. Bielefeld, 1910. Contains illustrations of works discussed.

2. Selected Letters

The volumes listed here are selected from a very large body of published letters. There are several editions of letters for some sequences of years; these do not always overlap completely, either in terms of time frame or in their contents. Those published under the supervision of Ruth Rilke and her husband are incomplete and fragmentary, having been expurgated by the editors for family or political reasons. It is hoped that there eventually will be an unabridged version of the letters.

Gesammelte Briefe. Edited by Ruth Sieber-Rilke and Carl Sieber. 6 vols. Leipzig: Insel, 1936–40. This is the basic edition of Rilke's letters. Vol. 1: *Briefe aus den Jahren 1892 bis 1904* (1939); vol. 2: *Briefe aus den Jahren 1904 bis 1907* (1939); vol. 3: *Briefe aus den Jahren 1907 bis 1914* (1939); vol. 4: *Briefe aus den Jahren 1914 bis 1921* (1938); vol. 5: *Briefe aus Muzot: 1921 bis 1926* (1940); vol. 6: *Briefe an seinen*

Verleger. 1906 bis 1926 (1936). Vol. 6 contains Rilke's letters to Anton Kippenberg, his publisher at Insel.

Briefe und Tagebücher aus der Frühzeit: 1899 bis 1902. Leipzig: Insel, 1931–33. Contains early letters, as well as the three diaries. This and the following five volumes are not part of the *Gesammelte Briefe.* They were published separately, and contain some letters not found in the corresponding *GB* volumes. These volumes were all edited by Ruth Sieber-Rilke and Carl Sieber.

Briefe aus den Jahren 1902 bis 1906. Leipzig: Insel, 1929–30.

Briefe aus den Jahren 1906 bis 1907. Leipzig: Insel, 1930.

Briefe aus den Jahren 1907 bis 1914. Leipzig: Insel, 1933.

Briefe aus den Jahren 1914 bis 1921. Leipzig: Insel, 1937.

Briefe aus Muzot: 1921 bis 1926. Leipzig: Insel, 1936.

Briefe an Nanny Wunderly-Volkart. Edited by Rätus Luck. 2 vols. [Frankfurt]: Insel, 1978.

Briefwechsel. Edited by Ernst Zinn. 2 vols. Zurich: Niehans & Rokitansky & Insel, 1951. Correspondence between Rilke and Marie von Thurn und Taxis.

Briefwechsel. Edited by Ernst Pfeiffer. Zurich: Max Niehans & Insel, 1952. Correspondence between Rilke and Lou Andreas Salomé.

3. Selected English Translations (alphabetized by translator)

Bly, Robert. *Selected Poems of Rainer Maria Rilke: A Translation from the German and Commentary.* New York: Harper & Row, 1981.

Boney, Elaine E. *Duinesian Elegies.* Chapel Hill: University of North Carolina Press, 1975. Dual language. Includes an interpretation of each of the ten poems.

Firmage, Robert. *Auguste Rodin.* Salt Lake City: Peregrine Smith, 1979. Illustrated.

Fleming, Albert Ernest. *Selected Poems.* Introduced by Victor Lange. New York: Methuen, 1986. Unrhymed. Selected from all the major cycles as well as collected poems from 1906 to 1926.

Hamburger, Michael. *An Unofficial Rilke: Poems 1912–1926.* London: Anvil Press Poetry, 1981. These skillful translations emphasize poems of the later years not included in the *Elegies* or *Sonnets.*

Houston, C. Craig. *Where Silence Reigns: Selected Prose.* Foreword by Denise Levertov. New York: New Directions, 1978. Includes *Cornet* and essays.

Leishman, J. B. *Poems 1906 to 1926.* New York: New Directions, 1957. Large (300-page) selection of poems with helpful introduction.

Leishman, J. B., and Spender, Stephen. *Duino Elegies.* New York: Norton, 1939. Dual language. A standard translation of the *Elegies* with extended commentary.

Linton, John. *The Notebook of Malte Laurids Brigge.* Oxford: Oxford University Press, 1984.

MacIntyre, C. F. *Duino Elegies.* Berkeley: University of California Press, 1961. Dual language. A standard translation.

————. *Sonnets to Orpheus.* Berkeley: University of California Press, 1960. Rhymed translation, with idiosyncratic and sometimes irritating notes. Dual language.

Mitchell, Stephen. *The Notebooks of Malte Laurids Brigge.* New York: Random House, 1983.

————. *The Selected Poetry of Rainer Maria Rilke.* New York: Random House, 1982. Dual language. Broad selection. Fresh, subjective introductory essay by Robert Hass.

Mood, John J. L. *Rilke on Love and Other Difficulties. Translations and Considerations.* New York: W. W. Norton, 1975. Poems focusing on love and praise.

Moore, Harry T. *Selected Letters of Rainer Maria Rilke.* Garden City, N.Y.: Doubleday Anchor, 1960.

Norton, M. D. Herter. *The Notebooks of Malte Laurids Brigge.* New York: Norton, 1949.

————. *Stories of God.* New York: Norton, 1964.

Phillips, Klaus, and Locke, John. *Nine Plays.* New York: Ungar, 1979.

Poulin, A., Jr. *Duino Elegies and The Sonnets to Orpheus.* Boston: Houghton Mifflin, 1977. Dual language.

Snow, Edward. *New Poems.* San Francisco: North Point Press, 1984. Sensitive and accurate translations.

Wettlin, Margaret, and Arndt, Walter. *Letters: Summer 1926.* Edited by Yevgeny Pasternak, Yelena Pasternak, and Konstantin M. Azadovsky. San Diego: Harcourt Brace Jovanovich, 1985. Correspondence between Boris Pasternak, Marina Tsvetayeva, and Rainer Maria Rilke.

SECONDARY SOURCES

The critical and biographical material on Rilke is vast. The following is an introductory sample and does not include works mentioned in the Notes and References.

Andreas-Salomé, Lou. *Rainer Maria Rilke.* Leipzig: Insel, 1929.

Baron, Frank; Dick, Ernst S.; and Maurer, Warren R., eds. *Rilke: The Alchemy of Alienation.* Lawrence: The Regents Press of Kansas, 1980.

Casey, Timothy J. *Rainer Maria Rile: A Centenary Essay.* New York: Harper & Row, 1976. Interesting look at Rilke and his critics a hundred years after his birth, and fifty years after his death.

Demetz, Peter. *René Rilkes Prager Jahre.* Düsseldorf: E. Diederichs, 1953.

Fuerst, Norbert. *Rilke in seiner Zeit.* Frankfurt: Insel, 1976. Attempts to place Rilke within a cultural and historical context.

Graff, Willem Laurens. *Rainer Maria Rilke: Creative Anguish of a Modern Poet.* Princeton: Princeton University Press, 1956.

Hähnel, Klaus-Dieter. *Rainer Maria Rilke: Werk—Literaturgeschichte—Kunstanschauung.* Berlin: Aufbau Verlag, 1984. A Marxist approach by a critic in the German Democratic Republic, where Rilke has been ignored.

Heller, Erich. *Nirgend wird Welt sein als Innen.* Frankfurt: Suhrkamp, 1975.

Hendry, J. E. *The Sacred Threshold: A Life of Rainer Maria Rilke.* Manchester: Carcanet New Press, 1983.

Holthusen, Hans Egon. *Portrait of Rilke: An Illustrated Biography.* Translated by W. H. Hargreaves. New York: Herder & Herder, 1971.

Leppmann, Wolfgang. *Rilke: A Life.* New York: Fromm International Publishers, 1984. Translation of *Rilke: Leben und Werk,* cited in notes.

Mandel, Siegfried. *Rainer Maria Rilke: The Poetic Instinct.* Crosscurrents. Carbondale: Southern Illinois University Press, 1965.

Meyer, Hermann. *"Rilkes Cézanne-Erlebnis."* *Zeitschrift für Aesthetik und allgemeine Kunstwissenschaft* 2 (1952):69–102. This and the following article provide excellent discussions of Rilke and modern art.

————. *"Die Verwandlung des Sichtbaren: Die Bedeutung der modernen bildenden Kunst für Rilkes späte Dichtung."* *Deutsche Vierteljahrsschrift für Literaturwissenschaft und Geistesgeschichte* 31 (1957):465–505.

Mövius, Ruth. *Rainer Maria Rilkes Stunden-Buch: Entstehung und Gehalt.* Leipzig: Insel, 1937. One of the most perceptive studies of *SB.*

Peters, Heinz Frederick. *My Sister, My Spouse: A Biography of Lou Andreas-Salomé.* New York: Norton, 1962. English version of *Lou: Das Leben der Lou Andreas-Salomé* mentioned in the notes.

————. *Rainer Maria Rilke: Masks and the Man.* Seattle: University of Washington Press, 1960.

Prater, Donald. *A Ringing Glass: The Life of Rainer Maria Rilke.* Oxford: Clarendon Press, 1986. Most recent, and extremely thorough, biography.

Stephens, Anthony B. *Rilkes Malte Laurids Brigge: Strukturanalyse des erzählerischen Bewusstseins.* Bern: Herbert Lang & Cie, 1974.

Index